The Artistry of the Homeric Simile

WILLIAM C. SCOTT

The Artistry
of the
Homeric Simile

DARTMOUTH COLLEGE LIBRARY
& DARTMOUTH COLLEGE PRESS
Hanover, New Hampshire

Published by
UNIVERSITY PRESS OF NEW ENGLAND
Hanover and London

DARTMOUTH COLLEGE PRESS
Published by University Press of New England,
One Court Street, Lebanon, NH 03766
www.upne.com
© 2009 by William C. Scott
Printed in U.S.A.
5 4 3 2 1

This work has been published simultaneously in print and in electronic form. The author, William C. Scott, asserts his rights as copyright holder for both print and electronic versions. The print version of this book is available from UPNE, One Court Street, Lebanon, NH 03766. The electronic version is available for download by the public, free of charge, at the website of the Dartmouth College Library: http://www.dartmouth.edu/~library/digital/publishing/scott2009.

Library of Congress Cataloging-in-Publication Data
Scott, William C. (William Clyde), 1937–
The artistry of the Homeric simile / William C. Scott.
   p. cm.
Includes bibliographical references and index.
ISBN 978-1-58465-797-2 (pbk.: alk. paper)
1. Homer—Literary style. 2. Greek language—Figures of speech. 3. Oral-formulaic analysis. 4. Oral tradition—Greece. 5. Rhetoric, Ancient. 6. Simile. I. Title.
PA4177.S5S28   2009
883'.01—dc22   2009016159

CONTENTS

Preface · vii

CHAPTER ONE
Similes, the Shield of Achilles, and Other Digressions · 1
    The Usefulness of Book Divisions · 10

CHAPTER TWO
The Simileme: The Background of the Homeric Simile · 14
    The Oral Nature of Homeric Verse · 14
    The Simileme · 18
    Homer and His Audience · 31
    Simile and Simileme · 37

CHAPTER THREE
Homer's Use of Similes to Delineate Character and Plot · 42
    Iliad, Book 2: Ironic Characterization · 43
        The Similes of Book 2 · 44
        The Role of Similes in Book 2 · 59
    Iliad, Books 21 and 22: Similes to Show a Thematic Contrast · 65
    Iliad, Book 11: Similes to Mark a Shifting Scene · 78
    Conclusion · 89

CHAPTER FOUR
Similes to Delineate a Narrative Theme · 94
    Iliad, Book 12: Direct Focus on a Single Theme · 94
    Iliad, Book 5: The Use of Parallel Similemes to Create a Unified Theme · 102
    Odyssey, Book 22: Similes to Interpret Typical Actions · 112
    Odyssey, Book 5: Thematic Similes · 118
    Conclusion · 126

CHAPTER FIVE
Problem Books · 130
    Iliad, Book 13: The Ordering of Conscious Chaos · 130
    Iliad, Book 17: Similes as Guides through a Series of Type Scenes · 145

    Iliad, *Book 16: Similes for Complexity* · 155
    Conclusion · 171

CHAPTER SIX
The Creative Poet and the Co-creating Audience · 174
    The Simile within the Narrative · 174
    The Poet's Choices in Forming the Individual Simile · 181
    The Creative Moment: Poet and Audience · 185

Charts of Similemes: The Basic Motifs · 189
Notes · 207
Bibliography · 247
Index · 257

PREFACE

The similes in Homer are treasure troves. They describe scenes of Greek life that are not presented in their simplest form anywhere else: landscapes and seascapes; storms and calm weather; fighting among animals; aspects of civic life such as disputes, athletic contests, horse races, community entertainment, women carrying on their daily lives, and men running their farms and orchards. But the similes also show Homer dealing with his tradition. They are basic paratactic additions to the narrative showing how the Greeks found and developed parallels between two scenes, each of which elucidated and interpreted the other, and then expressed those scenes in effective poetic language.

My earlier book, *The Oral Nature of the Homeric Simile*, identified series of repeated simile topics and common locations in the narrative with the goal of revealing the oral basis for the content of many of the similes as well as their placement. The current book, directed at the aesthetic qualities that Homer sought in forming each simile, represents that work's other side. The first study focused more on the traditional alternatives that occurred to Homer as he composed; this second study explores the variations and modifications to each of the topics that Homer employs in order to make similes blend expressively with the larger context. The focus moves from compositional modes to aesthetic choices—from the poetic background to the act of creation by the poet and the act of reception by his audience. The major question for the second study is: how does the artist translate his thoughts into his chosen language? He does so through the indispensable participation of a co-creating audience. Thus the two books are meant to be a unified study of Homer's similes as compositions derived from and dependent on an oral tradition.

The second study is rooted in the mixture of traditional materials present to the poet every time he considers adding a simile to his narrative. No name has been assigned to this conglomerate of topics and scenes, of previously successful placements of similes, of multiple choices available to the poet, of the alternate narrative techniques that poet and audience bring to the moment, and of the highly developed traditional language that was the birthright of every Greek. Poet and audience together used their understanding of the means of expression and their memory of tales from the past as mutually helpful partners in creating Homer's old-style "new" poetry.

The similes are not presented sequentially or in their order of appearance in the narrative; rather, they are grouped by books and then analyzed as they fit broad functional categories. The first chapter shows how Homer has used expository digressions widely and effectively in telling his stories and how the similes can be approached as parallel narrative devices. The second chapter will analyze the poet's and audience's inheritance from previous performances of epic in order to determine the choices available to Homer in shaping his similes to support the narrative. The next three chapters examine those books in the *Iliad* and the *Odyssey* that contain the largest numbers of similes — in other words, the books where Homer seems to have chosen to give the similes major significance in his design. Finally, the conclusion attempts to imagine how a poet could have juggled all the elements that went into the series of choices that produced the individual simile. Together these chapters demonstrate my major point: the individual simile — even the shortest one — is the result of a complex process that requires the participation of both poet and audience.

The translations are mine; I have everywhere tried to follow the original closely and have not added the Greek text of each simile.

Many friends have aided me in completing this study. E. M. Bradley, E. Bakker, M. Edwards, J. Foley, J. A. W. Heffernan, C. Higbie, E. Minchin, G. Nagy, R. Rabel, H. Tell, W. G. Thalmann, and L. Whaley have been loyal guides as the book took shape. To them and to the many other friends and colleagues who have offered generous criticism, I offer my appreciation.

The publication of this book in its double format has depended on close and friendly cooperation with the Dartmouth College Library and the University Press of New England. I wish to express my thanks for the interest and enthusiasm of Michael P. Burton, the Director of the Press, and Jeffrey L. Horrell, the Librarian of the College, as well as Phyllis Deutsch, William Fontaine, Elizabeth Kirk, and David Seaman.

Hanover, New Hampshire
W.C.S.

The Artistry of the Homeric Simile

CHAPTER ONE

Similes, the Shield of Achilles, and Other Digressions

> *Similes are often repeated with very little change, they accumulate when there is no need, and they compare where there is nothing comparable. Great art would consist in making one large and highly appropriate simile. Homer becomes too carried away with his own similes and forgets narrative.*
>
> M. DE LA MOTTE[1]

In the eighteenth book of Homer's *Iliad* Hephaistos makes a new shield for Achilles.[2] The description of this shield is justly famed as a small masterwork in its own right as well as being the prototype for later poets and writers who include art objects within their works.[3] The most notable ancient examples are *The Shield of Heracles*, the shields in the central scene of Aeschylus' *Seven against Thebes*, the cup in Theocritus' first *Idyll*, the tapestry in Catullus' epyllion on the marriage of Peleus and Thetis (c. 64), and the shield of Aeneas in book 8 of *The Aeneid*. These ekphrases occupy so large a portion of each work that they are necessarily major elements in the overall design.[4]

Homer often describes objects and implements in the course of his narrative, even pausing in the midst of events to present a detailed picture of some article drawn from the background. Book 11 of the *Iliad* contains three examples. The first and second are the descriptions of the breastplate and the shield of Agamemnon embedded in his arming scene (11.19–40); the third is "Nestor's cup" (11.632–37). The presentation of each object is sufficiently detailed that it has been possible to find fragmentary yet often rather precise remains that parallel the verbal descriptions.[5] These descriptions focus sharply on physical features. While they may interrupt an action, they do so only long enough to permit a listing of the elements that would meet the eye of the observer. Such quick sketches of a person's possessions, however, strengthen the characterization being developed in the larger passage. The

1

highlighting of Agamemnon's battle gear introduces the king as a heroic personage and reinforces his status as a major warrior at the moment he begins his aristeia.[6] The ornate cup that Nestor alone can lift endows him with extra strength and stature at the moment when he is going to give crucial advice to Patroclus.[7]

One such piece described in the poems, however, will never be successfully reproduced even with considerable effort and ingenuity, and that is the Shield of Achilles. Special problems abound: the figures are in motion and small vignettes are in the process of evolving; this shield will not hold still for a static modeling session but continues to shift and change before the eyes of the observer. Thus though several commentaries feature a basic drawing of the shield that locates the individual scenes within the surrounding border of the river Ocean, sketches of the events described in each scene are omitted.[8] The conclusion is inevitable: while there may have been shields that resembled the Shield of Achilles in basic shape and complexity, this particular shield never did and never could have actually existed because it is as much a product of the poet's imagination as the narrative itself. The people on the Shield live and breathe, events develop over time, and there is such a collection of varied subject matter that it probably could never have been arrayed in its entirety on the surface of any one weapon. In addition, the presentation of the Shield is complex. It is not only a verbal description of the contents; it also involves the medium, the process of creation, the maker and his motives, and the interpreter.[9]

Once it is clear that Achilles' Shield is more a creation of the poet than of the forge, a new set of revealing parallels can be sought. These would be imaginative constructs that interrupt the ongoing narrative in order to introduce a scene developed within its own clearly bounded framework. An obvious example is the tale of Odysseus' visit to his maternal grandfather, Autolycus, in book 19 of the *Odyssey* (392–466).

This story falls into three segments: the naming of the baby Odysseus, the reception of the young boy at his grandfather's palace, and his wounding by the boar. Each confirms an element in Odysseus' characterization that was present from an early age. Autolycus is known for being a thief and an oathbreaker, talents taught to him by Hermes, the god of thieves himself. This man gives his baby grandson the name "Odysseus" in memory of the pain and anger that he has caused to others. This name is Odysseus' first gift from his grandfather, a birthright that the *Odyssey* illustrates in many ways, most notably in the attack on the Cicones, in the raid on the Cyclops' cave, and in his continual baiting of the suitors. Later when young Odysseus visits Autolycus' palace, he receives gifts further identifying him as the heir of this wily and aggressive old man, and he is welcomed as a worthy member of the family at a great banquet. The next day when a boar unexpectedly appears during the hunt, Odysseus is eager to kill it. Although the boar wounds him with his tusk, he kills the animal with a single swift thrust. This small story embodies the basic characteristics of Odysseus: his aggressive nature, his eagerness to lead, his willingness to hurt, and his readiness to accept pain in the pursuit of victory—the very elements that Odysseus will draw upon throughout the second half of the *Odyssey* as he attempts to gain an advantageous position against the suitors.[10] This tale interrupts the narrative at the moment when old Eurycleia is washing Odysseus' feet and feels the scar. But there is no physical description of the wound or the scar; rather, the incident seems developed in order to provide an early foundation for the consistent behavior of Odysseus as a man of cleverness as he seeks and wins victories even against seemingly superior strength.

The scar is one token in a book of tokens—objects that contain signs portending events to come and therefore requiring interpretation. Book 19 opens with the removal of the arms from the hall. This is a revealing sign, but the suitors fail to understand; they accept the story that the arms are being protected from smoke damage.[11] Telemachus, however, correctly interprets the miraculous light that guides him and Odysseus, and Penelope repeatedly seeks to gather meaning from the clear signs that come to her. Odysseus as the beggar tells her of his cloak, his brooch, and his herald—all signs rich with meaning. Throughout their conversation Penelope questions and probes the beggar so deftly that she shows how deeply she has read and understood tokens which seem innocent on the surface. Although she refuses to hear the encouraging interpretation of her dream offered by Odysseus, the book ends with Penelope arranging the contest of the bow and preparing for a marriage that she and Odysseus hope will restore her to her husband. The beggar contains within him the combination of abilities and the spirit needed to make him the victor in the contest of the bow, but these qualities are evident only to those who know how to read the tokens as Eurycleia does openly—and Penelope does secretly.[12] Thus the story of the scar is formally an interruption in the narrative but, in fact, is another of the many objects in book 19 that call for interpretation to appreciate the strong underlying currents in events.[13]

Similes, the Shield of Achilles, and Other Digressions

Similar digressions include the parable of Meleager in book 9 of the *Iliad* (527–605) and Demodocus' song of Ares and Aphrodite in the *Odyssey* (*Ody.* 8.266–366). The story of Meleager is not just an abbreviated version of an older saga inserted into the *Iliad* as the static physical descriptions cited earlier are; rather, it presents behavior that has been sufficiently acceptable in the past to be cited as a normative story. As such, it is the very kind of argument that can be effectively brought to bear by a trusted old friend like Phoenix.[14] Demodocus' song could merely be an entertaining tale about the intrigues of the gods, yet the story of Ares and Aphrodite is developed to enhance the audience's understanding of the differences between the Phaeacians and Odysseus — the very contrast that is the major theme of book 8.[15]

These three passages — the scar, the parable of Meleager, and the song of Ares and Aphrodite, which I will call "expository digressions" — have certain similarities that distinguish them from the usual descriptions of physical objects or implements:

1. They are long digressions.
2. The poet creates a strong break from the locale of the ongoing narrative for digressions that develop their own stories in response to their own motivations.
3. Each digressive interruption is in motion; these tales have a beginning, a middle, and an end.
4. They are not simply enhancements to a feature of an individual scene but, rather, significant parts of each book's theme.[16]

This list provides critical insights into parallel passages. Homer's similes are especially open to such analysis — and especially the longest of all similes, the Shield of Achilles.[17]

There seem to be two simultaneous movements organizing the Shield's structure. In spatial terms the most general picture of the universe is placed in the middle and is surrounded by detailed images of various scenes from human life.[18] At the same time there is a temporal ordering: the Shield centers on the elements that are usually associated with primal creation — earth and heaven (Ouranos and Ge), sea, and day and night — and then opens out through stages of human development from basic communities and agricultural societies to gatherings of people for communal entertainment — art, music, and dance. When all of this is then bounded by the circling river of the Ocean, Homer has framed a view of the world in its full spatial breadth and temporal development; the Shield presents a complete and unified image of the varieties of life that mankind has developed. Antitheses provide a structure for the Shield—city and country, war and peace, work and festivity; these are basic, opposed forms of human life that are ordered by an inner polarity. As one critic notes, the whole image of the Shield is not intended to move the soul of the audience; it is more a rational construction.[19]

Book 18 splits easily into two halves: the first (1–367), Achilles' decision to revenge the death of Patroclus; the second (368–617), the provision and design of his new armor. Though the loss and the resupply of armor seems a relatively minor blockage to Achilles' decision to embark upon a suicidal death march, the whole scene of the Shield's manufacture and design is basic to book 18's larger theme. Achilles and Hephaestus are the dominant figures, each in his half of the book. Yet the differences developed between the two sections are important. The first scene emphasizes Thetis' concern for her son (382–411); in the second Charis welcomes Thetis graciously and Hephaestus wants to do what he can to repay the goddess' earlier favor—even expressing his willingness to hide Achilles from death. In the first section Achilles rejects the feelings of his mother, the *dysaristotokeia*, the woman who bore the best of men to her own sorrow, and thinks only of his wounded honor (18.86–93). In contrast, Hephaestus is a humane and genial host. He presides over a shop that is a veritable amusement park filled with wondrous robots—self-propelled tripods and golden handmaidens:

> in whose hearts is understanding, in whom there is speech
> and strength, and who know crafts by aid of the immortal gods.
> (18.419–20)

Under the touch of this divine craftsman machines have been made to act like humans and even have human features and qualities. Achilles is Hephaestus' antithesis; in the coming battle he will convert men into war machines. In book 19 he will not let the Greek warriors eat before the battle, in book 21 he will reduce Lycaon to food for fish, and in book 22 he will refuse any dealing with Hector as he plays out the end of a grim process. The major creation of Hephaestus is the Shield—another of his devices that make inert metal into a dynamic image of living men; Achilles intends to make men into inert matter.[20]

In book 18 Homer has juxtaposed two scenes that are otherwise linked only casually. If an audience were to hear a telling of one of these events without the other, they would find that each makes sense on its own but lacks the full import gained when they are juxtaposed. Only an awareness of the unified whole presents Achilles' choice in its broadest dimensions. As a result this book in its entirety is the appropriate introduction to the aristeia of Achilles — a campaign successful and sweeping, but also dehumanizing and repellent.

The Shield of Achilles is far more important in the design of the *Iliad* than the mere physical description of an object. It is a product of the poet's creative imagination; its content gives it a life of its own, and its position allows it to cast a shadow over the heroic code. Against this background it becomes easier to appreciate that by far the most common expository digressive elements in the Homeric epics are the similes.

The Homeric simile is easily recognized. It is based on the juxtaposition of two passages describing objects, persons, or events connected by the words "like" or "as," in which the subject of the simile may be developed as an independent picture. The similes vary widely in terms of length, form, structure, quantity of repeated phrasing, and the complexity of their relationship to the narrative context. Even the shortest similes reach outside the narrative for objects from a dissimilar area.

There is often development within the simile — the story seems to go back to an earlier moment that is set in motion and then catches up to the present. One example is the lion that started out attacking, but finally must change his direction and slink away:

> like a lion who leaves the farmyard
> when he is exhausted attacking the dogs and men
> who do not allow him to carry off the fattest of the cattle,
> staying awake all night. Craving meat
> he keeps attacking, but accomplishes nothing. For spears
> pour constantly from brave hands
> and lighted torches which he fears even though he is eager.
> Then at dawn he draws away sullen at heart.
> Thus did Menelaus, good at the war shout, go from Patroclus....
>
> (*Iliad* 17.657–65)

The narrative frame of this simile does not move while the poet is telling the vignette within the simile:

He [Menelaus] started to go like a lion....
[simile]
Thus did Menelaus, good at the war shout, go from Patroclus....

There are, however, several passages where the simile itself expands so far that it rejoins the narrative at a new point; the movement in the simile is so great that it seems to take the mind of the poet with it. The clearest example is at book 15 of the Iliad (lines 622–38), which would read as follows if the similes were extracted:

> The Greeks withstood the Trojans firmly and did not flee, but Hector leaped into the crowd. The hearts of the Achaeans were split in their breasts. Then the Achaeans were powerfully routed by Hector and father Zeus.

There is no doubt that action does develop in these lines, but there are gaps between the three sentences where questions are left unanswered. Hector leapt into the crowd, but why were the Achaeans so afraid? Was it just his reputation? Once Homer fills that gap with a simile, the question disappears:

> [Hector] *leaped into the crowd* as when beneath the clouds a rushing wave churned by the wind falls upon a swift ship. The whole ship is hidden in the spray, and the fearful blowing of the wind roars in the sails; the sailors tremble in their hearts, fearing — for only by a little have they escaped death.
> *So were the hearts of the Achaeans split....*
>
> (15.624–28)

Not one blow is struck by Hector, but Homer's description of the sailors' fear of the threatening wave makes Hector's effect on the battle clear — and explains how the hearts of the Achaeans can quite reasonably be divided. In the next sentence the Greeks are already in flight — how did that happen? The simile covers this moment in a different way than a factual report would:

> *So were the hearts of the Achaeans split in their breasts.*
> Just as a evil-minded lion comes upon cattle,
> that are grazing in countless numbers in the low land in a great marsh.
> Among them is a herdsman not yet experienced
> in fighting a wild beast over the carcass of a crooked-horned cow;
> but he walks with the herd, first in front

and then behind—while the lion leaping into the middle
devours a heifer, and all the rest flee. *Just so were the Achaeans
powerfully routed by Hector....*

(15.629–36)

By the time the cattle are fleeing in panic, there is little point in describing the specific deeds of Hector that turned the Greeks to flight. They can be imagined because the simile has already conveyed the nature of their fear so effectively that the poet can easily move on with his story.[21]

From such analyses it is clear that similes are not mere static descriptions of objects; they are smaller or larger vignettes that were constructed to suit their context so closely that the poet could rejoin the narrative either at the identical spot where he left it, or even slightly later, with no gaps or unexpected inconcinnities. As a result similes should be appreciated as being purposefully formulated within the creative mind of the poet to enhance his ongoing narrative. Instead of isolating favorite similes for comment, the whole series of similes within a unified section of the narrative must be coordinated with one another and with the thematic design of the unit; only then is the understanding of any one simile possible. Conversely, because similes have been incorporated by the poet within his story in order to provide support for his larger conception, they offer especially significant clues for the interpretation of longer passages.[22]

It is important not to overrate the words and phrases that the poet uses in attaching his similes to their narrative contexts (usually "like" or "as"). These words serve as markers to separate the narrative clearly from the simile, but they do not automatically indicate the major parallel joining narrative to simile. If the close conceptual unity between narrative and simile is to be clarified, a critic must be willing to focus on elements where the poet exercises choice in shaping the individual components of the simile, such as the placement of the simile, the choice of subject matter, the length of the simile, and the objects included in the extension of the basic subject. Here the poet could give each simile an individuality that would allow it to complement its context on a variety of levels.

The interpretation of the individual simile requires the constant participation of a co-creating audience, which has heard heroic songs sung in traditional language for generations. For the audience of a simile to participate in such complex communication it must share experiences with the poet. Such communication can occur between a speaker and an audience that is large or small. The full meaning of any simile can be accessible only to an audience that is intimately involved with the private life of the originator of the simile. A modern example is the simile "bend it like Beckham," which prior to the 2002 movie was almost unknown to all but devoted soccer fans. However, in the last scene of Aeschylus' *The Libation Bearers*, before a large Athenian audience Orestes asks the chorus for a proper definition of the robe and suggests a variety of contexts and experiences that would allow different descriptions depending on his hearers' familiarity with Agamemnon's death:

> And this thing: what shall I call it and be right, in
> eloquence? Trap for an animal or winding sheet
> for a dead man? or bath curtain? Since it is a net,
> a robe you could call it, to entangle a man's feet.
> Some highwayman might own a thing like this, to catch
> the wayfarer and rob him of his money and
> so make a living. With a treacherous thing *like this*
> he could take many victims and go warm within.
> (Aeschylus, *Choephoroi* 996–1004)

The phrase "like this" (*toiouton*) shows that he is listing various similes to describe the robe; the communicative power of the suggested comparisons depends on the audience's knowledge of the complex background.

The understanding of Homeric similes requires poet and audience to know well the long and deep tradition of oral verse-making, replete with stories, characters, and actions that are familiar by their frequent usage. The contexts in which similes occur have been sufficiently repeated that the audience would recognize junctures where a simile is a possibility and would be aware of the range of subjects which have been used in such a passage before. Further, the repeated recurrence of the same topic at similar narrative junctures implies that the audience should realize that certain contexts are likely to generate specific simile subjects and also should be able to recognize variations within similes of the same family. In suppressing or adjusting the scope of a simile to suit a narrative context, the poet creates the integral unity of each particular passage; the audience must know enough about his usual practice to evaluate the traditional alternatives that he has chosen.

Given an awareness of the resources of the poet, the act of communication does not so much produce continual amazement at the innovative power of the poet as arouse admiration at the poet's management of the audience's expectations. When the audience heard a simile—just as when they heard the presentation of the Shield or the scar—they would know from previous experience how to unify the elements of the full passage in order to derive the poet's full meaning. It is not difficult for them to realize that the new weapons for Achilles not only signal, but also characterize, his new resolve or that the story of the scar is yet another mode of describing the aggressive and dominating spirit of the returned Odysseus. Likewise, when they heard a warrior described by a lion simile, they would know the possible range of lionlike activities in the traditional simile language and would evaluate appropriately the specific content of the simile as an enhancement to the warrior's individual actions and spirit.

Similes are so important a device for Homer that it is possible to analyze his compositional technique in corresponding settings. This study will provide constant comparisons of parallel similes, long and short, peaceful or warlike, traditionally placed or seemingly unique in their position, repeated or sole exemplars. In addition, earlier analyses defining the methods of a poet raised in the oral tradition can be applied to the similes. They are not ready-made sparkly sequins to be attached to the narrative when the story slows, nor are they necessarily contemporary scenes from the poet's own world. The Homeric simile is so limited in its variety of actions and yet repeated sufficiently that it enables one to identify modifications designed by the poet to match different narrative situations. There are enough examples of parallel scenes to establish with some accuracy the poet's talent in manipulating and adapting Homeric language and structure. A continued awareness of the open communication between poet and audience allows a closer approach to the artistry of Homer himself.

THE USEFULNESS OF BOOK DIVISIONS

In studying the interdependency of the similes and their larger narrative contexts—thus, how a simile fits into its "book"—I have tried to select the books where the number of similes is the greatest. Stanley's chart shows the density of similes in the books of the Iliad; the highest is in books 2, 3, 4, 5, 11, 12, 13, 15, 16, 17, 21, and 22.[23] I will consider all except books 3, 4, and 15. I omit these because I have organized the discussion of simile-rich books by function:

Chapter 3 (books 2, 11, 21, and 22):
  Similes that aid in the delineation of character and plot
Chapter 4 (books 12, 5, *Ody.* 5, and *Ody.* 22):
  Similes as markers in shifting scenes
Chapter 5 (books 13, 17, and 16):
  Problematic books

In addition, I have ordered each chapter to show the clearest examples of the various functions of the simile within the narrative. Thus books 2, 12, and 13 provide the clearest models of similes used to support narrative strategies. In books 3, 4, and 15 the similes do occur in traditional places but do not seem to accompany the development of major themes. An example would be the series of similes in Agamemnon's review of the Greek troops in book 4. It is common for a character to be given a simile when he is introduced into the narrative.[24] In his march through the troops Agamemnon comes upon some Greeks who are not arming (fawns, 243), Idomeneus (boar, 253), and the Ajaxes and their soldiers (goatherd seeing a coming whirlwind, 275). These similes are placed where the tradition suggests the simile as one among many options and their subjects seem appropriate for the men described. However, they do not relate meaningfully with the earlier similes of the star (Athena, 75), the mother brushing away the fly (Athena, 130), or the woman staining ivory (Menelaus, 141). Because they lack compelling organization I have chosen to omit these books from major discussion because I cannot find narrative strategies that are equally compelling as those in the other simile-rich books.

At this point it is necessary to raise a problem. This study of eleven chosen books depends on demonstrating how closely the design of the similes follows broader thematic developments in each narrative section. For such a discussion it is necessary to identify the major structural units in the *Iliad* and *Odyssey*. Book 2 is designed differently than book 1: the locale changes, the entrance of Agamemnon's dream starts off a new series of actions, the focus shifts from individuals to larger groups, and the number of similes increases markedly. Although such contrasts make it easy to assume that most books contain a separately designed unit, it is impossible simply to accept the current book divisions as precise designators of Homer's narrative plan. Often the divisions do not seem reliable: some seem arbitrary, yet others clearly represent authentic breaks in the story that the poet has marked as his own.[25] The division between *Iliad* 1 and 2 seems to me unquestionably authentic, while that between *Iliad* 2 and 3 seems a matter of personal judgment. But the situation is even more confusing when one considers the number of books which end with scenes that suggest a natural break, such as "going to bed" and "having a meal"; the book division might occur with equal probability somewhere in the preceding fifty lines or in the following fifty lines in the next book.[26] Such "endings" often seem to depend on an unverifiable feeling that the number of lines is close to what a normal book should have; there is no narrative reason to pick one of these break points over another.

There have been several good suggestions for understanding the traditional book divisions by incorporating them into patterns that reflect larger systems. Stanley analyzes them as signs of a late switch from orality to a written text.[27] Heiden shifts the focus from narrative moments to the completion of a significant structure: "The placement of marked 'book divisions' in the *Iliad* follows a consistent pattern. It draws needed attention to scenes of high consequence for the story, as well as to scenes that invite thoughtful retrospection, and it encloses passages of narrative that are fairly coherent, although less so than some modern scholars find satisfying." Jensen presented her own version of more mechanical factors underlying the division of the poems into books, and her statement was followed by other scholars' responses.[28]

Rather than trying to settle this problem, I will use the customary book divisions as guides while not insisting that they authoritatively define the beginning and end points of basic narrative units comprising each of the epics. My assumption is that both poems are built from a collection of tales, each of which centers on an individual narrative that tells its story in its own way.[29] In other words, I will use the traditional book numbers as shorthand to identify a particular segment of the narrative while not attempting to justify the precise beginning and ending of that segment. Often adding twenty more lines (or even fifty) to the preceding book or taking twenty lines off the beginning of the book will not appreciably affect the discussion. I will treat the book divisions as suggestions that a unit is beginning somewhere in that area.

Let me illustrate the type of argumentation this compromise facilitates by discussing the difficulty in determining the division between books 5 and 6 of the *Iliad*. The question is clear: does the current book division mark precisely — or even suggest imprecisely — the boundary of two integral units, or does the aristeia of Diomedes continue into book 6 to be joined to the scene where he confronts Glaucus?

I will argue later that book 5 is a carefully constructed book in many ways, including the placement, subject, and extension of the similes. There are 21 similes in the 909 lines of book 5, or an average of one simile in every 43 lines; in book 6 there are 4 similes in 509 lines, or a comparable average of one simile every 127 lines. (If the length of the similes is calculated, 5.8 percent of lines in book 5 are similes vs. 1.7 percent in book 6.) In addition, in the initial 236 lines of the Glaucus-Diomedes scene there are no similes. On this evidence alone there seems a difference in the design of the two books; but the establishment of this difference is not dependent on book 5 ending at line 909, or at book 6.37, or later at 6.66, or at 6.72.[30] I feel that the contrast in the density of similes reflects a shift in the subject and theme of the two books. Book 5, the aristeia of Diomedes, is centered on his attacks on Aphrodite and Ares; book 6 is one where warriors refuse to fight and instead turn to broader considerations of family and friends:[31] Diomedes refuses to fight Glaucus, and Hector leaves the battle to visit his mother, sister-in-law, and wife. The book then closes with the return of Hector and Paris to battle. Thus the division between these two books signals a significant change in subject and style, and that change can be analyzed without insisting on the authenticity of the division at precisely 5.909.

CHAPTER TWO

The Simileme
The Background of the Homeric Simile

> *If Yeats's lines were really oral-traditional lines, and if you were in the traditional audience or its equivalent, you would not need to go back over them to savor them. The traditional diction would be familiar, known, understood, and appreciated on first hearing, because words and word clusters or configurations like them had been heard before.... Written poetry's technique is to seek a striking non-traditional image.*
> ALBERT LORD[1]

THE ORAL NATURE OF HOMERIC VERSE

It has been argued that insistence on a sharp division between orality and literacy in Homeric studies is misleading. In one sense orality implies an older, prewritten style; but it is equally clear that "oral" need mean only that words are spoken. In this second sense there is no advantage in conjuring up a written version of the utterance; such an imagined structure is inherently irrelevant to the understanding of the oral statement or the appreciation of its form. In our world oral utterances are being formulated constantly, and they are different than written compositions produced at the same moment. Bakker put this succinctly: "'Oral' denotes a *medium*, the way in which a discourse is realized. And as a *medium*, orality is not the absence of writing or its imperfect and clumsy ('early') use, but simply a way of using language that is different from, and opposed to, written communication."[2]

As a result, Homeric style itself authorizes the study of those qualities of the *Iliad* and the *Odyssey* that are deeply rooted in speech patterns. The studies of Milman Parry, his successors, and his critics make evident the special nature and extent of formulaic expression in a performance environment; others have focused on repeated typological scenes. Most critics agree that the poems were composed by a poet well grounded in the traditional diction, stories, and themes of early Greek oral narrative verse, and this familiarity is clear in virtually every line. More recent studies acknowledging the oral root to the means of poetic expression have identified an adaptability, an appreciation of the latent potential of the language, and a complexity in the design of the poems that bespeak a poet—literate or not—who uses traditional diction with a full awareness of its poetic power.[3] The poems are oral in nature, but not necessarily expressed in performance.[4]

In my earlier study, *The Oral Nature of the Homeric Simile*, I explored the components of the similes that seem most closely related to the techniques of oral verse-making. The extended similes, especially those that are repeated, do not seem to be solely the creation of a single poet but comprise expressions shared by Homer, his predecessors, and his colleagues. Many features of the similes in the *Iliad* and the *Odyssey* appear to arise from language and images that the tradition offered to the poet as he developed his narrative. The necessary foundation for a study of individual similes in the poems is the establishment of possible alternatives to similes—repeated suggestions that rise from a tradition developed and transmitted by poets prior to the period in which Homer created his two large epics.

The fact that formulaic diction has simultaneous generic and specific aspects is a major cause of difficulty in analyzing Homeric verse; each phrase must be continually understood both in its immediate context and in the larger semantic fields with which it is associated. Although the phrase "swift-footed Achilles" seems a gratuitous—at times almost contradictory—addition to most of the contexts in which it occurs, continual repetition suggests a past history where its honorific connotations were appropriate.[5] Before Homer there was a group of bards composing songs that kept alive tales from earlier centuries. In telling these tales they continually molded and honed their language to make it a highly expressive tool. As successive bards reshaped previously used phrases and lines, earlier associations were both extended and forgotten—and each further usage confirmed, adapted, modified, or replaced the previous phrasing. And Homer repeatedly used such subjects and phrases because they facilitated effective communication. Thus each detail within the extant similes is important because Homer chose that detail in place of others. To the extent that critics can incorporate the evolving nature of the traditional diction into their studies, they will move closer to understanding the poetic mind that created the individual similes.[6]

The simile is one of many traditional devices that are repeated throughout the *Iliad* and the *Odyssey*; examples include speech structures and speech language, repeated type scenes, the uses of general principles in argumentation, and variations in forms of address. Speeches have been studied in detail to determine the customary forms of direct communication. Griffin has shown the special terms, words, and emotive language that make Homeric speeches effective; Lohmann has outlined the repeated structuring of speeches; and Martin has studied the *mythos* as an authoritative speech act. All have demonstrated that the poet is able to move freely within these traditional forms to create especially moving and compelling statements. Armstrong, Krischer, and Foley have shown how type scenes can be fitted into the narrative. Lardinois has studied the use of *gnomai* and their expressive usage by various characters. Brown has shown how addresses can be modified to convey special meaning. All demonstrate Homer's mastery of traditional narrative style.[7]

Similes seem equally based in the tradition. This is clear in their customary placement and topics. Similes appear in repeated contexts but can also be suppressed in such passages; familiar objects and actions in the narrative suggest the use of the same simile subjects. Yet when the poet does use a simile, he has made a significant narratological move in choosing an indirect mode of presentation over a simpler, more straightforward description. In both modes he calls special attention to an action or an object, but in choosing indirectness he is inviting his audience to blend their familiarity with the narrative item and their understanding of the removed world of the simile in order to judge how each affects the presentation of the other. As a result, a responsible critic must not only be conscious of the poet's goals in choosing to use a simile within a tight narrative structure—but must also consider his reasons for avoiding a more direct presentation.

The strong contrast in narrative styles in the *Iliad* between book 1's description of the quarrel and book 2's preparation for the next day's activities makes the point. In book 1 there are only four short similes, but in book 2 there are twenty, many of them long and elaborate. In book 1 Homer wants to build the issues of the quarrel and its effects cumulatively. In book 2 he is eager to bring his audience to a deeper understanding of Agamemnon as the leader of the army; consequently, he introduces a series of similes—indirect descriptions of the Greek army's actions. Direct presentation of these actions would make the army look as though it were in chaos, but that is not Homer's point; the effect that Agamemnon's commands have on the army is more important than the clear structuring of their actions. The audience, which is familiar with the possible alternative ways of presenting the action of book 2, will realize that the poet's focused use of similes demands judgment. Because of their long experience of hearing epic traditions used and varied they will realize that here the customary similes for the movements of a great army disappear or are consciously weakened. Subliminally they are being told that the great Greek expeditionary army — the army that will appear in its full strength shortly in the catalogue, the army that is destined to defeat the Trojans — is no longer acting like a great army. In seeking reasons for this weak and confused performance the audience must realize that the opening of the book has put the focus on the inept commands of Agamemnon. The contrast between the numbers of similes in books 1 and 2 is sharp and follows closely the poet's plan for developing this theme.[8] My assumption is that no simile, long or short, appears by accident.

For the most part the subject matter of the Homeric similes seems to have been taken from a limited set of topics. The process of classifying the subjects of the similes as well as the contexts in which they frequently occur is made difficult both by the incompleteness of the oral record and the poet's freedom to make a choice. Yet it is possible on the basis of consistent usage to separate most of the similes in the Homeric poems into at least sixteen subject groups. In much the same way, the contexts in which Homer often placed similes can be determined by the regularity with which the simile was selected from among a small group of alternatives available at specific junctures.[9]

The poet chose such subjects in repeated contexts because they had proven apt for the stories he usually told, could be adjusted to suit scenes that frequently occurred in such stories, could be extended by drawing on the stock of phrases the tradition had developed, and — perhaps most important — were familiar to his audience.[10] Undoubtedly there were other simile families in existence that left only slight traces in the texts, and others that have left no trace at all. While it is impossible to construct a full classification of simile subjects used in the large body of early Greek narrative, at least in the repetition of these topics and the consistency of their employment in similar contexts there is evidence for significant influence of the tradition in the individual simile's formation. Such a tradition left the poet free to move in a variety of directions or to adjust emphasis by adding or deleting items. And, of equal importance, this ongoing tradition had been implanting itself continuously in the minds of the audience.

THE SIMILEME[11]

It is easy to respond to each simile as though it were a small, individually composed lyric. Among the many similes that have attracted numerous admirers, the most famous is probably the picture of stars at night describing the Trojan watchfires scattered over the dark field:

> As when in the sky the stars about the moon's shining
> are seen in all their glory, when the air has fallen to stillness,
> and all the watch places of the hills are clear, and the high shoulders,
> and the ravines, as endless bright air spills from the heavens,
> and all the stars are seen, to make glad the heart of a shepherd;
> such in their numbers blazed the watchfires....
>
> (*Iliad* 8.555–60)

Visualization is an important element in Homeric composition and communication.[12] But I would argue that the complex language of Homeric diction is no less important. Not only does it focus on pictorial features; it also carries meanings that have been derived from previous performances and are conveyed by the poet as the latest version of the larger picture he is painting. The nuances and the enrichment of each new presentation are dependent on the audience's recollection of the previous performance — and that performance drew both on the visual features necessary for a full appreciation of the poet's image and on their experience of previous verbal descriptions. Not only do they hear each phrase as a small component in the bigger picture; they also hear it in a framework of other phrases that have been tempered and shaped by previous usage. As filled with visual observations as this watchfire simile seems, it is also firmly based in oral tradition. Lines 557–58 are repeated as an identical two-line unit in book 16 in a different context (16.299f.);[13] the end of line 557 appears twice as a formula in the *Hymn to Apollo* (22 and 144), and in the first half of each line there is only a very slight remodeling of the Homeric line. In addition, the final line adding the rejoicing observer is repeated several times with a variety of different subjects (*Iliad* 11.683; *Ody.* 6.106; and *Hymn to Demeter* 232).

None of this analysis should lessen the emotional impact of the simile or dampen the response so strongly felt by its audience. Rather, this particular simile should be appreciated both as the expression of an individual poet and as a product of motifs which have been used in past performances. Homer's audience could avail themselves of their experience of these subjects in lines used elsewhere to enrich their appreciation of the constructed image; this more precise awareness of the traditional alternatives—verbal and nonverbal—available to the poet also deepens a critic's understanding of the poet's artistry in this and other similes. I will call the mental structure underlying each simile the "simileme"—in itself not fully expressible but composed of repeated actions and objects and alternative modes of expression, all of which have become associated through frequent usage. The individual simile is the single poet's particularized composition shaped to fit the full narrative passage; the simileme is the nonverbal background material shared by poet and audience—in other words, the full range of possibilities for dealing with the standard topics that have been developed through a long series of performances.[14]

Given the partial nature of the evidence for early Greek narrative, the definition of the simileme is inexact, but the attempt is supported by the impressive regularity with which discrete elements appear in separate simile families. Because these elements are not necessarily repeated in the same phrasing, it is not productive to use the type of close formulaic analysis developed by Milman Parry. In addition, Parry's studies depended on a formula of frozen meaning: every phrase, in the classic Parry definition, must have an "essential idea." While critics have had understandable difficulty in rejecting Parry's findings as a whole, there have been telling criticisms of his conclusions, especially in the area of the strictly univalent meaning of the formulas.[15]

As a simple instance, in book 22 of the *Iliad* Apollo mocks Achilles by asking:

> Why, son of Peleus, are you *chasing me with swift feet* [*posin tacheessi diokeis*]?
>
> (22.8)

Later Priam, looking from the wall of the town, says:

> Now again around the town of Priam
> is the divine Achilles *chasing him with swift feet* [*posin tacheessi diokei*] ...
>
> (22.172–73; my italics)

Later Athena in the guise of Deiphobos begins to encourage his brother Hector by saying:

> Brother, to be sure the fleet Achilles presses you
> around the town of Priam, *chasing you with swift feet* [*posin tacheessi diokon*].
>
> (22.229–30; my italics)

"Swift feet" does seem to be expressing an essential idea (= speed) in each of the above lines and does appear in a metrically identical position. In association with Achilles it gains added force from his famous epithet "swift-footed" in its various formulations[16] and is probably used pointedly on these three occasions in book 22 to enhance the threat to Hector.

It is possible that this phrase, *posin tacheessi diokeis/ei/on*, has special attachment to Achilles, perhaps deriving from a lost earlier story. There is, however, one other appearance of this formula, *Iliad* 8.338:

> As when a dog snatches at a wild boar or lion
> from behind *chasing him with swift feet* [*posin tacheessi diokon*].

Here the phrase has been deprived of all association with Achilles by being placed within the simile world, used to describe a dog, and applied to Hector.

As language develops through usage, words gain varied connotations, all of which are heard each time the word is used even though certain of these connotations will be immediately suppressed as irrelevant to the context. There will still remain a variety of meanings attached to the words and phrases in a simile, all of which must be coordinated to determine the poet's meaning. Foley calls such a collection of potential meanings "metonymic pathways."[17] These clusters of expanded meaning derive from what he describes as "traditional referentiality":

> Traditional referentiality . . . entails the invoking of a context that is enormously larger and more echoic than the text or work itself, that brings the lifeblood of generations of poems and performances to the individual performance or text. Each element in the phraseology or narrative thematics stands not simply for that singular instance but for the plurality and multiformity that are beyond the reach of textualization. From the perspective of traditional context, these elements are foci for meaning, still points in the exchange of meaning between an always impinging tradition and the momentary and nominal fossilization of a text or version.[18]

The expressive power of Homer's language is increased by its continual evolution within a narrative tradition.[19] The broad background of tales and heroes, which was developed over centuries, enriched the meanings of the repeated words and phrases and kept them fresh in the minds of poet and audience. Given the multivalent meanings that can be assumed for most words and phrases in the Homeric poems, the poet must limit these meanings to those he deems important. He has three means of accomplishing such limitation:

1. The suppression of elements that could be associated with the phrase but would be misleading
2. The enhancement of elements focusing on the desired meaning[20]
3. The combination of selected items from among the customary alternatives in order to control the meaning to be assigned by the audience[21]

Each of these methods allows the poet to refine his meaning by working within the traditional diction.

The four type scenes of arming in the *Iliad* provide good illustrations of all these methods. In the scene describing the arming of Paris (3.330–38) most of the particularizing elements elsewhere used to develop the basic form are suppressed; only the mention of his brother Lycaon as owner of the breastplate is added to the basic form of the type scene and, indeed, there is very little that is special about Paris as a warrior. However, more specific and targeted omissions are possible. In book 16 the stated rejection of Patroclus' ability to manage the Pelian ash spear is a particularly pointed removal of a customary item in order to emphasize his vulnerability and exposure in playing the role of Achilles (16.131–46). Many elements are added to the arming of Agamemnon, including the richly inlaid breastplate of Cinyras, the thick and elaborately decorated shield, the crested helmet, and the gleaming spears that excite the thunder of Athena and Hera (11.17–46). It is significant that all of these elements concern the external appearance of the Greek leader rather than his ability as a warrior—(as in the arming of Patroclus); while Agamemnon may look like a warrior, he needs Zeus' support. The arming of Achilles illustrates the third method, the combination of various alternative elements to accompany the best of the Achaeans (19.369–91): similes, enhancement of decoration, description of the hero's spirit, and the addition of the Pelian spear that was denied to Patroclus.[22]

These same methods are used in designing the individual similes. Repeated similes are evidence that there were some passages carried in the poet's mind as units, and repeated sections of similes and even individual lines reveal certain phrases or blocks of lines that could be added to or deleted from the basic form.[23] Thus the short lion simile, "like a lion," can be regarded as the basic lion simile with all elements but one—the subject—deleted; extended lion similes can likewise be considered adaptations of the basic lion simile made by deleting those elements that provide incorrect guidance to the precise meaning of the passage.

Such gatherings of customary elements were so present in the folk memory that the poet could produce a specific simile to suit his narrative with confidence that the audience would appreciate the adaptations he had made. To find the fundamental unity beneath the diversity presented by a series of similes requires, as a first step, the identification of topics used repeatedly and with sufficient frequency to be regarded as customary simile subjects.[24] An effective method must produce a list of the categories that the poet used in individual similes as well as alternative elements—even contradictory elements—within each category.

Most critics agree that there are simile families centered on the topics of lions and boars, fire, wind, trees, and gods. Yet the challenge, and the second step in finding similes' unity, is to define the qualities that mark separate similes as derived from a common simileme in the minds of poet and audience. A numerical test as the sole criterion is inadequate because the mere counting of surviving examples within highly selective original evidence will not produce compelling conclusions. There were undoubtedly other equally traditional simile subjects that are unrecognizable because they occurred only once in the two surviving epics. A more adequate method rests on the awareness that the poet chose one or two simile families frequently at specific narrative junctures; thus a major determining factor in the association of a simile family with a specific context is the subject.[25] The seven identically repeated similes that appear often in the same context offer strong corroboration of the principle that frequency of usage at a specific narrative juncture is significant in establishing a simile family.[26]

The third criterion in identifying families is the most stringent and enlightening of all: the use of common motifs for each simile in the family.[27] The tree similes, of which there are fourteen in the two poems, provide a model (thirteen in the *Iliad*, one in the *Odyssey*);[28] they appear only in contexts describing a warrior who is either dead (or about to die) or unmoving.²⁹ Thus tree similes seem a legitimate category on the basis of their frequent occurrence and also their consistent usage in defined contexts. However, they appear even more tightly organized as a family because they are constructed from a limited set of repeated elements. In chart 6 the fourteen similes are listed in the first column; then each element—essentially each noun and verb—within the simile is identified as the contributor of a generic type of information. For example, the simile of the poplar describing the fallen Simoesius at *Iliad* 4.482 can be analyzed into categories as follows:

Species = poplar
Locale = marsh
Action = tree felled
Agent or force = chariot maker
Tool = "shining iron"
Purpose of action = to make a chariot wheel

The chart shows that the other thirteen tree similes can be analyzed into similar categories. Three, 4.482 and 13.389 = 16.482, contain the full series of elements, but, more importantly, the nouns and verbs in all the tree similes can be easily assigned to one of the six categories. Of course, each simile has a few specific details that are not repeated, thus cannot be so categorized, and their status must remain indeterminate.

From this chart it seems possible to derive a simple list of the basic elements present to the poet's mind when he chose to employ a tree simile—thus, the tree simileme: a tree in a specific location stands or falls under the attack of an outside force that may employ a specific tool and may lead to a specific use for the tree. Of course, there is a fair amount of flexibility in the basic simileme for adding or deleting elements. Not only can the poet choose freely what items to include, but the choice of one specific item can limit or preclude the use of other variants: if the wind uproots a tree, then no purpose need be given for felling the tree, nor is any specific tool identified. As a result, motifs are assigned to separate columns on the chart when they seem to represent independent choices: the tree may be felled by means of a tool with or without the specific mention of a human agent or his purpose (13.178).

Pietro Pucci's analysis of the two lion similes at 12.299 and *Ody.* 6.130 offers a clear example of the degree of adaptation available to the poet and his audience in drawing on the simileme.³⁰ In both similes Homer chooses the lion to represent the hero, but when he comes to the lion's motivation to kill other animals, there are variants: in *Iliad* 12 he is ordered to kill by his bold heart; in *Odyssey* 6, by his belly (*keletai de he thumos / gaster*). Pucci writes: "We are encouraged to recognize the *same* animal in both passages, as if the divergence in the two descriptions was dictated by nothing more than their different contexts" (160). The role of the poet is admittedly crucial in the design of each simile, as is the ability of the co-creating, experienced audience to decode the intent of the different choices from the full simileme:

> And yet this reading faces an impenetrable opacity. Certainly the allusion is there and lets itself be read, but what sense should we grant it? Should we attribute to the *Odyssey* a humorous intent and imply that the *Odyssey* smiles at the high-minded lions of the *Iliad*? Or should we assume the timidity of the text and say that for its tradition a king is always comparable to a lion? Probably both answers are correct in the sense that the Odyssean "allusion" can mean at the same time the need for the poet to follow the traditional patterns and also his need to get out of them. (161)

It is clear that both the poet and his audience share the inheritance from the tradition. In analyzing Homeric composition scholars have compellingly supported a generative process dependent on mental constructs. Nagler has applied a model based in Gestalt psychology that explains how formulaic and typological scenes express general conceptions. But a Gestalt (or "mental template") has associations with innate knowledge shared by all audience members, while the simileme is solely man-made and thus in all cases can be changed and developed to suit narrative needs.[31] Fillmore developed a helpful concept in the "semantic frame," a "system of categories structured in accordance with some motivating context";[32] but such contexts include commonly known areas, such as the structure of the face, as well as elements learned from the broader experience of life. In similes the physical scenes (e.g., lions) seem mostly derived from poetic typologies. Thus while many features of simile composition are made understandable by parallels to both Gestalt structures and frame semantics, neither is a precise guide, fully adequate to define the Homeric simile as the product of customary placement and repeated topics, all expressed in a traditional diction.

In addition, there is a much more consciously creative, even possibly individualistic, potential to the form underlying the simile. The simile takes its being from the surrounding passage; in origin the mental construct underlying the individual simile was created and shaped to parallel the recurring actions of early Greek narrative.[33] Just as Homeric Greek is a specialized language developed to sing the old stories of Greece, so also the similemes were developed to provide easy comparison to the events that are customary in such stories.

For these reasons I have chosen the term "simileme" to represent the basic objects and actions that comprise each traditional simile family; this form is carried in the folk memory as an inheritance from previous generations of practicing poets but probably is impossible to express fully in any single example. Throughout decades of use the simileme remained an entity that was constantly developed by its redeployment in familiar contexts. The most important feature of the simileme is its flexibility; as similes are the product of human imagination, a wide variety of individual similes can be created by recombination, deletion, or addition of customary and familiar elements — and also, undoubtedly, at moments of creative innovation or discovery. Nagler has well described the special quality of Homeric expression: "All is traditional on the generative level, all original on the level of performance."[34] In drawing on the simileme, the poet is exercising his artistic choice within the traditional devices and language of early Greek narrative in order to tell his own story

Several general points should be made about the simileme using the chart constructed from the tree similes. First, the simileme is not a simple picture but a flexible and functional collection of variables that can be — and generally must be — adapted to a variety of situations.[35] The tree simileme contains both complementary and contradictory components that the poet can mold into an understandable scene on each individual occasion. Therefore the analytical category of "tree similes," which seems so neat as a classification, is in reality an unorganized gathering of relevant but not necessarily consistent components, all of which were present in the poet's mind anytime he chose to use this topic, but any one of which could be enhanced, diminished, or passed over as he considered the needs of his ongoing narrative. A short simile would best be defined as the suppression of all components of the simileme except one; the repeated similes are the product of the same series of choices — perhaps reinforced by the poet's recalling a striking image that he created on a previous occasion.

To deal with similemes one must understand the choice or rejection of variants. Nimis views a simile as an encoded passage that produces meaning only by being perceived through its intertextual parallels. He draws on Riffaterre in asserting that such a passage "is not an ideal configuration existing on a higher ontological plane than any of its 'realizations'; it is itself a system of signs whose poetic transformation results in the generation of variants of itself."[36] Yet there is one powerful element that I find missing in this reading of Homeric similes—the oral tradition. Any theory about Homeric expression must leave room for the seven identically repeated similes in the Homeric poems; in these similes Homer excludes all variants. The source of these passages is not necessarily a totally memorized model, but each passage can arise from the poet's recollection of having sung such a passage before—most likely in a situation that may not even survive for us. Thus the repeated horse similes used for Paris and Hector are not best interpreted as an original and a copy; rather, both similes have the same ontological status (6.506 and 15.263).

At the same time the mind of the poet contains a preexistent archetype that strongly influences the individual similes in the text. The horse simile, for example, has a consistent unwarlike tone that makes the whole suitable only for certain narratives. The audience of each passage will realize that there is a basic poetic unit of a certain length and tone that has a sufficiently fixed nature to withstand attempts to introduce variants.

This more fixed and lasting simile sketch is parallel to the basic type scene or even the shorter formulaic expressions that can be shifted within the line or split to accommodate new needs. The force preserving this archetypal simile is the conservatism of the oral tradition itself. The poet is not compelled to use one and only one form of a type scene or to keep the formula as a fixed unit in its position in the line, but the texts show a strong tendency to reuse the same formula unless there is a reason to change. It seems clear that at certain junctures of the narrative the use of the simile was a suggestion from the tradition which the poet could either accept, reject, or modify; similarly, at certain junctures the poet knew from experience that certain topics he had used successfully before were particularly apt. These suggestions led the poet to reuse simile subjects and phrasing—even to repeat certain long similes six times word for word.

Second, each simileme normally occurs to the poet in a limited number of narrative contexts. If the warrior stays fixed and unmoving, so does the tree; if the warrior falls, the tree falls. Even Achilles is proleptically described by tree similes when his mother realizes that his death is near; Telemachus receives the same simile when Eumaeus reports that his life is threatened by the suitors (18.56, 57, 437, 438, and *Ody.* 14.175). The tree simileme is not so much an analytical category as a description of the poet's repeated response on occasions when his story returns to familiar narrative junctures.

Third, neither the simileme nor its components are necessarily attached to repeated phrases; no one of the motifs listed on the chart is expressed through a limited set of formulae. There are four similes centered on the oak tree, all extended. In two (12.132 and 14.414) the oak is introduced in different phrases, neither of which is parallel to formulae in other parts of the Homeric poems. However, in the other two passages (13.389 and 16.482) the oak is included as part of a repeated three-line unit. The opening line of this repeated simile reveals alternative species of trees: "He fell as when an oak falls, or a poplar, or a tall pine." As a result the simileme offers different expressions to specify the oak tree; two of these expressions appear only once in the two epics, while the other two seem formulaic. Further, at 4.482 the poplar is introduced with a different word from that at 13.389 and 16.482, as is the pine at 5.560. The same is true for the words for leaves and shoots in the longer similes at 4.482, 13.178, and 17.53; yet the short similes at 18.56, 18.437, and *Ody.* 14.175 are identical in the choice of word, occur at the same position in the line, and are clearly formulaic. Likewise, there is little repetition of formulae in the element of the craftsmen, their cutting tools, their act of cutting, the mountain peak, or the intended use for the fallen tree. While the simileme depends for its existence on being expressed in specific words, the choice of those words is a separate act.

The most compelling proof for the nonverbal existence of the tree simileme is found in a two other passages that draw upon its elements even though they are not similes. Clearest is 11.86:

> at the hour when a woodcutter prepares his meal
> in the glades of a mountain when he has tired his hands
> cutting tall trees . . .

The elements shared with the tree simileme are the cutter, his act of cutting, and the mountain locale. Likewise, 23.117:

> but when they came to the valleys of many-fountained Ida,
> then in haste they cut the lofty oaks with their long-edged bronze;
> they fell with a great crash. . . .

Again the poet uses the elements of cutting, a cutting implement, the oak trees, and the mountain.[37] Each scene seems derived in its motifs, and occasionally in its phrasing, from the same model as the tree similes. However, in each of these passages—one an indication of time analogous to the formal independence of the simile, one a scene from the ongoing narrative—the poet has drawn upon categories contained in the tree simileme, but the passages do not occur in the limited contexts standard for tree similes, and in the first two cases they do not function as similes. Thus the word "simileme" is useful in a study analyzing similes but has applications to forms broader than and different from similes; in Homer's mind there seem to have been nonverbal collections of elements, each of which, in whatever words they are expressed, could be conjoined and adapted for a variety of purposes within the poem.

If the form and usage of similes developed over a long period, it is surprising that there are only seven identically repeated extended similes in the two poems,[38] but this number rises significantly if one considers repetitions at a level deeper than the verbal expression.[39] In other words, since simile motifs are often repeated in varied words and phrases, the simileme appears to exercise its force at a level that is nonverbal.

The tree similes derive from a simileme that is easy to analyze because there are relatively few examples in the Homeric text, but the characteristics of this simileme can be found in the other, more complex simile families: lions and boars, wind and wave, fire, and gods. The charts that appear in the appendix list the repeated motifs common to these similemes and show the flexibility available to the poet in choosing among and adapting these elements within a limited number of contexts.

In order to fully appreciate the achievement of the individual poet, it is necessary to develop a method that will not only allow critics to perceive the nonverbal form of the simile but also to be conscious of shadings the poet could assign to each component. If a poet chooses a lion simile, then all of the elements carried with the simileme are instantly present; he must decide either to include or omit each in forming the individual simile.[40] He is free to choose words that he has used or heard before—or he may manipulate his language to introduce new phrasing. Of course, context is always important. Since the poet is attempting to embed his simile within his story, he has good reason to use words from the surrounding narrative to express parallel features of the simile. Thus each simile is the result of a series of individual choices from among alternatives that are drawn from both nonverbal and verbal traditions, operating independently and together, and are heavily influenced by the context.[41] Any simile so produced is a unique and complex creation of the poet's imagination.

As the largest of the simile families, the lion and boar similes provide the best examples of the variables that the poet manipulates in bringing the simileme to verbal expression (see chart 2).[42] It is immediately evident that in seeking a parallel for his narrative the poet is thinking far more widely than the single point of comparison.[43] This simileme comprises at least five major motifs, other than the animal: number, attack or attacked, hunter or victim, time or place, and other variables.[44]

Number. The comparison is sometimes to one animal and sometimes to several. Generally the number in the narrative is repeated in the simile; often a precise dual matches a pair in the text. Yet these variations seem to make no difference in the list of motifs comprising the simile. And there are even occasions where the numbers between narrative and simile are in disagreement, such as 15.323, where Apollo's threat to the Greeks is compared to two animals.

Main Actions (attack/attacked). Many similes are linked to the narrative by a repetition of an action word:

> When Menelaus, dear to Ares, saw him
> striding forward before the army with big steps —
> as a lion *rejoices* coming upon a large carcass,
> finding either a horned stag or a wild goat —
> and he was hungry; he ravenously devoured it,
> even though swift dogs and sturdy young men rush upon him —
> just so Menelaus *rejoiced* seeing Alexander. . . .
>
> (3.23; my italics)

It would be easy to define the function of Homeric similes if their main action verbs were always drawn from the surrounding narrative; the components in the lion/boar simileme would be almost automatically generated by parallel verbs of attack. But such direct linkage does not occur often enough to define the narrative action as the major source of the simile's phrasing.

It is not uncommon for the action in the simile to be so complex that it is compared to at least two movements in the narrative. For example, the simile at 5.554 sketches the lifetime of two lions: they were raised in the mountains, preyed on cattle and sheep, and finally are slain by men. The surrounding narrative contains a precise parallel to this whole story: Crethon and Orsilochus were two fighters, well trained in warfare; they came to fight at Troy, and now they are slain by Aeneas. The verbs in the simile, however, do not repeat those in the narrative: in the narrative the stages of growth are marked by *genesthen, hebesante, eis Ilion hepesthen, telos thanatoio kalupsen, damente kappeseten*; in the simile the verbs marking the parallel stages are *etrapheten, harpazonte . . . keraizeton, katektathen*. The verbs in the simile describe quite precisely three stages of development, yet the emphasis of the simile is on the single action of being slain. In addition, several similes are built from two different points of comparison in the narrative (11.61, 12.145, 13.137, 13.491, and 15.623). These are important observations because they indicate that the poet seeks parallels for full scenes in the narrative rather than creating tight comparisons to individual actions or words.

Supplementary Figures (victims/hunters). Although a variety of other forces confront the lion/boar, the similes of this family present only two basic scenes: the lion as predator (in which case the opponents are limited to sheep, cattle, oxen, goats, or deer) and lion/boar defending his own life from those who hunt or stalk him (farmers and herdsmen, hunters, or dogs). Of course, the major subjects are distinguishable in that the boar is not a carnivore and thus does not prey on other animals for food, although he does confront the same hunters. And there are some similes where the lion challenges a boar in a fight for their lives. Generally the actions in lion/boar similes are quite limited; there is no mention of the lion at play, or asleep, or standing majestically in a king-of-the-beasts pose, or in a family scene among his mate and cubs. This restriction of the breadth of scenes results from the simileme's status as the major source of the lion similes: that is, the poet usually tended to work within the poetic tradition and did not draw on broader observations of nature.[45]

Time or place. Chart 2 reveals only three further standard components in the lion/boar simileme: the confidence or fear of the animal, the location in space or time, and his hunger or thirst. In each case there are alternatives. The locations are most often mountains; otherwise farms or folds, a roadside, a marsh, a wood or thickets, the lion's lair, over a victim, or over young lions; night is the only time cited, probably because night is the time for animals' hunting and stalking activities. Such a variety of alternatives offers the poet many choices in generating individual similes. The phrasing for several locations and times is familiar from other simile families as well as narrative scenes—another indication that the decision to include the element of location was taken independently of other choices; the phrase *nyktos amolgoi* is shared by both similes and narrative, and *pannychoi egressontes/a* occurs only three times, twice in a repeated simile and once in the narrative in Athena's words to Odysseus (*Ody.* 20.53). The traditional diction was adapted to the needs of the simile just as easily as to those of the narrative.

HOMER AND HIS AUDIENCE

This exploration of the complex traditional material underlying each simile shows the necessity of including the audience as a reliable co-creating participant in the production of the Homeric poems. First, the audience could appreciate Homer's choice to sing a simile because they knew that there were other customary ways of continuing the narrative that had been passed over. From a lifetime of hearing previous performances the audience could hear the enrichment of the narrative that Homer created through the indirectness of the simile as well his adjustments for its length or shortness. They could then evaluate the choice of subject, since they were aware of the various alternate similemes that the tradition made available to the poet for specific narrative junctures. The audience would not only listen to the details of the individual image and appreciate its contribution to the whole passage; their awareness of the basic sileme would also make possible a complex kind of coded communication—not only through words and phrases but also through silent communication (e.g., repeated motifs with conventional connotations, consciously excluded options). Homeric epic was a joint creation of a trained poet and an experienced audience, in which the skill of the poet was judged not on the basis of free invention but rather on the effectiveness of his choices from among known alternatives.[46]

One of the clearest examples of this silent communication occurs at *Odyssey* 4.791. Penelope is in her bed wondering whether her son has been slain, and then drifts off to sleep:

Such things as occur to a lion in his [*deisas*] fear in the midst of a crowd
of men when they draw a treacherous ring around him,
these are the things which she [*hormainousan*] pondered as sweet sleep
came upon her. . . .

The Simileme · 31

This simile occurs at an appropriate juncture: one of the standard uses of the simile is to provide a parallel scene through which the poet can express the psychological state of a person in the narrative.[47] In addition, the simile is molded to suit the situation of the beleaguered Penelope, who is virtually imprisoned in her own chamber by the suitors. Yet though it may seem unsuitable for the poet to have chosen the subject of the lion, with its customary battlefield associations, that is precisely the point. Both poet and audience knew that the simileme of farm animals was readily available, as well as those of deer or birds,[48] all of which would provide a tone more consistent with the unwarlike narrative. Yet the poet rejected these topics in order to use an image that provided more than a superficial parallel. With no overt explanation he has drawn upon his audience's familiarity with the tradition to describe a Penelope who may be entrapped and threatened but who is also a lioness in character — a fit mate for Odysseus, the lion.[49] The men in this simile may momentarily have the upper hand, but they are contending with a lion (note the acknowledgment of the tradition in the use of the masculine, *deisas*), and there are many similes that testify to the resourcefulness and strength of other lions who emerge victorious over men and hunting dogs. When the poet suppresses any suggestion that the lion is killed or the lion is triumphant, he leaves his audience to imagine the continuation with an enhanced respect for the capabilities and resources of Penelope.

Or, the reverse — the poet may use scenes from more lyrical, gentler nature to describe warlike elements in the narrative:

> As a star appears among other stars in the darkness of the night,
> the evening star, which stands as the fairest star in the heavens,
> just so was the gleam from the sharp-pointed spear which Achilles
> balanced in his right hand devising evil for the noble Hector.
>
> (22.317)

Again, knowledge of the tradition enriches communication. Similes are constantly used to describe the gleam of weapons[50] — here the death weapon at the final moment of the battle between Achilles and Hector. Homer has gone out of his way to present this star as "the most beautiful star in the heavens," in contrast to the language used of Achilles, which focuses on his monomaniacal, ugly pursuit of vengeance. The simile highlights the difference between Achilles, the aberrant force, and the background of the wider world of nature that was introduced with the long description of Achilles' shield and has been developed by a combination of settings and similes throughout his aristeia.[51] Against this background of nature as normalcy, the motivations of the warrior appear distorted and grotesque—a judgment that will be confirmed by Achilles in book 24, though at this point he is too enmeshed in his own limited concerns to see it. At the moment when Hector is fatally wounded, the poet places a traditional simile at a customary juncture in the narrative but fills the broader passage with meaning by emphasizing the contrast between nature's beauty and Achilles' destructive intent. Such communication is silent but effective.

Evaluations of individual similes depend on the audience's recognition of the formal features of similes as well as explicit parallels between simile and narrative. Similes are attached to the narrative by a limited and constantly repeated set of phrases (e.g., "just as when," "like a [lion] who," and so on) and usually share at least one parallel element with the narrative. It is important for the audience to realize through an explicit marker that the poet has begun a section that requires experience of the simile tradition for full appreciation. In addition, a prominent point may serve to anchor the simile tightly—and perhaps mechanically—within the context both before and after the simile and thus contribute to the surface impression of "threaded speech" that is so common a characteristic of Homeric verse. Yet all the time the simileme as an independent whole has been present in the poet's mind, continues to offer many alternative motifs to be developed, and provides the poet with opportunities to draw multiple connections to the narrative.

A clear example of a simile framed by standard linking phrases, presenting only a single point of connection, and significantly enriching the full passage through artful extensions is the famous lyric simile at *Iliad* 8.555 describing the numbers of the Trojan watchfires at night (cited earlier). Formally this simile is introduced with the customary "just as when" and is reattached to the narrative by an equally familiar "so many were the fires." The single point of comparison is the number of stars that describe the number of fires; this is made clear through an explicit A B A structure of quantitative words: "*many* fires," "*all* the stars," and "so *many* were the fires" (554, 559, and 560f.). This single point of connection, however, scarcely explains the effectiveness of this simile either as an image in itself or as a marker of this pivotal point in the story. The poet has chosen to express a fuller form of the fire simileme by adding a series of details to the picture. As the audience experiences each added phrase, the scope is widened. First, there is the narrow view of bright stars around the moon; then the vision widens to include the landscape of peaks and thickets on the hills. Next the clear air pours forth from the heavens and all the stars are seen. Finally the poet puts a viewer into the scene: "and the shepherd rejoices in his heart." Only at this moment does the movement of the simile emerge. Each element in the widening scene has been revealing the view of the whole as it comes clear to the shepherd. First he sees the brightest stars; then—as his eyes adjust—he begins to pick out the less distinct landscape; then he is able to see all the stars through the clear air, and this wider scene stirs joy in him. The poet has not only used his language to tell his audience that number is his concern; he has molded the nonverbal elements in the simileme to create in his audience the experience of one man as he progressively grasps the fuller scene. It is almost a time-lapse image; the poet leads his audience from a formulaic beginning to the profound experience of a lone man whose eyes only gradually arrive at a broader and finally almost infinite vision.[52] Then when the poet leads this audience back to the narrative with the simple formulaic phrase "so many were the fires," he will have given no literal number but will have created the feelings stirred in an observer who lets his eyes dwell on a whole heaven full of stars. Confining interpretation to the single point of comparison will ruin the effect of this powerful interaction between simile and narrative.

In general, Homer's literal phrasing, while seemingly indispensable to the poet, is only one guide to his thought processes.[53] Homer has themes, conceptions, and imaginative passages that must be expressed within the language that he inherited from the tradition, a language that is largely designed to describe concrete objects and physical actions. The consistency with which the poet is able to make a simile respond significantly to the larger narrative movement reveals a mind striving to create a particularized complex image from preexistent building blocks.[54] A number of similemes are so firmly fixed in the minds of his audience that the poet can include in one simile a series of suggestive comparisons to the narrative from the literal to the metaphoric; the devices he uses repeatedly are the components of the simileme that he then must express in specific phrasing. In putting the simileme into words he creates a vivid picture both by including complementary objects and suppressing alternatives that he felt were inappropriate. It is the role of the audience to appreciate the individual simile as the mental product of suppressed alternatives—and then to fit the decoded comparison into the developing larger narrative.[55]

Above I defined a short simile as a version of the simileme in which all the components but one had been passed over. While short similes are often treated as virtually meaningless formulaic filler, Homer seems to have employed these similes with the realization that they conjure up the full pattern of the simileme for the audience even though only one component is mentioned. The organizing force of the simileme underlies all similes in that family, long and short, and the full awareness of the background is vital if these similes are to be effective in their context.

A compelling example of the allusive potential in a short simile occurs at *Iliad* 24.572, where Achilles leaves old Priam and goes to arrange the return of Hector's body:

> The old man grew afraid and was obedient to his words,
> but the son of Peleus went forth from the tent like a lion. . . .

In the final books of the *Iliad* Achilles has been compared to a lion three times: 18.318—the grieving lion that tracks a hunter who has snatched away his cubs and seeks vengeance (= Achilles mourning for the dead Patroclus); 20.164—the angry and dangerous lion (= Achilles going to fight Aeneas); and 24.41—the cruel lion who attacks the flocks to get dinner (= Achilles savaging the body of Hector). The poet has formed each of these similes by choosing to enhance certain features of the simileme and to suppress others. Through this process of adaptation the details in each simile come to contain several connections to the surrounding narrative, and the tone of each simile is appropriately warlike in describing Achilles' attitude and actions.

By the time Achilles meets Priam in book 24, he has decided to return the body, and in a quiet and private conversation he and Priam find a wider conception of mankind's interdependence. At the end of the *Iliad* Achilles transcends his society—yet this development is not supported by that last simile of the lion. It is only a short formulaic simile; yet even this short mention of the lion should evoke the whole simileme for the audience. They will be reminded of the usual warlike context for such subjects and may even recall the three lion similes that have already described Achilles in his aristeia. There is no way to avoid the conclusion that the lion simile on the surface (i.e., without the contribution of the co-creative audience) is inappropriate when Achilles is trying to renounce the demands of the warrior ethic, yet this inappropriateness echoes the ambiguity involved in the ending of the *Iliad*. Achilles is a tentative member of a new generation. He is not presented as the full-fledged spokesman for a different code or a new world; he is still the hero who will fight and die before Troy. Priam protests the inevitability of war when he tells Achilles that they will all fight again after the truce for Hector's funeral "if it is necessary"; and Achilles in his brief response merely acknowledges that the war will continue (24.665–70).

In the speech immediately preceding the short lion simile Achilles has shown his familiar impatience:

> No longer drive my spirit in its grief,
> old man, lest I not leave you alone in my tent
> even though you are a suppliant, and I violate the commands of Zeus.

These are the words of a recently converted and uncertain new man; the reflex of the warrior code is strong in him and will break out with disastrous consequences if he is pushed. He is openly telling Priam to respect the fragile nature of his newfound behavior. Thus the lion simile, though short, does incorporate the full simileme of the lion/warrior with overtones appropriate to a hesitant, tentative action based only on an inchoate sense of the appropriate response.[56] A longer lion simile would overemphasize the usual spirit of the bold warrior; here the short simile with the exclusion of the murderous activities of the lion and other features that are associated with warriors is a subtle yet effective means of presenting the warrior king who finds himself guaranteeing high honor for his enemy.

In form short similes often share the same formulaic beginning as extended ones, since long similes are usually phrased as a series of motifs that are added to the initial brief statement of the subject. Thus the presence of a simile is marked clearly, even though the audience does not know whether it will be long or short. Once their attention is caught, the short simile effectively fulfills clear poetic purposes:

- introduction of the simileme without retarding the narrative movement for a full pause (best illustrated by the sequence of god similes in *Iliad* book 5, which, though short, do repeatedly emphasize the confusion of men and gods, one of the major themes of the book — 5.438, 459, and 884)[57]
- introduction of a subject that will appear later (cross-referencing or framing — e.g., 18.56–7 = 18.437–38; *Ody.* 6.231 = *Ody.* 23.158)
- introduction of a subject with no need for developing it into a small story paralleling or predicting the direction of the narrative — in other words,

the poet can invoke the subject while leaving room for his audience's speculation.⁵⁸

The widespread usage of the short simile demonstrates its usefulness in providing another bit of flexibility for an audience well versed in traditional technique.

SIMILE AND SIMILEME

In summary, the simileme exists powerfully in the minds of both poet and audience even though it can never be fully defined or represented in any one concrete simile. The usefulness of similemes in poetic composition is evident in the frequency with which the poet draws upon them—although their power is no greater than that of any other element in the traditional diction. The contexts in which the similemes appear are sufficiently confined that they seem subject to many of the same rules that have been defined for type scenes; one can even meaningfully speak of a modified economy and extension in the usage of the simile. But the greatest piece of evidence for the existence of the simileme is the regularity with which similes of a single family are developed from a series of motifs that are repeatedly used together; it is this consistency that makes possible the construction of the charts of simile families. Such similemes are highly flexible and complex collections of nonverbal components that give poet and audience an extranarrative device dependent on a coded language and capable of providing the narrative with reinforcement, nuance, and subtlety.

The poet's most powerful compositional technique in shaping the individual simile is suppression—the choice to do less. Both framing and selection, processes vital to the composition of the simile, are products of the poet's need to include and to exclude. The expressive potential of conscious framing is often unnoticed, yet it is a technique used broadly in the arts, most obviously in painting and filmmaking. A painter is surrounded with the disorderly collection of paraphernalia typical of a studio, and a movie director sits among the chaos of his crew and equipment; each is attempting to create a small patch of order, and in both cases the frame is crucial in isolating the area in which a controlled design can be realized. Selection of the objects to include within the frame is of equal importance. In addition, objects and the modes in which they will be presented offer major opportunities for selection, modification, and exclusion: the tones or shades of color, the harmonies or disharmonies, the juxtapositions or disjunctions, or the relative weighting of objects in the design of the whole. The artist endlessly refines and reworks his material to express with precision the idea that justifies his creative effort.[59]

Homeric criticism has produced many comments about the power of the existing text based on the poet's decision to include, rather than assessments of his choice to exclude. But the decision to add to a composition is the inverse of the choice to reject; the creative process encompasses both in a simultaneous decision. The identification of the simileme allows a critic to construct sets of alternatives considered by the poet at each parallel juncture. It is just as significant to discover that the poet did not include a simile in one passage as that he did in another; the effects of the two scenes can be quite different and should offer clues to the design of the larger narrative. Likewise, it is vital for the interpretation of a passage to know why the poet created a simile that contained a large number of categories, while at other places he omitted many of these in order to produce a shorter version. There are even possibilities of evaluating the relative harshness or calmness, the crudeness or refinement, the bleakness or brightness within the phrases the poet has chosen; such comparative evaluations become possible once the alternatives that were not chosen for each passage have been made clear.

In addition, the simileme places several standard problems regarding Homeric similes into new perspectives:

1. The delineation of the simileme's motifs permits a clearer understanding of the process of poetic composition in regard both to the similes and to the larger epics. The similes provide a unique body of evidence within the Homeric epics that is identified by features inherent in their basic form: their relative shortness and separateness, their clear demarcation as discrete poetic units, their close references to a parallel scene, and their flexibility. In forming the individual simile the poet makes many artistic choices similar to those made in composing other less well defined and delimited elements of his larger epic. The paralleling of two radically different subjects or actions juxtaposed and placed in like settings permits a critic to see the artistic processes of the poet with a clarity available at few other places in the poems. First, the poet is describing the same moment twice in different words and from different perspectives; second, it is possible to compare parallel passages in the narrative where the poet employs a different subject or even chooses not to use a simile.

2. There is reality to the classifications of simile families that various critics have developed. However, if critics are to deal with Homer's creative processes, they must avoid statements that are based solely on the phrasing and language of the individual similes, that is, classifying similes only by the first animal mentioned or the active subject. To analyze an individual simile properly one must compare the maximum number of similes composed of parallel elements. While there is no law prohibiting the continual subdivision of the individual simile into increasingly discrete units, the establishment of elements that are repeated through a series of similes should enable critics to come closer to dealing in the broader categories in which Homer himself thought.

3. Scholars have long felt that there was more being expressed through certain similes than the simple surface meaning of the words. The discovery that the simileme is the shared property of poet and audience allows more open discussion of silent, but powerful, nonverbal communication; it also permits a measure of control over impressionistic responses to those similes which have been appreciated as though they were freestanding small lyrics of high emotional charge. In spite of the limitations of the traditional diction, which usually ties the simile to the narrative through one and only one contact, it becomes mandatory for a critic to press for a broader interpretation that acknowledges that the simileme as a whole was present to both poet and audience whenever its subject was introduced.

4. The difference between long and short similes is not as important as some have thought. The choice is aesthetic: a short simile can add a degree of emphasis to the narrative without injecting the full weight of an expanded simile into a passage.[60]

5. Most similes seem to be told from the point of view of the narrator—but there are repeated methods for introducing others' points of view. It is even possible for the poet to allow the audience to perceive the action with the eyes of a character in the narrative.[61]

Homer's creative process can never be adequately defined; therefore it is easy for critics to speak in ways that diminish it. The talent, poetic brilliance, and remarkable abilities shown by later poets should not be denied to Homer even though he was dependent on those modes of expression prevalent in his own time. To the extent that his verse-making is viewed as a mechanical process, the fault is ours for underestimating his creations on the basis of criteria developed from the study of later and more familiar poetry. The derivation of traditional modes of expression and categories of thought from the *Iliad* and the *Odyssey* themselves comes as close as possible to establishing the phrasing, typological classes, and customary associations that were in the mind of Homer as he composed his two epics—and in the minds of his audience as they interpreted them.

There is no simple way to limit the holdings of the human mind from which a poet can draw. Such a stock is built through experience, and we are so ignorant of Homer—his home, his workplace, his method and occasion of composition, significant facts about his life and the time in which he lived—that it is impossible to specify the experiences that formed and were re-formed in his mind and in that of his audience. Studies of the broader traditional background to the epics suggest that various sets of information were coded and available to the poet; they operated simultaneously at several different levels and could be formed into a variety of combinations in the process of verse-making and verse-hearing. The easiest of these sets to identify, analyze, and quantify has been the pervasive formulaic language in the two epics. Homer was not enslaved to these formulae, but he did choose to use and adapt formulaic speech as the basis of his expression. In addition, some typological scenes were repeated word for word in the poems and seem to have been maintained in his mind as virtually preexisting units.[62]

Of equal interest are the traditional features that were not carried in verbal form but were images, ideas, or concepts that could be brought into the poems through a variety of expressions; these existed separately from the system of formulaic language. They vary widely in subject and use—the standard actions of epic verse, narrative stories of individual heroes and incidents that could be transferred among several heroes, the basic tales of the ancient kingdoms, the customary norms and qualitative values accepted by all members of the society, devices for developing a narrative, and—among the latter—the similemes. Most of these nonverbal conceptions were shared by Homer, his fellow poets, and his audience as basic elements of their culture.

Of course, both poems were composed to express Homer's individual and independent thoughts on his society and culture. He drew from earlier legends and stories that he carried in his mind, organizing his selection through the poetic devices that he had learned from years of listening and performing. To express this personal statement to others he turned to the preexistent formulaic language and worked to make this language tell the narrative in the way he wanted it told. Of course, this is too diagrammatic a scheme to represent the associative way in which the human mind works. Because many of these elements would have instantaneously suggested new modes of organization and the poetic mind can continually borrow traditional elements and recombine them to make new forms, the categories of thought can never be so neatly defined. Such a creative process, with its continuous interaction between differing subjects and plots, can never be fully defined in itself, but it can be described to some extent through the careful analysis of existing passages. Because the similes are discrete units and seem to arise from this type of creative process, they offer a particularly fruitful area for the investigation of Homer's compositional style.[63]

CHAPTER THREE

Homer's Use of Similes to Delineate Character and Plot

In the practice of traditional storytelling the poet combines elements of plot and character in a productive balance, and as he develops his story, they become mutually reinforcing. At the beginning of book 11 the Greeks begin a new day of fighting. Dawn breaks, Eris shouts a shrill call to battle and makes the Greeks eager for war, and Agamemnon encourages his troops and arms among them. He then leads the Greeks onto the battlefield in a series of encounters that are destructive, vindictive, and bloody, but this rampage is the appropriate introduction to a book of Greek setbacks. He is the right character in the right place at the right time; his wounding and retreat from the battlefield are the appropriate beginning to Hector's day of glory. In other words, the needs of the plot often seem to call forth a specific character, and individual characters mark developments in the plot.[1]

Such tailoring of tradition has been analyzed and discussed often enough for critics to acknowledge the storyteller's freedom to shape his tale by selecting elements from an earlier pattern, expanding and condensing material, and adjusting the amounts of speech mixed into the narrative.[2] Characterization in the Homeric poems is equally complicated. It seems certain that Homer did not invent his major characters;[3] rather, he repeatedly borrows them from earlier tales by accommodating and adapting their salient traits to the needs of his continuing narrative. In addition, a large number of minor figures appearing only once or twice in the Homeric poems probably had roles in local sagas, but their stories were never sufficiently significant to earn them a major part in the more widespread narrative tradition.

There are two sections of the *Iliad* where a relatively large number of similes are major features in presentation of the motives and values of major characters: in book 2 they underline the characterization of Agamemnon, and in books 21–22 they heighten the contrast between Achilles and Hector. In these books the characters dictate the development of the narrative. In book 11, however, similes provide a necessary and continuing focus on a plot that roams widely over the battlefield and is vaguely structured around the shifting strength of the Greeks and the Trojans.

ILIAD, BOOK 2: IRONIC CHARACTERIZATION[4]

Book 2 of Homer's *Iliad* contains twenty similes, a large number.[5] Some books contain even more; book 11 is the winner with thirty-two. And because of book 2's length there are other narrative sections where similes are more densely concentrated: again, the first part of book 11 (1–596) offers the densest gathering of similes in a continuous narrative. But book 2 is a better beginning point for testing the poet's choices in designing similes because here Homer employs a large number of them in a wide variety of forms. This book not only contains a collection of different simile subjects and a mix of similes ranging from the highly traditional to the uniquely structured (e.g., 144 and 478); it also presents the greatest simile cluster in the Homeric poems (455–83) and three rare juxtaposed similes (144 + 146, 468 + 476, and 780 + 781).

Book 2's series of extended similes concentrates on the major character, the army. The subjects are taken from familiar similemes—wind, fire, birds, gods, and insects—and tradition firmly underlies the placement of each simile. Yet there are signs that Homer significantly adapts traditional features of the similemes to enhance his story. And, of course, it is important to the interpretation of the individual similes to acknowledge that the audience had a firm knowledge of the alternatives the poet considered and thereby could evaluate what he was accepting, modifying, and suppressing in structuring his narrative.

Book 2 of the *Iliad* falls easily into two narrative units: (1) efforts to organize the army (1–483) and (2) its final marshalling and marching to meet the Trojans (484–877). The division between these sections is clearly signaled in lines 441–52, when Agamemnon orders his heralds to summon the Greeks for battle; leaders encourage their men, and Athena marches with the army to rouse its spirit. This division of the book is echoed by the differing poetic strategies in each part. The first section describes the Greek leaders' frenzied attempts to establish a direction for the army, while in the Catalogue the army is presented straightforwardly as a unit of impressive and unified power. The organization implicit in, and imposed by, the catalogue form itself presents the army for the first time in the epic as a potent fighting unit; the names of men and the numbers of ships are listed as components of corporate strength, and individual lives and fates are mentioned only briefly.[6] After the Greek Catalogue the narrative continues to move toward battle as the Trojan heroes and troops are also listed.

While the narrative of book 2 develops from the army at rest to the army marching to its first battle in the *Iliad*, the theme of the book is leadership. In neither books 1 nor 2 does Agamemnon mold his troops into a strong fighting unit.[7] Of course, the Greek army is big—the length and scope of the Catalogue exhibit the massive power that the Greeks possess at Troy;[8] but this force must be organized to move effectively toward a single goal if the war is to be won. When Agamemnon misinforms the troops about his dream, he misreads the spirit of the army and causes extreme disorganization.[9]

In order to understand the functioning of the similes in supporting the theme of ineffective leadership it is necessary to examine each simile closely as the product of the poet's choice. There is good evidence that the inherited language of early Greek narrative suggested a limited number of subjects at certain common junctures; on some occasions the poet chose to follow these prompts, often he made modifications, and at times he opted not to use a simile at all.[10] On each occasion his aim was to make the choice that allowed him to tell his story most effectively for an audience who also knew the similemes and could appreciate the poet's art.

The Similes of Book 2

2.87
just as the swarms of thronging bees
flow ever anew from a hollow rock;
in clusters they fly to the springtime flowers—
some flitting here and some there

This simile, describing the army gathering for the assembly, is drawn from the insect simileme.[11] In the other two bee/wasp similes (12.167 and 16.259) the insects are stirred up to attack their provokers or else to defend themselves;[12] appropriately, in each passage the narrative describes the fierce spirit of warriors. At 2.87, however, the army is only marching to a meeting where they will sit down and listen to their leaders; the poet has fitted the insect simileme to this calmer context by removing any threat from the bees. They leave their homes only to seek the flowers of spring; they fly in different directions and gather in clusters wherever there is a flower. The crucial idea of an organized and spirited self-defense, so central to the other two similes, is deleted.

There are few parallel descriptions of groups that gather but do not go to war immediately; usually armies are mustered to attack each other or at least to advance to battle. In such scenes the similes center on lions, wind and waves, fire, and rushing rivers.[13] At 16.156 the simile of bloodthirsty wolves stresses the gory aspects of their attack on a stag—even though the Myrmidons are only arming themselves. Perhaps the closest parallel to the movement of troops not directly involved in battle occurs in the *Epipolesis*, where Agamemnon encounters the two Ajaxes and their followers readying themselves for war:

> as when from a cliff a goatherd sees a cloud
> coming across the sea driven by the blast of the west wind;
> as it moves over the sea, it seems blacker than pitch
> to him even though he is far away, and it brings a great whirlwind.
> Seeing it he shudders and drives his flock into a cave....
>
> (4.275)

In this case men in armor are on the move and war is imminent; the simile emphasizes the goatherd's fear as he sees danger threatening his flock.

By choosing insects for the first of many similes describing the army in book 2, the poet prepares his audience, well aware of the traditional possibilities in the insect simileme, to focus on the fighting spirit of the Greeks. Yet at the same time, when he rigorously suppresses the available warlike elements to create a spring scene of untroubled bees, he counts on that same audience to realize that he has eliminated the aggressive element of the simileme in order to present the least ready army in the *Iliad*. The disorder and uncertainty in its movements are made clear in their random clustering (82 and 89) and their lack of direction (90).[14]

2.144, 147, and 209
like the long waves of the deep,
the Icarian Sea, which the East Wind and the South
rouse rushing from the clouds of father Zeus,

> and just as the West Wind comes to a deep field of corn,
> blowing briskly, and sets the ears to bobbing.

> just as when a wave of the sounding sea
> thunders on the long beach and the sea roars

The unplanned and chaotic rush of the army to the ships and back again to the assembly is described by three wind and wave similes, two of which are juxtaposed and closely parallel in structure.[15] Because the subjects of winds and waves are complementary components of the same simileme and often accompany the charge and attack of a warrior or of the whole army, it is possible to assess degrees of intensity. The clearest example of the destructive potential in this simileme is:

> as a fast-moving wave
> swollen by the wind from beneath the clouds
> falls upon a swift ship; the whole ship is hidden by the foam,
> the terrible blast of the wind roars in the sail,
> and the sailors tremble in fear—for only barely do they escape death
>
> (15.624)

13.795 also expresses nature's power, even though it does not specifically mention the threat of sinking the ship or destroying the men:

> like the blast of harsh winds
> that rush over the plain driven by the thunder of father Zeus
> and stir up the sea with a gigantic roar; many waves
> of the loud-sounding sea boil up,
> arching high and white—some before and some following after

By comparison, the three wind and wave similes in book 2 present an image of nature offering little threat or danger. At 2.144 waves on the sea are mentioned briefly in a phrase; then the second line locates the scene and names the winds that clash; the final line gives the source of the winds. For the most part, proper names displace the direct description of the winds' powerful action. But the phrasing also softens the scene: the winds rushing down from the "clouds of father Zeus" seem less dramatic than the winds that come to the plain "driven by the thunder of father Zeus" (13.796).

The second simile describes a wind blowing through a cornfield. For comparison there is a simile of winds blowing through a forest at 16.765:

the East and South Winds battle one another
in shaking the deep woods in the ravines of a mountain,
beech, ash, and smooth-barked cornel.
These whip their sharp-pointed branches against one another
with an unbelievable noise and there is a crashing of shattered limbs.

This storm is a major event; the winds are strong enough to break branches. In contrast, the bobbing ears in the cornfield recall an everyday scene on the farm that should only arouse delight.

Each of the two similes in book 2 (144 and 147) is drawn from one of the most traditional subjects, but the poet diminishes the dangerous potential of the winds by omitting those parts of the simileme that menace or destroy. It is further significant that these two similes are joined with no intervening line, and the full unit is framed by the same phrase in the narrative: "The council was moved" (144 and 149). Juxtaposed similes are found elsewhere at 2.478–81, 2.780–81, and 14.394.[16] In each case the tone of the joined similes is complementary and the extending elements present the same level of violence and power. At 2.144 and 2.147 Homer has not only suppressed the most powerful and threatening scenes available within the wind simile family but has also, by the device of juxtaposing two separate scenes, underlined the army's moderate and unwarlike qualities.[17]

At 2.209 the poet describes the noise of the army returning to the meeting place. The previously mentioned simile at 16.765 also presents the noise of a destructive windstorm. In book 2 the waves thunder on a broad beach and the sea roars. This is a scene that could well attract picnickers and hikers — not much threat compared to the violent whirlwind that is present elsewhere in the simile repertoire.[18] 13.795 presents the strengthened form drawn from the simileme.[19]

Still, the poet has not chosen the mildest descriptions of wind and waves for book 2. There is no calmer picture of winds than that of the fog hanging over the mountaintops when the winds are asleep (5.522), and no more placid country scenes than the wind blowing the chaff around the winnowers (5.499) or the gusts that raise clouds of dust on dry country roads (13.334). The second half of the book will present the army's full power and at the moment the possibilities inherent in the simileme keep that power alive — though in a simile that the audience would realize expressed only medium strength. Most of the similes in book 2 present only middling or weak support to the actions of the army by a like diminution of the strongest traditional features within the simileme. It does not seem possible to identify a "base" form for the simile families; rather, the memories of both poet and audience recall a range of descriptions from the most powerful to the weakest and evaluate the individual simile by placing it within that range.

2.394
>   the Argives cried aloud just as a wave
> against a high cliff when the South Wind drives it
> against a jutting crag that the waves driven by every wind
> from this side or that never leave once they rise

The Greeks shout their approval of Agamemnon's order to fight and then return to their camps. This simile is curious because it seems to have two focuses in the narrative, neither of which is directly supported within the simile. It is introduced by the phrase "The Argives cried aloud" but rejoins the narrative with the troops being scattered among the ships. In the simile there is no word for sound, and the only support for the scattering of the Greeks is the winds that blow "from this side and that." Context controls the audience's application of the simile; sound is only implied in the simile scene.[20]

The emphasis within the simile seems to be on steadfastness. The rock itself is a "high, jutting crag that the waves never leave"; in support of this reading, there is a parallel passage in which both narrative and simile use the image of the crag to underline the steadfast resistance of a group:

> like a towering, huge crag, nearby the gray sea,
> which endures the swift blowing of the whistling winds
> and the swelling waves which break against it;
> thus fixed did the Greeks await the Trojans and did not flee[21]
>
> (15.618)

In book 2, however, steadfastness does not seem relevant — especially since the assembly is in the process of scattering, each man to his own ship.

Even with this change in narrative situation, the simile in book 2 is not as strongly phrased as that in book 15. In book 2 the headland is high; in book 15 the crag is towering.[22] In book 2 only one wave breaks against the headland, which is daily subject to waves from this direction or that; in book 15 the winds are shrill and the waves are swollen. The crag simile in book 2 is formed by choices that diminish the force that such a simile can express and is set in a narrative that it is only tangentially prepared to support.

The Clustering of Similes 2.455–83

The marshalling of the Greek army for its grand presentation in the Catalogue is a major moment. In no other passage is the power of the largest expeditionary force in Greek legend made so explicit, with the names of heroes from all parts of the Greek world joined in one panoramic display. This display of the Greek forces provides a moment of order from which the maelstrom of the *Iliad* will be generated; only in book 23 will the characters of the Greek heroic world be regathered.

The Catalogue is introduced with appropriate weight by the unique prelude of seven similes in twenty-nine lines:

455: a fire burns in the distance
459: flocks of birds fly here and there on the plain
468: the numbers of troops are like leaves or flowers in spring
469: flies swarm around milk pails in springtime
474: goatherds separate goats in the pasture
478: Agamemnon's appearance is like Zeus, Ares, and Poseidon
480: a bull stands out in the herd

Simply stated, there is no short passage of Homeric narrative that is as densely packed with similes. The effect is even greater because none of the seven similes is short.

2.455
just as a destructive fire burns an immense forest
on the peaks of a mountain and from afar the glare is seen

The repertoire of fire similes contains two basic types: one fire is frightening in its ability to destroy; the other is beautiful and bright, an object of wonder. The destructive fire is nowhere better exemplified than at 17.737, where it describes the Trojans assaulting the two Ajaxes:

like a fire which suddenly rises and rushes
against a city of men and burns it, and houses fall
in the giant glare. The force of the wind sets it roaring

Homer's Use of Similes to Delineate Character and Plot · 49

But there is also the more lyrical fire that describes the gleam from the divine arms of Achilles:

> just as when the gleam of a burning fire appears over the sea
> to sailors—a fire which burns high up in the mountains
> in a lonely farmstead. The winds carry them all unwilling
> far from their friends over the fish-filled sea
>
> (19.375)

In this simile the gleam of a distant fire is so far away that the sailors are more concerned over friends left behind than any threat of storm damage.[23]

Fire is a common comparison for the activity of warriors, alone or in groups, often describing a strong attack or an impassioned spirit. The simile in book 2 is a mixture; even though the fire is presented as *aïdêlon* ("destructive"), its threat is diminished when compared with a simile describing the fighting of Agamemnon:

> As when a destructive fire falls upon a thick forest,
> and the wind whirling it around bears it in all directions, and thickets
> fall uprooted when they are attacked by the force of the flames
>
> (11.155)

The simile in book 2 starts with the same formula, "a destructive fire," and continues with a similar idea, "burns/falls on a vast forest"; but here the parallel ends. While the simile from book 11 directly focuses on the wind that whips the fire, the simile in book 2 merely defines the location of the fire, "on the peaks of a mountain." Then the absence of danger is reinforced by placing the unnamed observer at a safe distance.

Again a traditional subject, fire, is designed by the poet to express far less than full strength. The range of power within the simileme is large; there is an extreme diminution of force at *Odyssey* 5.488, where Odysseus, having barely survived the storm at sea, crawls ashore stripped of all but his life. Lying in his nakedness beneath a thorn bush and an olive tree, he is compared to an ember, "saving a seed of fire"; the hero's fire still burns but has been reduced to a mere glow.

2.459
as the many families of winged birds,
of geese or cranes or long-necked swans,

fly here and there rejoicing in their wings
on the Asian plain near the streams of the river Kayster
as they move forward with loud cries, and the plain echoes with sound

When the actions of warriors are compared to birds, the simile usually focuses on the strength of the attack.[24] Birds of prey attack smaller birds or small animals that are driven in fear before them: a vulture pursues geese, a falcon chases after starlings, an eagle swoops after a hare (17.460, 16.582, *Ody.* 24.538, and 17.674). In addition, there are similes where whole groups of attacking warriors are compared to birds of prey; for example, Odysseus and his friends attack the panicked suitors in the final battle at his palace:

as vultures with crooked talons and hooked beaks
coming from the mountains rush on small birds
who dart over the plain fleeing away from the clouds,[25]
but the vultures diving down slay them and there is no defense
or flight. And men rejoice in the hunt

(*Ody.* 22.302)

The simile at 2.459 is far different. These birds seek no prey; they fly randomly here and there as they delight in the openness of the meadow. In addition, the species cited are traditionally victims. Both Penelope and Telemachus see an eagle attack a single goose or geese, and later the interpretation is immediately offered that Odysseus is the eagle that will overpower and take vengeance on the weaker suitors (*Ody.* 15.160 and *Ody.* 19.536–50); Automedon attacks the Trojans like a vulture in pursuit of geese (17.460). At 3.2 cranes do bear death to Pygmy men, but in this case only the small size of the men allows even these weaker birds to be attackers. Because line 460 is repeated elsewhere in a similar context, it is probable that it is a traditional listing of victims:

just as a yellow eagle plunges
upon a flock of winged birds who are feeding by the river,
geese or cranes or long-necked swans,
so did Hector rush at the ship

(15.690)

Thus, another dilution of a traditional subject by selecting the weaker features in the simileme. Once again the low end of heroic potential within the simileme is reached when Achilles complains of his disadvantaged position in the Greek army: "as a bird brings food to her unfledged chicks whenever she catches it, but it goes ill for her" (9.323).

2.468 and 469
as many as the leaves and flowers in spring.

just as the many swarms of dense flies
which crowd around the sheep farm
in the springtime when the milk splashes into the pails

Homer juxtaposes these two similes with differing subjects to illustrate the vast number of troops marching against the Trojans. The passage is united internally and externally: it is composed of two juxtaposed springtime similes, and the narrative's emphasis on number is directly expressed both before and after (*myrioi hossa ... tossoi*, 468 and 472).²⁶ The two similes join to present an enhanced scene of countryside peace, an effect parallel to the earlier intensifying similes at 2.144 + 147. The short simile of leaves and flowers seems a standard comparison repeated at *Odyssey* 9.51, where the poet describes the numbers of attacking Cicones. Flies also seem a typological subject for this context: there is another simile at 16.641 where the phrasing is similar, and its last line is identical to 2.471.

The poet's choice of topics at such a narrative juncture is limited if he wishes to remain within the traditional alternatives. In the places where he uses a simile to illustrate numbers of troops, the tradition—as far as it can be defined—offers only two subjects of consistent usage: insects and leaves.²⁷ While the subject of leaves is not present often enough in the poems to establish a reliable scaling among its customary elements, the earlier discussion of the insect simile shows that the poet has chosen features that present these insects as an image of nature at peace.²⁸ Rather than bees or wasps, he uses harmless flies that flit purposelessly through the farmstead; the rest of the simile diverts attention from them by focusing on the season.

2.474
as goatherds easily separate the widely roaming flocks
of goats when they have mingled together in the pasture ...

This simile describes the leaders among their men, a scene that occurs often in the *Iliad* and *Odyssey*, several times with a simile. In almost every case the tone of the simile reflects the surrounding narrative. If the men are involved in active fighting, the simile centers on a subject that can be developed into an appropriate parallel for warfare. As the battle-starved Myrmidon commanders arm themselves around Achilles and Patroclus, they are compared to wolves:

> flesh-eating wolves,
> in whose hearts is unquenchable fury,
> who having killed a great-horned stag in the mountains
> rip him with their teeth. Their cheeks are red with blood,
> and in a pack they rush to lap water
> from the surface of the dark spring with their slender tongues,
> vomiting up bits of bloody gore. Their spirits
> are unrelenting and their stomachs, full
>
> (16.156)

Equally appropriate analogues for a war context are the comparisons of Idomeneus to a boar, of the two Ajaxes to a dark cloud that causes the goatherd to drive his flock to safety, of the men thronging around Diomedes to lions or boars, and the appearance of Hector among his followers as an evil star (4.253, 275; 5.782; and 11.62). In peaceful scenes the tone of the simile usually matches the narrative: Proteus among his seals is likened to a shepherd among his sheep; Nausicaa among her handmaidens is like Artemis sporting in the mountains; and Odysseus' men gather around him like calves around a mother cow (*Ody.* 4.413, *Ody.* 6.102, and *Ody.* 10.410). In the *Iliad* even Odysseus, when he is not actually fighting, is compared to a ram walking through a flock of white ewes (3.196).

The simile in book 2, however, presents a striking discrepancy between the warrior world of the army and a scene of peaceful nature, a discrepancy paralleled in the aristeia of Idomeneus. Aeneas gathers his comrades to confront Idomeneus, and the soldiers follow along:

> as sheep follow after the ram
> going to drink from their feeding place, and the shepherd rejoices in
>   his heart,
> thus did the heart rejoice in the breast of Aeneas....
>
> (13.492)

Because this tranquil scene introduces some of the goriest fighting and crudest woundings in the *Iliad*, the effect of the simile emerges only from a view of the wider passage. The aristeia of Idomeneus is an episode in the larger battle stretching from the beginning of book 13 to the return of Hector in book 15, a long narrative section directly under the control of Poseidon as he strengthens the Greeks. Throughout this section the two armies are contrasted: the Greeks, with the irresistible support of Poseidon, versus the Trojans, who have momentarily lost the attention of Zeus. The scene from 424–95 emblematically opposes Idomeneus to Aeneas: the Greek awaits the Trojans like a bristling boar that is eager to defend himself against hunting dogs and men opposed to Aeneas, the leader of the weakened Trojans, who is like a ram among his ewes (13.471 vs. 492).

Likewise, in book 2 the mustering of the army for combat would naturally call for a simile appropriate to a warlike context. Instead the poet has developed the simile to stress the non-warlike features of the Greek leaders: the goatherds control the flocks easily, the scene is a pasture, and the flocks have idly mingled together.

2.478 and 480

         among them mighty Agamemnon
like Zeus, who delights in thunder, in his eyes and head,
Ares in his waist, and Poseidon in his chest.

Just as a bull is by far preeminent among all in the herd,
for he stands out among the gathered cattle

Agamemnon is presented as the supreme king of the Greek army with two more juxtaposed similes. In the first the poet chooses to focus on Agamemnon's appearance as he prepares for battle; the simile of a god at 7.208 describing Ajax before his single combat with Hector provides a parallel for both context and subject:

thus Ajax moved forth like giant Ares,
who goes to battle among men whom the son of Cronos
has sent to fight in the violence of soul-devouring strife.[29]

The simile at 2.478 has several unusual features. First, though there are other similes in which alternatives are offered as comparisons, here Agamemnon is simultaneously likened to three different divinities.[30] Second, while heroes are commonly compared to a specific god, they are never said to be like that god in regard to a particular physical feature. With the sole exception of Hector, who has the eyes of a Gorgon or of Ares when he is in the act of routing the Greeks (8.349), warriors are not complimented on their eyes, their heads, their waists, or their chests. Usually the comparison is to the action of the god, as in the simile describing Ajax, rather than to his physical appearance. Thus though there are precedents for the simile subject at 2.478, the passage is odd in stressing the surface appearance of the warrior, in identifying him with several gods at once, and in focusing on uncustomary features. Once again choices in the extending elements drain the potential warlike qualities from the simileme.

There is even a lowered intensity in the choice of the simile form. The simile by its nature is an indirect description.[31] While Homer does not often offer physical descriptions, the strong effect of a direct presentation is evident in the image of Hector as he advances on the Greek ships:

> foam appeared around his mouth, his eyes
> shone from under his ferocious brows, and his helmet
> shook fearfully around his temples as he fought
>
> (15.607–10)

Book 2 does not present such a fearful image of Agamemnon.

The second simile centers on a bull, an animal familiar from the simile repertoire. Bulls are usually victims, especially of lions.[32] The simile describing the last moments of Sarpedon is typical:

> as a lion going into a herd destroys a bull—
> a tawny, spirited bull among the shambling cattle—
> who bellows as he dies in the jaws of the lion
>
> (16.487)

Similes of farm animals usually describe warriors who are helpless or dying (13.571 and 20.403). The simile of the mother cow lowing over her calf that describes Menelaus taking his stand over the body of Patroclus at 17.4 illustrates how effective such a simile can be. Menelaus is always a warrior who causes concern to others when he is exposed to danger. His strength is immediately shown to be sound when he slays Euphorbus just as a tempest uproots a young olive tree (53), and he is compared to an enraged lion as he terrifies the Trojans cowering around him (61). But then Hector confronts him; he quails and retreats to seek Ajax, who returns with him to guard the body of Patroclus. Ajax's action, parallel to the earlier stand of Menelaus, receives a powerful lion simile (133–36). Thus the simile of the mother cow is the first part of a parallel structure intended to underline the inadequacy of Menelaus as Patroclus' defender.[33]

A related use of the farm animal simileme occurs in the passage where Paris returns to battle as a horse racing to the pasture (6.506). When the wounded Hector recovers his strength and reenters battle, he receives the same simile to express his renewed energy, but it is immediately enhanced with a second simile of a lion (15.263 + 271). Though the horse simile is repeated word for word, the effect is totally different; when the second simile is missing, Paris seems a frivolous creature interested only in warrior-like posturing.

The tone of the bull simile in book 2 can be further contrasted with alternative comparisons at similar junctures. The closest parallel is at 12.41, where Hector urges the Trojans to cross the ditch—another picture of the leader among his men; he is likened to the courageous lion that terrifies the men around him. Also 11.62: Hector stands among the Trojan leaders like an evil star, and his armor flashes like the lightning of Zeus (66); elsewhere both subjects stress the impressive appearance of an effective warrior.[34]

From this brief survey it appears that warriors are usually compared to farm animals when the poet presents them as weak, helpless, or pathetic—and there is no warlike word or serious threat added to the image of the kingly bull amid the cattle that describes Agamemnon.

The farm animal simile that is most like that in book 2 occurs when Odysseus returns from Circe's palace to his companions awaiting him on the beach:

> as when calves on a farm jump around the herd of cows
> returning to the farmyard when they are full from grazing—
> all together they frisk around them and the pens no longer hold them,
> but lowing endlessly they run around their mothers
>
> (*Ody.* 10.410)

This simile suits the infectious joy of men who have been weeping disconsolately on the beach. In addition, the day's activities are done, and the returning herd provides an appropriate parallel for the leader who will now neglect the voyage home to settle in with the sorceress. His leadership has ebbed to the point where his men will have to remind him of their goal. A like tone of failed leadership describes the commander Agamemnon as he musters his troops for the Catalogue.

If a simile cluster is defined as a grouping of at least three long similes within thirty lines, all of which are focused on a single scene, then there are only three other identifiable simile clusters. In book 11 after Agamemnon departs wounded from the battle (280–83), Hector advances for the day of glory promised by Zeus. To mark Hector's entrance Homer employs a cluster of four similes, both short and extended:

> 292: a hunter sets his hounds on a boar or lion
> 295: Ares, the destroyer of men (short)
> 297: a blustering wind churns the sea
> 305: two winds clash, raise heavy swells, and the waves scatter spray

Second, in book 15 when the Trojans are on the verge of burning the Greek ships, thus fulfilling the plan of Zeus and putting crucial pressure on Achilles (592ff.), there is a cluster of six similes, two of which are short comparisons:

> 592: the Trojans are like flesh-eating lions (short)
> 605: Hector is like Ares (short) or a destructive fire (extended)
> 618: the Greeks remain fixed like a cliff that is battered by wind and waves
> 624: Hector attacks the Greeks like a wave that so threatens to sink a ship that the sailors barely escape death
> 630: Hector attacks like a lion that harasses the inexperienced herdsman[35] and kills a heifer, scattering the herd

The third cluster falls at the end of book 17 and describes Menelaus' and Meriones' struggle to remove the body of Patroclus to the Greek camp. In this passage similes respond to the balanced battle between Greeks and Trojans:

> 725: hounds (Trojans) viciously attack a wounded boar (the two Ajaxes) that scares them away when he turns to fight
> 737: a fierce fire (Trojans) is driven against a city by the wind and destroys it
> 742: two mules (Menelaus and Meriones) drag a large beam along a rugged path
> 747: a ridge (Ajaxes) holds back several rivers (Trojans) that threaten to burst through
> 755: a falcon (Aeneas and Hector) attacks smaller birds (Greeks), bringing the threat of death

These four passages in books 2, 11, 15, and 17 establish the simile cluster as a form familiar to the poet. Two rules prevail in such clusters:

1. The tone developed in the extended similes is subordinated to the direction of the narrative.
2. Each simile acts independently in reinforcing the others in order to underline that direction.

Similes in such passages are derived from a variety of similemes, but there is no need to coordinate the subjects within the cluster so that one will suggest or lead to the next, nor is there any necessity for a framing or linking structure.[36] The grouping of such similes is a clear and economical means of introducing striking poetic background into the narrative. The simile cluster in book 2, the largest and most impressive in the *Iliad*—whether analyzed as a series of individual comparisons or as a structured whole—obeys these rules in presenting a consistent poetic background of the more lyrical and peaceful qualities of nature, even though in this book Homer's goal is to present the army gathering for attack.

The Final Similes: 2.780 and 781

as if the whole earth were swept with fire.

the land groans just as when Zeus who delights in thunder
is angry and lashes the land around Typhoeus among the Arimoi,
where they say lies the couch of Typhoeus

While these two similes describing the Greek army on the march are not joined as closely by verbal links as those at 144 + 146 and 468 + 476, they are juxtaposed, and their combined effect is greater than either would be alone. The word "groan" (*stenachizo*) occurs before and after the second simile— and the repetition gives simile and narrative a common focus. The sound of the fire is not directly reported by *nemoito* ("were swept"), but there is no necessary incompatibility between the idea of a large fire sweeping the earth and a great sound.[37]

Since these two similes immediately follow the Catalogue of the Greek ships, they are parallel to the earlier cluster of seven introductory similes. However, they present two images—massive fire and earthquake/thunderstorm—that are radically different from the milder, more restrained pictures throughout the previous lines of book 2.

Fire is a traditional simile subject accompanying the army on the march or in battle.[38] Yet though 2.780 is relatively short, it threatens destruction by stating so openly that all the earth was being consumed by fire; this is no small blaze seen at a distance by disinterested observers. This simile does not have to be extended to a great length to emphasize the change in tone, both because it is responding to the first simile in the earlier cluster at 455 — the far-removed fire that offered little threat — and because it is immediately reinforced by 781.

The image of Zeus lashing the land is insufficiently paralleled in Homeric poetry to construct a pattern of a simile family, but the story is told by Hesiod:

> When Zeus gathered his strength and took up his arms,
> thunder and lightning, and the smoking thunderbolt,
> leaping down from Olympus he struck him [Typhoeus].
> He burned all the wondrous heads of the terrible monster.
> But when he had overcome him and lashed him with strokes,
> he fell lamed and the great earth groaned.
> The flame from the king who was struck by the thunderbolt
> shot forth in the dark rugged ravines of the mountains.
> Much of the huge earth was burned by the amazing heat
> and it melted like tin. . . .
>
> (*Theogony* 853–62)

Both the Hesiodic passage and the simile present a scene of massive destruction. Probably the simile refers either to a powerful lightning storm, reminiscent of Zeus' victory over Typhoeus, or an earthquake created by Typhoeus moving under the mountains.[39] In either case the poet has chosen to end the Catalogue with two mutually reinforcing images of nature as overwhelming and awesome in its destructive might.

The Role of Similes in Book 2

For the most part the confused and perplexed reactions of the army to Agamemnon's commands are physical actions through which the theme of ineffective leadership is presented; but the focus on the army's response to its leader is continuously intensified by similes. Of book 2's twenty similes, fourteen are placed within the first five hundred lines, a rate of one in every thirty-five lines. In addition, since only four of those fourteen are short, similes play an extraordinarily important role in the telling of this tale. It is further significant that the first twelve similes describe the Greek army: its mass, its movements, the noise it makes, and the gleam from its weapons — all topics for which the tradition offers similemes that can be designed to fit war contexts. Yet in developing each of these similes the poet consistently chooses unwarlike features: harmless insects, random winds, wandering flocks of small birds, unthreatening farm animals, leaves, and flowers. The topic of insects traditionally illustrates both the number and ferocity of a group, but both insect similes (87 and 469) stress peaceful, pastoral qualities. The series of wave similes (144, 209, and 394) emphasizes both the vastness of the sea and its chaotic qualities; in 144 it is unclear which wind is moving the waves, the East or the South Wind, and this confusion is continued immediately in the simile at 147, where the West Wind blows through the cornfield. At 394 the waves roll "now here and now there."[40] Such similes suggest that the Greek army moves in no coordinated manner or in any specific direction; thus there is no meaningful threat to humans in either simile or narrative. The fire simile (455) describes a blaze that is seen from afar by men who are unthreatened, and the birds at 459 have no goal — they too fly "here and there." Not even the locales mentioned in the similes are related to war: the plain with spring flowers, a farm or pastureland; the army musters for the Catalogue "in the flowering meadow" (467). Even two short similes used in speeches to describe the army are highly unwarlike; both Nestor and Odysseus call the warriors children or widow women (289 and 337).[41]

Because the tone of the similes sharply diverges from the war preparations in the narrative, their consistency strongly supports the theme of weakened leadership. From its first scene book 2 is built from intrigue, deceit, and mistaken judgment. The book opens with Zeus instituting the plan that will accomplish his promise to Thetis; he sends a dream to Agamemnon that urges the exact opposite of that promise: arm the Greeks and seize Troy. However, Agamemnon proposes a stratagem to the Greek leaders; he will test the army's mettle by proposing that they abandon the expedition and return home. When the troops seize upon his words and rush to the ships, their actions and thoughts threaten to abort the mission and thus run contrary to the plan of Zeus. The disabling and weakening of the vast army, which is conveyed through its backward and forward movements, is repeatedly described by similes that make the troops seem harmless.[42]

This ironic undercutting reaches its climax in the cluster of seven similes before the Catalogue. Homer introduces this section with these words:

> [Athena] gleaming rushed through the mass of the Achaeans
> urging them to march. In the heart of each man
> she roused unshakable strength for war and fighting.
> And war became sweeter to them than returning
> to their beloved homes in hollow ships.
>
> (450–54)

But this firm war spirit is immediately dissipated by the similes — the fire that gleams but does not threaten or destroy, the birds that glory in the freedom of disorganized flight, the leaves and the flowers in springtime, the farmyard flies, and the goats roaming the pastureland.

Once the Catalogue has tallied the actual military might of the Greeks and they begin to move to war, the theme of inadequate leadership ends, and the size, talent, and inherent quality of the united mass of the Greek army lends credibility to the terrified Polites/Iris, who rouses Hector and his fellow Trojans. The similes closely accompany this change. At 780 and 781 the similes describe massive destruction as Zeus enters the simile world by hurling his thunderbolts at the earth, lashing the land. Now there is no mention of springtime or harmless movements. Here the forces of nature run amok as fire sweeps the land and the earth groans.[43]

The deliberateness with which similes support the narrative of book 2 becomes even more apparent in examining those junctures where the poet chose other means to continue his narrative even though the simile was a traditional option. While it is impossible to know the poet's mind sufficiently to construct a full list of such passages, eight such occasions can be identified in book 2.

1. *16ff. and 35f.* — *the coming and going of the Dream*. The tradition suggested four standard means for describing the journey of a divinity: a simple two-line statement (leaving/arriving), the preparation for the trip, the listing of the route, or a simile.[44] For the journeys of the Dream to and from the Trojan camp Homer chose the simplest form of description.[45] Since the theme of the book is the leadership of Agamemnon, the poet introduces the Dream succinctly so that the audience can concentrate on the directions from Zeus to Agamemnon, the key to understanding Agamemnon's "clever" device in leading — or misleading — his troops.

2. *42ff.* — *Agamemnon enters the action by initiating his plan*. The Homeric text provides similar ways to bring an important hero into the action, includ-

ing the simple entrance, the statement of the hero's preparation, the ponderings of the hero on possible success or failure, and the simile.[46] In this passage Homer describes Agamemnon's appearance as he prepares to go through the camp—his tunic, his cloak, his sandals, his silver-studded sword, and his ancestral scepter—rather than his status, valor, or emotions. At this point an extended simile would offer a parallel scene to deepen the audience's understanding of the king.[47] Projections of success or failure would produce a subtler, more sympathetic character, perhaps capable of inner doubt; the Agamemnon of book 2 is misguided and stubborn. Homer chooses a description of his entrance that penetrates no deeper than his clothes and equipment in order to direct attention toward the conduct of his office.

3. *93f.—Rumor urges the Greeks.* As the Greeks gather to hear the message of Agamemnon, "Rumor blazed forth in their midst urging them to go to the meeting." Several divine forces in the Homeric poems are described by similes, such as the river Xanthus, the old man of the sea in book 4 of the *Odyssey* (413), or the god Sleep (14.290). Rumor, as the messenger of Zeus, could be emphasized if Homer were stressing the role of the divine plan in the action of this book.[48] But, just as with the Dream, a strong emphasis on divine intervention would destroy the focus on the book's theme. Therefore Rumor enters in a two-line factual report. Such restraint allows Homer to present the eagerness of the army succinctly without diluting the immediately preceding four-line simile describing the human response of the army.

4. *100ff.—the scepter of Agamemnon.* This scepter is important in the first two books of the *Iliad*. It is cast to the ground by Achilles in book 1 (234), Agamemnon leans upon it as he addresses the Greek army making his misguided proposal to the troops (2.100), and Odysseus takes it up when he attempts to stop the chaotic rush to the ships, even beating Thersites into silence with it (2.186 and 265). An object of such significance is often marked by a simile.[49] In this passage Homer has chosen to detail the genealogy of the scepter, tracing it back through the House of Atreus to the gods Hermes, Zeus, and Hephaestus. By such an extended description Homer presents the divine and ancestral authority associated with the scepter, the very qualities that Agamemnon betrays in his unfortunate plan. By rejecting a simile in this passage, Homer isolates the king and expresses his lack of depth against the list of previous divine and human authorities.

5. *166ff.—the arrival of Athena.* As the Argives rush to their ships (invalidating the plan of Zeus), Hera complains that Troy may go unpunished because

of the inept machinations of Agamemnon; Athena descends from Olympus, asking Odysseus to urge the Greeks back to the assembly. The alternatives are the same four mentioned in regard to 16ff. and 35f. above; here, as there, Homer chooses the simplest of descriptions. Since it has been made clear that Odysseus knows Agamemnon wants the army to advance spiritedly toward Troy, he needs no further motivation from Athena to bring the Greeks back from the ships. Therefore her advice to him cannot be intended to introduce new motivation from another plane; rather, the accent provided by the divine message shows that even heaven has been upset by Agamemnon's clumsy scheme. In this case there is not much point in stressing Athena's journey from heaven to earth through a description of elaborate preparation, or by a listing of her route, or by a simile; it is more important to demonstrate widespread dismay with Agamemnon's actions.

6. *182ff. — the entrance of Odysseus.* At this point the narrative spotlight falls directly on Odysseus as he takes the scepter from Agamemnon, rallies the Greeks, squelches all opposition, and finally makes a major speech of encouragement to the whole assembly. Odysseus, more than any other leader, provides new direction to the narrative. Often major figures receive a simile marking their entrance into the narrative,[50] but Odysseus is not parallel to other entrants, since he largely seeks to resist a massive movement. Homer describes Odysseus' feelings as he watches the Achaeans stream toward their ships, summarizes his thoughts in Athena's speech, has him take the symbol of authority from Agamemnon, and shows the variety of means that he employs to rally the Greeks. A simile would only call attention to Odysseus, diverting the audience's minds from the complexity of the situation. Odysseus, as rallier of the Greeks, is the contrasting figure that exposes Agamemnon's folly; therefore it is important to focus on the effectiveness of his leadership in order to make him a weighty foil to Agamemnon.

7. *212ff. — the entrance of Thersites.* Much the same could be said of Thersites in his section of the narrative; he also could receive a simile as he emerges from the background to resist the movement surrounding him. However, since he carries Achilles' criticisms of Agamemnon into this book, it is more important for the poet to emphasize those thoughts over the fact of his resistance. A simile would merely shift attention from the continuing inadequacy of the Greek leader.

8. *265ff. — Thersites' tear.* When Odysseus strikes Thersites with the scepter, a tear falls from his eye and he sinks to the ground. A simile is often effective

in presenting emotions,[51] but in this passage Homer does not call attention to Thersites' emotions. The narrative requires that the audience focus on the actions of Odysseus that will reinvigorate the Greeks' spirit. In addition, by enhancing the sorrow of Thersites through a simile, Homer would build sympathy for a character whose subjugation is cheered by the other Greeks.[52] The continuing focus on the contrast between Agamemnon and Odysseus as leaders directly furthers the theme of the book (2.270–77).

The major literary device of book 2 is irony, the constant exploitation of the gap between reality and illusion. In the Greek universe the plans of the gods are always stronger than those of humans. If heroes struggle against the established tide, they will suffer and perhaps die; but if they can catch the flow, they can move painlessly — even effortlessly — forward. To follow that irresistible direction they will often have to repress their own plans and highest goals. The hallmark of Greek heroism is the willing sacrifice of one's life for a fragile illusion, but in doing so heroes gain the sympathy and approval of all mortals, for their effort provides a noble model.

Book 2 of the *Iliad* is rooted in this split between the overwhelming strength of the gods and the frailty of mortals. Zeus intends to kill numbers of Greeks and lures them into cooperating with his plan by telling them a lie. Agamemnon, eager to promote this plan, misreads his men and foolishly brings them into opposition to Zeus' command. Odysseus, the voice of cool intelligence and perspective, and Nestor, the voice of authority and inherited wisdom,[53] organize the Greeks to march on the Trojans — thus furthering Zeus' plan and unwittingly guaranteeing many deaths. Such is the confusing situation in which humans find themselves under the reign of deceptive gods.

The situation in book 2 would present the familiar struggle of mortals attempting to interpret the riddling comments of god were it not for the intervention of the vain and haughty Agamemnon. As the king reverses the clear pronouncement of Zeus, his troops struggle to find the direction of events. Following their best judgment, they place themselves in an even weaker position than if they had obeyed the simple command of Zeus that, though misleading, at least gave them a clear direction and did not attempt to manage them through psychological games.

The similes in book 2 consistently support the pervasive irony of the strong-but-weak army directed by the powerful-yet-inept commander. They are repeatedly placed to emphasize the reactions of the army as the visible signs of Agamemnon's folly, and are avoided at junctures unrelated to this theme. Homer's audience would recognize that the similemes are in most cases the ones used throughout the *Iliad* to describe a strong fighting force. Yet in the individual extended similes the strength possible in each subject is so diminished that the army, which should be ennobled by similes of fire, winds, and birds, seems only to be mocked—the fire is safe, the winds are harmless, and the birds are tame. Although the design of the similes in book 2 is deeply conditioned by the tradition, the master poet—aware how effective the concentrated use of poetic background can be in developing his theme—is at every point in control—and the co-creating audience has been prepared to follow his direction.

ILIAD, BOOKS 21 AND 22:
SIMILES TO SHOW A THEMATIC CONTRAST[54]

Book 21 of the *Iliad* is built from four disillusioning actions—events that reveal unpleasant and unexpected truths about the situations of the heroes:[55] Achilles kills Lycaon, a warrior he thought he had permanently removed from the battlefield (1–135); the river god Xanthos, intent on drowning Achilles, is forced to retreat before the overwhelming power of Hephaistos (136–382); gods descend to the battlefield only to become involved in personal bickering while men continue to die (383–513); and Achilles, in pursuing an enemy, suddenly finds that he is fighting a phantom (514–611). In these four scenes the poet undermines the actions and intentions of men and gods in order to provide a meaningful introduction to the battle between Hector and Achilles; by the end of book 21 Achilles has evidence that his pursuit of honor will deprive him of all humane standards and offer him no worthwhile reward.[56]

In the first section (1–135) Achilles leaps into the Xanthos River to continue slaying Trojan warriors and seizes twelve youths for human sacrifice, perhaps his most inhumane act. Killing enemy warriors or capturing them for ransom are familiar and suitable activities in the *Iliad*, but few warriors take prisoners to be living sacrifices. To emphasize the savage quality of his attack, Homer sketches a contrasting lyrical background:[57]

> But when they had come to the crossing of the *fair-flowing river*,
> the *swirling Xanthos*, which immortal Zeus begat
>   Half of the men
> were crowded into the *deep-flowing, silver-eddying river*

> Thus at the hands of Achilles was the *sounding stream*
> *of the deep-swirling Xanthos River* filled with horses and men.[58]
>
> (21.1–2, 7–8, and 15–16)

This mix of pastoral nature and bloodshed is extended when Achilles suddenly encounters Lycaon, a warrior that he had previously captured and sold into slavery; on the earlier occasion Achilles came upon him at night in his father's orchard as he was cutting young shoots from a wild fig tree (36–38).[59] Now Achilles is so astounded to find him on the battlefield that he wonders openly whether all the Trojans slain by him will soon begin to rise from the underworld (56–63). This first questioning of the effectiveness of war as a human pursuit is ironically absurd; later questions in this book will be more realistic. Lycaon supplicates Achilles, who responds harshly, an answer foreshadowing his brutality in book 22.[60]

In the second section Achilles slays Asteropaeus, the son of the river Axius, and many of his comrades. The river Xanthus becomes so choked with corpses that it begs Achilles to stop, but he continues his bloody rampage (136–297). The juxtaposition of these first two sections firmly establishes Achilles' uncompromising intent. In the first scene Achilles meets a weaker warrior and not only denies him the humane treatment that he gave him on an earlier occasion but also refuses his request for supplication; in the second scene a force of nature itself rebukes Achilles for his arrogant behavior. But no sooner does the river begin to pursue him than Poseidon and Athena—with the approval of Zeus—protect Achilles and encourage him to continue fighting until he pens the Trojans within their walls and slays Hector. Although he will be triggering his own death by this act, he fights ceaselessly even against the river god because of the honor code's demand that he avenge Patroclus and the gods' promise of glory (294–97).

Achilles has become a pawn in the hands of powerful divinities who carry the battle to a cosmic scale (298–382). Hera's goal is the defeat of Troy; Achilles is the device through which she can most easily accomplish her individual desires. Hephaestus sweeps the plain with fire to drive back the river, and finally a number of gods are drawn into battle—leaving the concerns of men far behind. Even though Poseidon encourages Achilles to pursue his own desires in slaughtering Trojans, the god is more interested in pursuing his own more personal cause (288–97)—and such self-interest characterizes other gods' clear motivations for the remainder of the book.

At line 383 the third section begins as a variety of gods enter the battle, and it is explicitly stated that Zeus laughs as he watches the scene (388–90). Divine emotions throughout this section are typical of the petty jealousies and vindictiveness that motivate the gods in their dealings with one another. Athena and Ares trade insults, and she lays him flat with a large boundary stone. Aphrodite tries to lead Ares away, but she too is struck by Athena. Poseidon urges Apollo into battle by reminding him how thankless the men of Troy have been to their patron gods, but Apollo curtly replies that men are not worth fighting over. Artemis tries to shame her brother into fighting with Poseidon, but Hera grabs her by the hands and whips her with her own bow until she flees in tears from the battlefield. Throughout this section the serious toils of humans are ignored as individual divinities vie for momentary prominence. The utter disdain of gods for men's activities is clear in Apollo's famed lines:

> Mortal men, pitiful wretches — like leaves, at one moment
> they are full of the blazing fire of life, eating the fruit of the field,
> but suddenly they shrivel away to death.
>
> (464–66)

Finally, at line 514 the focus returns to men's actions on the battlefield. Apollo enters Troy to plan the final deception of the book; he rouses Agenor, whom Achilles now chases in his insatiable pursuit of glory. But this pursuit is futile on all fronts. Apollo himself had urged Agenor to distract Achilles so that the other Trojans could flee safely into the city. Though Agenor considered fleeing or facing Achilles, this was senseless; Apollo had no intention of letting him actually confront the Greek hero. Both Achilles and Agenor are openly manipulated.

The four sections of book 21 all present war as an unworthy — even irrational — pursuit for men. Achilles' words to the corpse of Lycaon show how distorting the single-minded pursuit of honor can be to a warrior's basic humanity:

> Lie there now among the fish who will care little for you
> as they lick the blood from your wound. Your mother
> will not lament placing you on a bier, but the swirling Scamander
> will carry you to the broad bay of the sea.
> And a fish swimming in the wave will rise up above the black ripple

> and feed on the white fat of Lycaon.
> Die on, all—until we reach the city of sacred Ilium.
>
> (122–28)

Achilles then so pollutes the river that nature itself rebels against his intrusion. In section 3 it is made clear that divinities are so obsessed with their own prerogatives that they treat the decisions and debates of humans as frivolous. The gods insult and strike one another in an almost comic scene;[61] they brag and boast, but typically none of them are deeply concerned about mortals' deaths and sufferings on the battlefield. The book closes with a divine game in which Apollo sets all the rules, deceitfully hindering mortals from pursuing their own goals.

In this book two separate dramas are going on at once; the earthly drama takes place on the battlefield around Troy. Men respond to their thoughts and feelings in choosing the most rational course; the result may be an unfortunate and ugly war, but its heroes are actively striving to gain honor within their own value system. The second drama is among the gods, a drama that produces no profound or lasting results because of their continual quarreling and jockeying for position.[62] When these two opposed dramas conflict, the interests of the more powerful Olympians predominate.[63] Warriors who have planned and committed themselves to a set course of action are compelled to replan and pay the price for their natural inferiority. If humans could learn the lessons of book 21, they would make commitments only on the understanding that all such planning might be futile.[64] As it is, men live on and die on as best they can only to find that such thinking is useless; they can devote themselves to pride or purity, righteous anger or the seeking of individual honor, but in the larger world none of these decisions matter because the gods will manage affairs to suit themselves. The heroic code, the continual seeking to maximize one's honor and avenge hostile actions, is a defensive ethical system developed by mortals that allows them to make sense out of an existence dominated by chaotic and often malignant gods.[65] It is important that Homer presents these four scenes focused on mortal insignificance as an introduction to the battle between Achilles and Hector, in which the extreme demands of the heroic code will be exposed. The similes reinforce this interpretation of book 21 by continually picturing the actions of men as dangerous and destructive while the events sponsored by gods are presented as risk-free—and finally comic.

In the first section, centering on Lycaon (1–135), the similes describe a world where overwhelming powers (= Achilles) threaten small, innocent victims (= Trojans).[66] Achilles is immediately compared to a threatening fire before which locusts cower in the river hoping for safety (12). Fire has described Achilles since his reappearance on the wall in book 18, and he will be defended by the irresistible fire of Hephaestus later in this book. At line 22 he is compared to a killer dolphin who scares small fish back into their holes; and at 29 in a short simile the twelve captured Trojans are described as fawns. Each of these three similes is built around a traditional subject: fire and fish to describe warriors, and fawns for the victims.[67]

In addition, at line 18 the short simile describing Achilles as "equal to a god," a common simile for a fighting warrior, points directly to the theme of this book—men versus gods.[68] At line 34, when Lycaon enters the narrative, it would be possible to use a simile because he will be such an important character in the first episode, but instead Homer tells the story of his previous meeting with Achilles.[69] A simile would be so indirect that it would blunt the narrative's focus on Achilles' change of judgment in his second meeting with the defenseless warrior.[70] The following speeches could contain similes, but the issue between Lycaon and Achilles, the worth of human life, is so fundamental to the theme of the book that Homer avoids outside comparisons in the rest of this episode. The "god" simile is repeated at 227 to describe Achilles' destructive attack against the Trojans—the moment at which the river Xanthus chides Apollo for forgetting Zeus' command to support them. The two early similes of a god represent Achilles as a hero, but they raise him only to prepare for his fall; at the end of the book the only man compared to a god is cheated of victory by the clever and effortless stratagem of a real god.

In the second section (136–382) the warlike actions of Achilles are accompanied by juxtaposed similes from the world of risk and loss at 251 and 252; the topic of the first is a spear cast, and of the second, the attack of the hunting eagle, the strongest and swiftest of the birds.[71] The actions of the river god and Hephaestus, however, are accompanied by similes of a different tone. At 237 the river bellows like a bull, and in a longer simile (257) the river threatens to overtake Achilles just as water in an irrigation channel runs beyond a man who is guiding it through his garden. This scene is the equivalent of a Wordsworthian country tale[72]—and the same tone underlies the next simile, at 282, where Achilles fears that he, the very model of the heroic warrior, may now be drowned like a swineherd boy swept away as he tries to cross a large river.

Achilles reduces his own situation to a scene of absurd futility—making such a death equal to the passive result of a child's mistake. When Hephaestus battles the river Xanthus there are two similes presenting the effectiveness of the fire god, both drawn from scenes of nature at peace working in an orderly and nondestructive way. At 346 the plain of Troy is parched by Hephaestus' divine fire just as the North Wind at harvest time dries out an orchard and makes men glad. At 362 the river boils just as lard bubbles over a fire.

In the next two sections the similes continue this pattern of nature at war for Achilles versus nature at peace for his opponents. When the gods confront one another, in the third section (383–513), there is only one long simile at 493: Artemis flees like a dove that escapes a falcon; this scene eliminates killing while stressing the continual competition among species of animals.[73] When two gods discuss men, they evaluate them as leaves on trees that come and go in their seasonal cycle (464).

In contrast, in the last section (514–611), where Agenor is made to confront Achilles, the similes portray the hazards and destruction involved when two humans take warfare seriously. At 522 Achilles continues his rampage of death, causing grief to men just as though their city was being destroyed,[74] and Agenor meets him as a fearless leopard that confronts hunters and will not stop fighting until he is slain (573).[75] It is, however, explicitly stated that this is a carefully managed battle that can have no result:

> [Apollo] thrust courage in his heart, and the god himself
> stood beside him so that he might keep off the heavy hands of death
> (547–48)

This divine devil's game is the appropriate ending for a book in which continuing warfare, slaughter, destruction, terror, and grief only produce victories that are trivial or meaningless when seen from the gods' perspective. This theme, the insignificance and futility of men's pursuit of war, is developed in the carefully orchestrated series of four sections until the final absurd action where one man risks his life to fight a phantom and the other is whisked away in a cloud of smoke. In each section the poet chooses similes that underline the opposite ways in which men and gods perceive war. Because the book is designed to contrast these two attitudes, most similes are drawn from the extreme options within the similemes. Those that describe men's fighting present war as overwhelming and total in its destruction; those that describe the gods' actions and attitudes are drawn from simple country scenes where risk and danger are minimized and there is even room for quiet humor.

The transition between books 21 and 22 is so smooth that it is difficult to identify either closure or opening.[76] Achilles continues to pursue the image of Agenor, the geographical setting does not change significantly but only moves closer to the city, and the action does not turn immediately or directly to Hector; thus the challenge to the worth of men's heroism continues as the major theme. Yet the beginning of a new section of narrative, different from the four-part structure of book 21 and designed to express its own individual theme, brings Hector into sharper focus.[77] Book 22 is arguably the most complex section of the *Iliad*, since the major threads of the preceding narrative are finally joined in the battle between Achilles and Hector—a confrontation anticipated from the beginning of the epic, openly stated as a desired goal in book 9, and pursued with total dedication by Achilles after the death of Patroclus.[78] Each warrior is driven by the urgent values that he carries into this contest—and yet this contrast of values injects confusion and ambiguity into the very act that should mark a clear and final triumph for Achilles. Even though he kills his enemy, he cannot rest with this victory and must finally renounce its results. Hector, though defeated, gains sympathy as a tragic victim who in his noble and brave acceptance of death earns respect.[79] Never has it been made so clear in the course of the *Iliad* that the act emblemizing the heroic code, the slaying and plundering of the weaker by the stronger, is an act which is equivocal, even bewildering, to the humans who pursue that code.[80]

Although Hector's parents beg him to return within the walls, he succumbs to heroic urges seeking to avoid the reproach of his fellow citizens, especially of Polydamas. Yet at line 136 Hector feels the full weight of this decision and, seized with trembling, he runs. Even the heroic code, with all its powerful sanctions, cannot overwhelm the human and reasoning side of Hector; he has known both victory and defeat, and he may sense the hopelessness of confronting a warrior who wears immortal armor. Zeus cannot save Hector from death; when he raises the golden scales, Hector's fate sinks. Yet his fear and hesitancy are the very qualities that allow him to be an exemplar of an appealing type of heroism. He must fight for two purposes that are contradictory or—at best—held in an uncomfortable tension: Hector yearns for glory, but at the same time he must defend his family, his friends, and his city. He alone in the *Iliad* understands the dilemma of the hero who must balance every decision against the necessity of protecting what he regards as dear. Even as he debates engaging Achilles, his instincts move toward conciliation. He is consistent in this humane attitude throughout the book, and appropriately the similes describing the actions of Hector reflect the complex tensions that he brings to this contest.

In contrast, Achilles is unrepentantly the grand and assertive hero. When he views the miraculous armor brought by his mother from Hephaestus, he sees only fire; though encouraged to take food, his lust for vengeance is so intense that he himself will not eat and even attempts to forbid food to his men. Achilles remains uncompromising and stiff-necked, hard and cruel to a degree that will make him an inhuman monster, a war machine created as the perfected product of a perverse code. For Achilles war is a game in which men are mere counters. He twice refuses Hector's proposal for the victor to return the stripped corpse of his enemy to his countrymen in exchange for compensation. Although there have been previous single combats presented in the *Iliad* where terms satisfactory to each of the participants have been worked out as part of the code of the battlefield,[81] Achilles, having already stated that he would devour Hector's flesh raw, refuses all accommodation and ties Hector to his chariot to drag him back to his tent. The shamefulness of this act is stated directly by the poet (22.395), lacks parallels in the *Iliad*, and is powerfully dramatized in the reaction of Andromache, who first faints but when revived describes the death of Hector as the end of civilized life for herself and her child (22.487–507).[82] Yet since there is such a discrepancy between Achilles' self-definition as a warrior who seeks maximum honor and the poet's judgment of his actions, the similes designed to accompany the hero's words and actions often convey this irony.

In book 22 similes occur frequently to lend tone or color to the quality of action and the words of the warriors—but only up to the point where Achilles kills Hector.[83] Afterward the poet uses more direct techniques: speeches, significant actions, and gestures (like the fainting of Andromache).[84] Before the two heroes meet (up to line 135) there are separate similes describing each. Hector is compared to a snake swelling with wrath waiting for a man to come by his lair (93), an appropriately warlike simile, although comparable passages about snakes are too few to construct a simileme;[85] in contrast, Homer describes the other Trojans huddling in the town like fawns—a customary simile of frailty and timorousness (1).[86] Hector himself adopts a gentler tone when he considers dealing with Achilles, but he immediately realizes that the kind of dialogue held between a young man and a girl could never occur between them (127). Such a simile reveals a world of tenderness and trust that evaporates when exposed to the harsher realities of combat; it is Hector's presence that brings the possibility of a more civilized tone into the narrative.

However, as soon as Hector begins to run, acknowledging both his doubts of defending Troy and Achilles' tremendous power, his role in the similes becomes that of a vulnerable competitor, often the weaker and lesser victim in a threatening situation. The two champions are described in a series of similes with two actors: at 162 they are like racehorses contending for a prize in funeral games;[87] at 189 Hector is like a deer fleeing a hunting dog; and at 262 he is cast as a man or a lamb opposed by a lion or a wolf. The only simile in which Hector is presented as an equal is that of the two men in a dream in 199: the pursuer cannot catch his victim and the victim cannot get away—but, in fact, this equality is only a dream.

The simile at 308 in which Hector is compared to the eagle against the tender lamb seems a telling exception:

> [Hector] ... swooped as a high-flying eagle
> which dives to the plain through black clouds
> to seize either a tender lamb or a cowering rabbit.[88]

This simile, however, immediately follows Hector's decision to face Achilles and die. To support this final show of courage Homer does include the simile stressing as much as possible the strength of this warrior[89]—yet the next lines present Achilles' overwhelming counterattack with a description of Hephaistos' armor. At this point Achilles receives the balancing simile of the finest star in the heavens, and immediately kills Hector. The eagle simile allows the complex figure of Hector to be presented as a powerful warrior at the end, but only for an instant.

In choosing simile topics for Hector, Homer used some similemes that are traditional (the deer, the racehorse, and the lamb), yet he also selected others that have no parallel in other similes—the dream figure and the boy and girl, all of which are unwarlike creatures and suggest small, helpless beings. The subjects describing Hector parallel the other devices—his actions,[90] the active presence of his family, the scales of Zeus—that stress his exposed humanity as opposed to the unconquerable, divinely shielded force of Achilles.

The presentation of Achilles offers Homer a more complex challenge. In the course of book 22 he has chosen some of the most traditional subjects in his repertoire to describe Achilles: Ares, the helmeted god of war at 132; a fire or a sun at 134;[91] a bird of prey at 139;[92] a hunting dog at 189; and a lion or a wolf at 262. These topics—especially the lion, the fire, the god, and the bird—are the most frequently used similemes in Homeric poetry, and they usually describe warriors. Each simileme is appropriately developed to present not only the quality of Achilles' fighting but also his obsessively driven soul: he is devoted to pursuing the traditional role of the heroic warrior to its fullest.

Yet, in addition, there are several similes from the world of more peaceful nature.[93] At line 22 Achilles is compared to a racehorse lightly galloping across the plain; all tone of warfare is deleted from this simile. This peacefulness is underlined later, when the subject is continued at 162 to include two horses rounding a turning post on a racetrack.[94] Star similes occur at 26 and 317. At line 26 Achilles is compared to the dog star, which shines the brightest of all other stars in the sky and yet is a sign of coming evil. Such a description provides a complex parallel for Achilles, since it involves the coldness and remoteness, the purity and beauty of a distant shining star but also portends evil for men.[95] The second star simile falls at the moment when Achilles is about to kill Hector (317): the gleam from his spear point shines as the fairest star in all the heavens. In this case a lyrical scene of nature's beauty describes the most warlike of the heroes at the moment when he kills the most human of the defenders.[96] This discrepancy between peaceful simile and warlike narrative echoes the simile of the two men running in the dream at 199. Again, most of these similes describing heroic fighting are taken from traditional similemes (the horse and the star), while only one seems new (the man in the dream), but the shaping of each expresses a tone calling for an audience reaction that is more than usually complex.

This peaceful perspective injects into the tale of depraved war-lust a reminder of a more permanent and unthreatening world inhabited by civilized men. This world surrounds Hector daily in his home and his city; Achilles, although now blinded by his heroic myopia and pursuing a single-minded vendetta, was earlier aware of its existence. As Achilles sinks to an ugly level of inhumanity in his conduct of battle, scenes of nature at peace add a poetic background that forces the audience to measure his actions against the more normal day-to-day world. The final simile in book 22, the second star simile describing the gleam from the spear point that will pierce Hector's throat, is jarringly—but appropriately—one of the most peaceful similes in the whole *Iliad*:

> As a star comes from among the stars in the darkness of the night,
> the evening star that is the most beautiful star in the heavens,
> so shone the point of the sharp spear which Achilles
> poised in his right hand thinking evil thoughts against Hector. . . .
>
> (317–20)

The similes of book 22 are among the most complex and subtle in the Homeric poems because this narrative, which presents the culminating confrontation of two heroes different in character, in situation, and in their pursuit of the heroic code, has several layers of meaning. First, Homer presents Achilles, the maniacally committed warrior, in such a way that the audience cannot avoid evaluating his actions. Hector, who must temper his heroic reflexes, is constantly described as a humane warrior and tragic victim of the heroic code.[97] When Achilles kills him, the civilized world is diminished by this crude assertion of raw brutality. Hector's body is treated insultingly by the Myrmidons and Achilles, he is lamented movingly by his parents, his wife foresees and enacts the fall of the city, and her prediction of their innocent child's ruined future closes the book. The audience not only hears this tale of the two heroes' conflict as a major moment in the development of the narrative but also sees the results of the opposed values represented by each. Achilles is the purest of the warriors created by the heroic code; Hector is the first archaic man who constantly sees within himself an individuality that must be a crucial part of any decision. Their confrontation is introduced by the powerful questioning of humans' attempts to pursue consistent values and guiding purposes in book 21. The death of Hector and the insults to his body lead directly to the eventual reconciliation of Achilles with his fellow men in book 23 and 24.

A listing of similemes in book 22 seems to jump randomly from one topic to another, but when joined with the structure of the narrative, the individual similes support the design of the story effectively. First, the heroes are apart—Achilles rushing toward the city and Hector near the wall pondering single combat (1–134). Then the two men are in contact, Hector running and Achilles pursuing (135–246); finally, they directly confront one another (247–363). In the first part of the book, up to line 134, Hector and Achilles each receive individual similes. After 134 the poet chooses similes that include two elements—one representing Achilles and the other, Hector: Achilles is the falcon while Hector is the dove; Achilles is the hunting dog while Hector is the deer; Achilles is the lion while Hector is the man or the lamb.[98] The point of contact with the narrative is specifically made double by using a plural or dual (162), by making Achilles the point of origin for the simile but rejoining the narrative with Hector (189), or by using a coordinated two-part sentence to reenter the narrative (136 and 199). In each case a traditional simile subject suggesting overpowering force meets an object that is customarily associated with vulnerability, hesitancy, or helplessness. In addition, Achilles is even drawn into Hector's area of weaker forces: two racehorses are used in one simile, and two men run in the dream. This alternation of similes that describe Achilles—at one time the most warlike subject, at another a peaceful scene—is only superficially disordered; within the design of the narrative it is a strong device for expressing the ambiguity of Achilles' own position as seen by the poet—and as it will be seen by Achilles himself by the end of the epic. Opposed to this alternation is the consistency with which Hector is compared to the weaker creatures in each simileme.

It is pointless to discuss junctures where Homer chose not to use a simile, because the battle section of this book contains one of the densest collections of similes in the Homeric poems. At almost every opportunity similes reinforce the scene, which is in every way the essential statement of the epic's theme—the unavoidable, inevitable battle between Achilles and Hector, the perfected hero versus the humane hero.

Books 21 and 22 together support this theme, although each is composed differently. The juxtaposition of their differing content and style is echoed by Homer's conscious design of the similes to reinforce and supplement the narrative units. The books are joined closely when the narrative moves directly from book 21 to book 22 as Achilles continues his pursuit of Apollo/Agenor. Yet the game Apollo plays with Achilles is the appropriate conclusion to book 21, since it is the most cynical misleading of man by god in the *Iliad*, thus exemplifying the insignificance of mortals' pursuits of honor in a final brief episode. Similarly, the exposure of this ruse is the proper introduction for the major confrontation of the poem, for in being tricked, Achilles is shamed; he feels "robbed of great glory" and wishes that he could seek vengeance against the god (22.18f.). This enhanced need to seek maximum honor even at the cost of exceeding normal human limits is the appropriate beginning for the contrasting characterizations in book 22.

As the books have different themes, so also the narrative is structured in different ways. Book 21 is composed of a series of four discrete incidents:

Lycaon, the battle with the river, the general battle among the gods, and Apollo's deception of Achilles. Throughout these scenes the heroes' thoughts and plans decrease in importance from the moment when one mortal warrior offers another the chance to choose humanity on the battlefield to the final scene in which one warrior is effortlessly duped by the overwhelming power of a god. The causal linkage between scenes is sufficiently slight that Homer appears more interested in juxtaposing a series of individual units than in structuring a unified, linear narrative. For example, after Hephaestus has overcome the river, there is virtually no transition:

> But when the fury of the river Xanthus was overcome,
> the two stopped, for Hera — though she remained angry — checked them.
> But among the other gods there fell a heavy strife. . . .
>
> (21.383–85)

Similarly, Apollo proposes to withdraw from the fighting at 466ff. and then does disappear from the narrative with no response to his sister's angry outburst; yet within thirty lines he is entering the city of Troy, and soon he is back on the battlefield deceiving Achilles in order to save the Trojans. Appropriately, the similes throughout this book are designed to emphasize the radically different views and behaviors of gods and men in the four juxtaposed episodes.

Book 22, however, develops a carefully motivated linear structure within a balanced framework. The spotlight shifts between the two champions as they move closer to one another and then focuses on the final combat. The final scene of lamentation by Priam and Hecuba repeats the configuration at the beginning of the book where they both appeal to Hector (33–89 and 408–35); and Hector's monologue on the possibility of confronting Achilles and saving the city is balanced by Andromache's lament for his death, with its heavy implication of the city's downfall (99–130 and 460–515). Even in the last sections of lamentation, divided areas of activity are carefully joined; Andromache looks out over the battlefield to see the body of Hector disappearing in the distance toward the Greek ships. The scene within the wall and outside shows simultaneous action in the two areas. To a large degree it is the similes in this book that provide the sense of a narrowing chase; as a result the moments focusing on the main characters can be devoted to the development of personal motivations and contrasting purposes.

The placement and development of the similes in these two books corroborate their individualized themes, structures, and designs. There are, of course, obvious connections between similes when the poet repeats a subject late in the book that he has used earlier or continues to choose the same subject several times.[99] But rather than hearing each simile solely as an addition to its own passage shaped to match the surrounding scene, the audience, drawing on its knowledge of the diverse similemes, can interpret them broadly as integral components of the book's design.

ILIAD, BOOK 11:
SIMILES TO MARK A SHIFTING SCENE[100]

Homer made similes an important element in the design of book 11.[101] Not only does this book contain the largest number of similes in the Homeric poems, but several are among the most forceful descriptions in the simile repertoire. There is a plan in their distribution: they are concentrated in the battlefield section of the book and almost totally suppressed in the scene between Nestor and Patroclus. In addition, simile subjects are often repeated, suggesting that Homer sought to create cross-references and to invite comparisons within his narrative. Four times similes are juxtaposed to intensify their effect. As a result, an exploration of the dense array of similes in this book can lead to further definition of their role in Homeric narrative — especially in regard to placement, choice of subjects, and extension.

The complexities of book 11 are rooted in its role as a pivotal book in the *Iliad*.[102] Schadewaldt has compellingly demonstrated how many of the elements of the evolving epic converge in this book: the decisions of individual warriors, the consequences of their actions, and the importance of Zeus' plan in shifting momentum to the Trojans — all bring pressure on Achilles to reevaluate his strategy. The narrative begins with the dawning of a new day as the Greeks are freshly inspired for war (1–2 and 50); but it ends with the despairing words of the wounded Greek warrior, Eurypylus:

> No more, godborn Patroclus, will there be a defense for the Greeks,
> but they will fall back against the black ships.
> For all those who before were our champions
> lie near the ships struck and wounded
> at the hands of the Trojans. Their strength grows greater.
>
> (11.823–27)

More broadly, the book is structured to show the increasingly urgent situation of the Greeks caused by Zeus' vigorous pursuit of his plan (begun in book 8) and the results of their failed appeal to Achilles in book 9.[103] Whether the *Doloneia* precedes book 11 is a problem external to this discussion. If it is genuine, then it provides the success that motivates the reinvigorated attitude of the Greeks; the transition to the beginning of book 11 is smoother. Yet without book 10 the Greeks can equally well grow eager for battle in response to the cry of Eris (10–12) and to the rousing challenge of Diomedes at the end of book 9.[104]

Book 11's narrative is organized around three major characters: Agamemnon, Hector, and Patroclus. The book opens with the reinvigoration of the Greeks, Agamemnon's highly elaborate arming scene, and his initially successful aristeia.[105] The audience, however, remains aware of Zeus' promise to Thetis in book 1, the ominous external pressure that has begun to steer the battle and is responsible for Agamemnon's withdrawal. The agent for Zeus' plan is Hector, who in the course of book 11 emerges to be an effective leader for the Trojans as they force a series of Greek heroes to retreat. His success on the battlefield, though artificially enhanced, heightens his role as the commander of the Trojans in the service of Zeus. Finally Patroclus, the most crucial secondary figure in the epic, is brought into the narrative to report the dangers pressing on the Greeks—the very result that Achilles prayed for and Zeus promised to support. Patroclus' emotions run deep, and the number of wounded Greeks arouses his compassion, thus motivating angry and frustrated tears when he delivers his message to Achilles at the beginning of book 16.

Not all commentators elevate Hector to the level that I have suggested. The majority of modern critics agree that the structure of book 11 is based on a series of Greek woundings and reverses—Agamemnon, Diomedes, Odysseus, and Ajax—all of which lead to the bleak situation that brings Patroclus to Nestor's tent;[106] only in book 12 does Hector emerge to lead his troops relentlessly forward until they break through the Greek wall. But I would argue that Homer has organized book 11 to support the development of the narrative from book 8 through 18.242, Hector's promised day of preeminence.[107] Agamemnon is clearly portrayed as the center of attention in the first section of book 11 (1–283), but Hector is given an equal introduction even in that section, and in various ways the narrative foreshadows his importance when he becomes the agent of Zeus' plan. In the next unit (284–596)

Hector reenters the battle with the introduction of a hero entering his aristeia and is a constant presence as the Trojans gain strength. That strength is illustrated by the sequential wounding of the Greek heroes, whose combined suffering at the hands of the Trojans shows the clear emergence of the plan of Zeus. Hector as leader is the only proper carrier of that theme even though he does not accomplish all the killings; he is mentioned thirteen times after he enters the battle under Zeus' promise, while the focus shifts between the three Greek warriors. In addition, the motivation for the meeting between Nestor and Patroclus is the general fear of a Trojan success. Achilles says on sending Patroclus to Nestor:

> Noble son of Menoitius, dear to my heart,
> now I think that the Achaeans will stand around my knees
> begging; for a need has come which is no longer endurable.
>
> (11.608–10)

Surely the need he sees is not caused solely by the removal of Machaon from battle, which is the subject of the following lines.[108] Even though Patroclus at 648–54 cites Machaon as his only interest, Nestor seems to realize that Achilles has larger concerns on his mind and easily expands those concerns to include the more widespread weakness of the Greeks in his speech at 655ff.

Homer often uses single heroes to present the prevailing direction on the battlefield. Between such individualized scenes he will insert general lines summarizing the status of the battle, but the situation of the armies is derived from the results of previous encounters. In this case the role of Hector presents the beginning of the relative weakening of the Greek army through a series of individual woundings by various Trojan heroes; the more normal battle scene would focus on the dominating hero rather than the threatened enemy.

The main structural sections of book 11 are clearly marked by the sequential entrances of the three major characters—Agamemnon, Hector, and Patroclus—each as the dominant figure in his part of the narrative. Consistent with the enhanced role for Hector, the second section contains divisions that are centered on a principal Greek hero:[109]

1. 1–283: the aristeia of Agamemnon
2. 284–596: the entrance of Hector
   a. 310–400: the wounding of Diomedes

    b. 401–88: the wounding of Odysseus
    c. 489–596: the fighting of Ajax
3. 597–848: the mission of Patroclus

Two points of significance for the development of Homer's theme stand out in this outline. First, in Agamemnon's aristeia the spotlight follows him as the single active agent moving from victory to victory. In contrast, Hector appears only sporadically as the leader of the Trojan effort. The spotlight does not follow him; rather, the focus shifts from one Greek hero to another. Since he is explicitly supported, instructed, and guarded by Zeus, this form of presentation is highly expressive; to present him as an independent hero scoring a series of personal victories would be false.[110]

Second, in the final section of the book Patroclus becomes entangled in a series of events that leads inevitably to his death. Homer marks the moment:

> Immediately he [Achilles] spoke to his comrade Patroclus,
> calling from the ship. And when he heard, he came from the hut
> like Ares — and this was the beginning of evil for him.
>
> (602–4)

At this point there are major changes in content and style: the scene shifts from the battlefield to a more intimate setting in a removed camp, the plot is developed more through speeches than actions, and similes disappear as complements to the narrative.

Since this book presents a turning point in the battle, it appropriately puts many heroes in the foreground — mainly Agamemnon and Hector, but also Diomedes, Odysseus, Menelaus, Ajax, Achilles, Patroclus, Nestor, and others. In contrast, book 2 focuses on Agamemnon and book 22 opposes the responses of Achilles and Hector to the heroic code's demands. The major problem of book 11 is maintaining a clear direction in a narrative that threatens to break apart. There are almost too many characters in book 11, and they seem to get in each other's way. Agamemnon is so powerful a warrior that Hector must be removed for his own safety, but once Agamemnon is gone Hector is offered a clear path to the Greek ships. However, this turn in the battle disturbs Achilles sufficiently that he seeks information — thus involving Patroclus. In essence, all these characters are called upon to play the role of preeminent warrior that only Achilles can perform, but he is unwilling, and they lack his ability and focus.

As a result, the theme of book 11 does not depend on one or two individual warriors but, rather, concerns the complex interconnections of these characters with each other under the plan of Zeus. The book has scarcely begun with the arming of Agamemnon when Homer abruptly postpones the Greek advance to present Hector amid the Trojans.[111] Later Zeus removes Hector from the battle as the Greek leader presses on after him (163ff.).[112] But when Agamemnon is forced to withdraw, Hector is given an entrance equivalent to Agamemnon's — an appropriate opening to the second section: Hector shouts a rallying cry to the Trojans boasting that Zeus has promised glory to him, he receives four honorific similes, and the poet lists a catalogue of his victims (283ff.).[113]

Dominating the two contrasting sections (1–283 and 294–596) is Zeus' constant presence. He makes his plan obvious to all when he sends Iris to speak his will to Hector:

> As long as [Hector] sees Agamemnon, the shepherd of the people,
> raging among the front fighters and killing rank after rank of men,
> let him withdraw and order his troops
> to fight with the enemy in the strong conflict.
> But when struck by a spear or hit by an arrow
> Agamemnon leaps behind his horses, then shall I grant Hector
> power to kill until he comes to the well-benched ships,
> and the sun goes down and sacred darkness appears.
>
> (11.187–94)

Later at the beginning of book 13 Zeus will relax for a moment, but at this point his presence is pervasive. In line 3 he authorizes Eris to rouse the Greeks to battle. The breastplate of Agamemnon is described as being adorned with dark blue serpents, "like rainbows, which the son of Cronos has placed in the clouds to be a portent for mortals" (27–28). Hector's bronze armor flashes like the lightning of Zeus (66). As the battle is about to begin, Zeus sprinkles the ground with bloody drops of dew, and later he is reported to be sitting apart from the other gods watching the battle around Troy (52–55 and 80–83). At 163 Hector is taken off to a safe position by Zeus and then warned to avoid battle while Agamemnon is still fighting. At 336 Zeus, as he continues to watch the conflict from Mount Ida, makes the opposing lines even. Ajax fights like a torrent driven by the rains of Zeus as he enters this carefully managed battle (489–97). Only in the third section, when the scene switches to the Greek camp near the ships, does Zeus fade as an active force, but by this point he has so organized the battlefield that men will carry his intentions forward.

In the first two sections similes constantly reinforce the narrative. At the book's opening it is important to celebrate Agamemnon, who strives to be a leader and hero in order to reinvigorate a situation that has been disintegrating since the end of the previous day (book 8); his fighting is successful enough to overcome recollection of his despairing words at the beginning of book 9. The morning battle is described as fierce and balanced. Similes enhance the fluid situation: Agamemnon's breastplate is decorated with serpents that gleam like ominous rainbows (27),[114] while Hector appears as a baneful star and his armor shines like lightning (62 and 66). The first battle of the two armies is described in opposed similes of peace and war that reflect the ambiguous conditions on the battlefield: the warriors are like workmen in a wheat field, but simultaneously they rage like wolves (67 and 72).[115]

The description of the weary woodsman closes the morning's battle and initiates the presentation of a contrasting atmosphere of raised expectations and resolute fighting (84–93). Agamemnon begins to dominate as he pursues the cruelest and most bloodthirsty mode of combat in the *Iliad*: warriors who vainly beg to be taken alive are ruthlessly slain, even though they were formerly freed for ransom by Achilles; the woundings are physical and gory; Agamemnon decapitates and mutilates the enemy; when he strips men, they are left to be carrion for vultures; his pursuit is ceaseless, and even Hector must be pulled to safety.[116]

The similes reinforce this powerful style of fighting. Agamemnon's initial series of killings concludes this way:

> as a lion easily crushes the gentle young
> of a swift deer, snatching them with his strong teeth,
> once he has entered into their lair, and he devours their tender hearts;
> and even if the mother happens to be near,
> she cannot give them aid, for a severe trembling comes over her.
> Swiftly she darts through the thick brush and woods,
> rushing and sweating beneath the attack of the powerful beast
>
> (11.113–19)

Agamemnon is described three more times as a lion (129, 172, 239)[117] and once as a raging forest fire (155). In both of the extended lion similes the description presents the helplessness of the victims before the lion's power with special emphasis on his killing the young, breaking up families, and doing physical damage (113 and 172).[118] These are all extreme elements from the lion simileme.[119]

The fire simile at 155 emphasizes the completeness of the destruction; the audience would know similarly extreme passages derived from the fire simileme. When Agamemnon strikes off the head of Hippolochus and sends it rolling on the ground, there is a simile to call attention to the vicious oddity of his death (147).

After this series, the simile that describes the wounding of Agamemnon, sufficiently painful to cause him to withdraw from battle, is perhaps the most ironic in the Homeric poems: the manslayer is compared to a woman in childbirth (269). In contrast to the preceding similes, the destroyer of young deer, thickets, and cattle suddenly becomes a mother figure.[120] The distance between this simile and the brutal descriptions of Agamemnon's killings emphasizes the absurd abruptness of the change on the battlefield — thus highlighting the artificiality of a war scene controlled by Zeus.

The entrance of Hector is presented as a lesser event, even though Zeus has specifically promised him a moment of glory. To be sure, he enters the battle as a leader, accompanied by four honorific similes.[121] He is compared to a hunter setting his dogs on a boar or lion,[122] to Ares the war god, and twice to a tempestuous wind that whips up the sea (292, 295, 297, and 305):

> as when a hunter drives his white-toothed dogs
> against a wild boar or a lion
>
> (11.292–93)

> like a strongly blowing wind
> which falling downward stirs the violet-hued sea
>
> (11.297–98)

The hunting simile, however, lacks the detailed and gory descriptions of the strongest versions — for example, 20.164–73:[123]

> He rushed against him like a rapacious lion,
> that men are eager to kill, the whole town,
> once they have gathered. He ignores them
> going on his way, but when one of the young men, swift in battle,
> strikes him with a spear, then he crouches down with open mouth,
> foam appears around his teeth, and his brave spirit groans in his heart,

    and he lashes his ribs and flanks with his tail
    on both sides, urging himself to fight.
    With glowing eyes he charges forcefully
    to see if he will kill one of the men or himself be slain in the crowd

In the same way the power of the wind simile is diminished in comparison to many others familiar to the audience; for example:

    as a fast-moving wave
    swollen by the wind from beneath the clouds
    falls upon a swift ship; the whole ship is hidden by the foam,
    the terrible blast of the wind roars in the sail,
    and the sailors tremble in fear—for only barely do they escape death
                                                        (15.624)

13.795 also expresses nature's power, even though it does not specifically mention the threat of sinking the ship or destroying the men:

    like the blast of harsh winds
    that rush over the plain driven by the thunder of father Zeus
    and stir up the sea with a gigantic roar; many waves
    of the loud-sounding sea boil up,
    arching high and white—some before and some following after

In contrast, at 11.297 the simile's force is confined to the adjectives "strongly blowing" and "violet-hued" rather than the series of action verbs in the cited parallels. Because the wind and wave simileme is used so frequently, the audience would recognize the relative weakness of the similes Homer has created to accompany Hector's fighting.[124]

Immediately the promise in Hector's entrance is cut short as a series of Greek heroes occupies the spotlight. The story now no longer presents a series of effortless killings by a cold-blooded, efficient warrior; Hector has to work to gain appropriate visibility in the battle scenes. In addition, the characters from Agamemnon's similes spill over into those that describe the Greeks' resistance. Hector's introductory simile describes a hunter sending his dogs against a lion (292);[125] even though Agamemnon has departed from the battle, not only does the lion remain the opponent, but the principal character of the simile, the Trojan, is a single human.[126] He may win, but that is uncertain, since the conflict is at best a battle between equals. When Odysseus and

Diomedes appear, the imbalance is repeated as they are compared to two boars that attack hunting dogs; later Diomedes even describes the Trojans as goats who tremble before a lion (324 and 383). When the Trojans approach the isolated Odysseus, they are again presented as hounds and young men around a boar who refuses to give way, and Ajax comes to aid Odysseus like a lion who scatters cowardly jackals (414 and 474).[127] By the end of the second section the Trojan attack stalls as Ajax refuses to give way, and Hector avoids a confrontation. Appropriately, Ajax attracts a simile that is typical for a warrior: a rampaging river (492).[128] This simile comes after a brief catalogue of the Trojans slain by Ajax — a customary marker of an aristeia — and also provides Ajax with the same type of introduction that Hector had earlier received at 299ff. Ajax's effort does not develop into an aristeia, but Hector's potential sweep is stopped. Ajax's strength is described by three juxtaposed similes, each of which progressively focuses on his characteristics as a warrior: he is like a wild beast, a persistent lion, and a stubborn ass (546, 548, and 558).[129]

In the simile concluding the second section the two armies fight like blazing fire (596), a shared image appropriately closing the two battle sections of book 11, since the fighting has been equally intense for both sides.

The two main characters in the first sections are carefully drawn. Agamemnon is a dominating warrior, bloodthirsty in his pursuit of victory; the similes support this characterization economically and effectively. The similes of section 2 picture Hector and the Trojans as weaker opponents, likening them to dogs, goats, a woman or a child, hounds and young men, jackals, oaks and pines, dogs and country folk, and small boys — subjects never used to describe impressive power in Homeric epic. Those subjects that traditionally represent the decisive might of a warrior are boars, lions, and rivers — precisely the topics used to describe the Greeks in a series of similes (324, 383, 414, 474, 491, and 548). Before Agamemnon is compelled to retreat and Zeus gives power to Hector, the Greek king receives similes in which the opponents are overwhelmed. After this point, each time another strong warrior appears in Hector's area the similes delineate the equalized or even uncertain strengths of the Trojans, most precisely at 474:

> The Trojans followed like bloody jackals around a horned stag
> that has been wounded in the mountains — a stag that a man has struck
> with an arrow from his bow. The stag escapes fleeing

as long as his blood flows warm and his limbs move.
But when the swift arrow wears him down,
the flesh-eating jackals devour him
in a shadowy mountain grove. And a divinity brings a hungry lion
    upon them.
The jackals scatter and the lion feasts on the carcass.
In this way then around the wise and crafty Odysseus
did the Trojans crowd, many brave ones, but the warrior
darted forward to keep off the fatal day with his weapon.
Then Ajax came near bearing his shield like a tower
and stood near him. The Trojans all scattered in different directions.
(11.474–86)

    Throughout the first two sections of book 11, similes respond to the strategy of the narrative in their placement, the choice of subject for each simile, and the design of the extensions. In addition, all similes in book 11 occur in places where the tradition would have suggested the use of a simile and suitable similemes among the alternative ways of continuing the narrative. Homer chooses to use similes when they enhance the presentation of his theme, and he extends them to fortify this strategy. In the first section similes are drawn from the traditional families that accompany warriors in battle, but in addition, each consistently contains the most physical and bloodthirsty alternatives from its simileme. In the second section the Greeks are not made weaker; they are presented as being forced to retreat when confronted by opponents who have the force of Zeus behind their attack. The poet uses his similes to show the undiminished power of the Greek warriors, who thus retain sufficient strength to reverse the direction of the battle in books 13–15.

    This imbalance in strength should not seem unusual. Throughout the *Iliad* Hector is regarded as a warrior whose bravery will be fatal. In the earlier meeting between Hector and Andromache she tells him that his power (*menos*) will kill him (6.407)—a prediction that is fulfilled at 22.96, where the same *menos* compels Hector to confront the charging Achilles. She develops this idea further when she becomes aware that Hector is already dead:

> [Achilles] has made him cease from the painful courage
> that was his alone since he never did remain with the mass of men,
> but always rushed forward yielding to no man in his power
> (22.457–59)

Not only does Zeus aid him to gain victories in contests that he would not necessarily win on his own; Hector is willingly complicit in seeking greater risk. Even the simile for Hector at 12.41 describes a lion whose "courage kills him."[130]

Book 11 contains more similes than any other book in the Homeric poems, and they are densely packed; on average there is a simile every nineteen lines throughout the first two sections of the book. Even this statistic is misleading, since multiple similes often cluster around a single event, thus intensifying their effect. Agamemnon is introduced with a direct comment on his heroic status by the lengthy arming scene; this arming scene is balanced by the immediate introduction of Hector through two similes and a catalogue of his fellow Trojans (55–63). Even in this small way the relative merits of the opposed warriors are made clear: Agamemnon is given an honorific introduction through his actions and the quality of his armor, but Hector is described only indirectly by similes and a listing of his associates. At the beginning of the second section Hector enters the battle with four juxtaposed similes and a list of those he kills; but this lavish introduction collapses as Homer fails to develop a formal and glorious aristeia. In fact, the next set of juxtaposed similes accompanies Ajax, who steadfastly protects the faltering Greek cause and opens the way for a series of quieter scenes where men consider their responses to the pressures that have blunted the Greek attack (474–95 and 497–542).

It is difficult to specify other incidents in this book that might have received a simile. The structure of the book is relatively simple, and the details in the narrative all seem to support that structure. Similes are so common that the addition of yet more comparisons seems unnecessary; the problem is not to find places where further similes might have occurred, but rather to judge whether this book, with its high number of colorful and vigorous similes, could allow any more.

The final section of the book describes the response of Achilles to the Zeus-driven results of the battle: he sends Patroclus to Nestor's tent. The report of his mission is of a totally different nature from the two battle sections and highly important to the book's major contribution to the *Iliad*'s design. As the narrative shifts to Nestor's quiet tent, Homer invites his audience to witness the private meeting of the two Greek warriors. There is no reason to order or rank the battle skills of various kings or to define the momentary shifts in the directions within the ongoing battle. Similes fall away completely—with two exceptions: Nestor's servant is "like the goddesses" (638), and he describes his own fighting with a familiar simile, "like a black whirlwind" (747). Perhaps Homer uses these similes to hint at the rough-and-tumble world outside this quiet inner scene; if so, the short similes reaffirm the calm discussion of the two men as they try to bring order to the inconstant world of battle that the earlier sections of the book have portrayed.[131]

In a variety of ways it is clear that this is a carefully crafted book—central to many of the themes in the *Iliad* and containing incidents that will later prove of enormous significance. Not only does this book have the largest number of similes in the Homeric poems, but several are among the most forceful descriptions in the simile repertoire. Book 11's similes play a major role in emphasizing and organizing shifts in the balance and complexity of the hard-fought battle. As a result they are closely coordinated with the narrative themes:

1. The ever-dominant power of Zeus in aiding the Trojans.
2. The clear demonstration that the Trojans are forcing the Greeks back to the ships, but only with the divine force temporarily given to them by Zeus. The Greeks are not being portrayed as weak even though they retreat.

Although all similes in book 11 occur in places where the tradition would have suggested them, it remains Homer's choice to use these similes because they enhance the presentation of his themes, and he consistently extends them to fortify this strategy.

CONCLUSION

The broad traditional background of the Homeric poems allows plot and character to have separate lives. They can function independently because each is based on discrete areas of the traditional storytelling material. The plot of book 1 of the *Iliad* presents two characters who argue with increasing fervor and bitterness until they seem to reach an impasse. The plot calls for a summary position of both sides, but both characters are so hot-headed and intense that they are not likely to pause to sum up their case; therefore the plot needs a third party to come forward to slow the action in order to let characters and audience take a breath before those final statements. But the plot does not dictate the character to play the role of intermediary. Depending on the direction Homer wants for his narrative, he has a large cast of characters who are well known to the audience. He chooses Nestor. But it is important to remember that Nestor existed as a character who could cool down a scene before book 1 was formed — and the same could be said for the various other types of warriors that make up the traditional storyteller's collection.

Most probably Homer's creative process allowed him to develop the plot and choose the appropriate characters in an instant. But he did have a reliably typical quarrel scene between leaders and "insubordinates" that would fulfill his narrative needs: Hector/Polydamas, Zeus/Hera, Hector/Achilles, Odysseus/individual suitors, Telemachus/Antinoos. Each scene occupies a position in an ongoing narrative that calls for a certain tone and argumentative style. The tradition also supplied Homer with a series of characters that provided varied styles and coloration.

As a part of this creative process Homer also drew upon a series of traditional similemes, which through repeated use came with suggestions for choice of topics, placement in the narrative, and possible extensions. In book 2 Agamemnon's plan actually weakens the Greek army that finds itself roaming the battlefield in confusion. Similes are used repeatedly to show a strong army brought to weak action by the misperceptions of their leader. In books 21 and 22 the plot structures are completely different. The similes support individual sections of book 21 in stressing the varied qualities of the fighting among different participants, but then in book 22 they programmatically follow the developing scene between the two champions until Hector is finally killed. In book 11 the narrative centers on Agamemnon and Hector — but also on Zeus. Both plot and characters are interwoven in the complexities of this book, but the similes are a reliable guide to the continuing reality beneath the narrative.

The important role that similes can play in such settings is best illustrated by contrasting parallel scenes. First there are two passages where the reaction of the army to a leader's encouragement is obedience, but with a very different spirit. In book 2 Agamemnon concludes his first speech of instruction to the troops:

> But come now, even as I say, let all be obedient.
> Let us flee with our ships to our dear native land;
> for no longer shall we capture Troy with its broad streets.
>   So he spoke, and he moved the hearts in their breasts

for all among the multitude, as many as had not heard his plan.
The gathering was moved like the long waves of the deep,
the Icarian Sea, which the East Wind and the South
rouse rushing from the clouds of father Zeus,
and just as the West Wind comes to a deep field of corn,
blowing briskly, and sets the ears to bobbing;
just so was the full gathering moved. They with shouting
rushed to the ships, and the dust rose up high
from beneath their feet; they urged one another
to lay hold of their ships and to push them into the sacred sea,
and they cleaned out the launching tracks. The shout rose to the heavens
from the men eager to return home. And they removed the props from
    under the ships.

(2. 139–54)

In book 15 Ajax urges his men to take heart even though the Trojans are about to burn the Greek ships:

My friends, be men, and put shame in your hearts,
have respect for one another in the strong fighting.
When men have shame, more live than die;
when men flee, neither glory nor valor is present.
    So he spoke, and they were eager to defend themselves;
they took his word into their hearts, and they fenced off the ships
with a wall of bronze.

(15.560–67)

It is clear from this comparison that direct description is the strongest form of Homeric expression. There is no clearer mode of showing agreement than the speech-into-action pattern in book 15. And of course the audience is aware that the poet could add many elements that would provide a mood or imply resistance to direct action. The passage from book 2 shows how the injection of a simile between the command and the performance can be crucial. The wind and wave simile is not the most powerful or intense within the simileme; the movement is confused by the force of conflicting winds, and there is no destruction involved. The second simile of the bobbing ears of corn offers little purposeful activity. As a result, the army performs the actions

Homer's Use of Similes to Delineate Character and Plot · 91

ordered by their commander only after images of disorganization and purposelessness introduce their responsive action through the similes.

Contrasting similes provide another revealing comparison of the powerful contribution that each can make. In book 14 Hector is disabled by a stone thrown by Ajax:

> then great Ajax, son of Telamon, struck him as he withdrew
> with a stone, for many — as props for the swift ships —
> rolled at the feet of the warriors; hoisting one of these
> he hurled it at his chest above his shield just by his neck;
> striking him he twirled him around like a top, and he spun about wildly.
> Just as an oak falls beneath the blast of father Zeus,
> uprooted, and a dreadful smell of sulfur rises
> from it, and no man standing near sees this
> and keeps calm, for terrifying is the lightning of great Zeus;
> just so did the powerful Hector fall immediately to the ground in
>   the dust.
> He dropped his spear from his hand, and his shield and helmet
> were thrown from him, and his shiny bronze armor rang about him.
>
> (14.409–20)

Notice the contrast when Agamemnon's wound forces him to withdraw in book 11:

> But when the wound grew dry and the blood stopped flowing,
> sharp pains overcame the might of Atreus' son.
> Just as when a sharp pang seizes a woman in labor,
> stinging, the pain which the Eilithuiae send, the goddesses of childbirth,
> the daughters of Hera who supply bitter pains;
> just so did sharp pains overcome the might of Atreus' son.
> He leaped into his chariot and ordered his charioteer
> to drive to the hollow ships; for his heart was pained.
>
> (11.267–74)

Every element of the scene around Hector stresses the danger presented by his attacker and his weapon; the stone is a prop for ships, Ajax takes careful aim, the force of the blow spins Hector around and lays him to the ground, he drops his weapons and is left defenseless in the middle of the battlefield. The simile is a perfect complement to this tone; the oak is proverbially sturdy, the power of the lighting bolt is stressed, and the observer is shaken at the sight. These descriptive elements leave no doubt that this is a serious wound to the Trojans' leader.

When Agamemnon is wounded, all the elements are softened. Iphidamas fails to harm Agamemnon in his attack (12.234–37); Agamemnon still kills this opponent and strips away his armor. Coon, Iphidamas' brother pushes a spear through Agamemnon's arm, but Agamemnon continues to fight and kills him too. Then the wound begins to draw down his strength. The simile responds to this scene: there is no question of a moment of total destruction leaving a warrior defenseless. In fact, he is only momentarily weakened and needs to withdraw. There is deep irony in using the image of a woman in childbirth to describe the temporary affliction of the warrior who had been the bloodthirsty, unsparing killer of so many Trojans.

Wounding scenes vary widely in their effect, ranging from sheer misses to instant deaths. The similemes of lions and boars, winds, fish, and farm animals are often repeated topics for such scenes.[132] In these two passages Homer has gone to extremes to contrast the most serious of wounds and an insignificant, healable wound. The completely opposed tones of the two passages show the degree to which similes can be developed to follow the needs of each narrative scene.

In these matched comparisons the use of similes to parallel the shifts in characters and plots demonstrates the flexibility available to the poet within the areas of topics, placements, and the various extensions possible — in addition to the choice to use a simile at all.

This chapter has largely treated Homer's use of similes to reinforce his narrative. While not as directly involved in the decisions of plot and character, the co-creating audience had already learned, by hearing decades' worth of tales, how to decode the poet's choices in forming similes from similemes. In the books treated in the next two chapters this audience is increasingly vital in more interpretive areas of determining and organizing the themes, deriving significant meaning from typical actions, and finally using simile topics to comment on the broader action.

CHAPTER FOUR

Similes to Delineate a Narrative Theme

Many sections of Homeric narrative are not focused on one or two characters in a single, developing situation. Several books have a broader scope; either they describe one situation within which several warriors are highlighted, like the assault on the Greek wall in book 12, or else attention is focused on one character in a series of special situations, such as Diomedes in *Iliad* 5 or Odysseus in *Odyssey* 22 and 5. In these books the theme is important both in the structure of the individual book and in its contribution to the greater plan of the poem. Without Hector's breaching of the wall the anger of Poseidon would lack motivation, as would the jockeying for position among the various gods who attempt to influence the battle in books 13–15.[1] In *Iliad* 5 the poet sketches the problems that Diomedes, as a model hero, must resolve in conducting his aristeia, thus introducing critical problems that Achilles will explore more deeply in his radical challenge to the heroic code. Throughout the battle book of the *Odyssey*, book 22, blood is shed and vengeance taken in a series of scenes, yet it is made clear that forces greater than the heroic code are motivating the combatants. In *Odyssey* 5 the terms of the hero's choice to return to Ithaca are made clear in the two separate panels of Calypso's island and the storm — the choice that will motivate Odysseus' perseverance through the rest of the epic as he regains his wife, family, and throne. In these books the similes join with familiar compositional devices, such as diction, formulaic expressions, and type scenes, to form highly individualized narratives focusing on a major theme.

ILIAD, BOOK 12:
DIRECT FOCUS ON A SINGLE THEME[2]

Although book 12 presents strong efforts by both sides in the battle, at the end the Trojans finally break through the Greek defensive wall.[3] There are enough references to this wall throughout the book to establish it as the narrative's principal framing and organizing element.[4] At the beginning of the book, Homer develops the motif of the gods' anger against the wall's builders into a major statement that Poseidon and Apollo will join the force of many rivers to sweep it away once the war is concluded. Later Sarpedon comes close to breaking through the wall, and finally Hector bursts open the gates with a large stone and leads the Trojans inside the wall as the battle moves ever closer to the Greek ships.

Behind this structured Trojan advance the plan of Zeus is constantly visible;[5] the terms of this plan were presented earlier, in book 11, when Iris reported Zeus' pledge to give Hector glory in battle throughout the day "until he comes to the well-benched ships, and the sun sets and sacred darkness comes on" (11.208–9). Hector, putting his own trust completely in Zeus' promise, upbraids Polydamas for his fastidious advice (12.200–250). Following this speech Zeus sends a wind from Mt. Ida blowing dust into the eyes of the Greeks, bewildering their minds and gaining glory for Hector and the Trojans (252–55). Subsequent Trojan successes are dependent on the enhanced strength of Hector, who assumes undisputed leadership as he opens the way through the Greek defenses. Even though he surpasses Sarpedon in his achievement, it is explicitly stated that Zeus made it easy for him to lift the rock with which he breaks through the wall (450). The interwoven and mutually reinforcing themes of book 12 are the plan of Zeus and the focus on Hector as he directs the battle and finally breaches the wall. All this is stated succinctly at 173–74, when the Trojan Asios complains about the unexpected Greek strength:

> Thus he spoke, but his words did not persuade the mind of Zeus.
> For his will was to give glory to Hector.

The book moves purposefully through six sections, organized around the failed attack of Asios, the partial success of Sarpedon, and Hector's final victory:

1. 1–33: the description of the wall
2. 34–107: the introduction of Hector as leader of the Trojans
3. 108–94: the frustrated attack of Asios
4. 195–289: general battle stressing the successful resistance of the Greeks and the determination of Hector

5. 290–412: the attack of Sarpedon against the wall[6]
6. 413–71: Hector breaks through the wall

The narrative is structured with care and precision.[7] The wall stands as a continuing mark of success or failure for both sides. The opening and final lines of the book are designed to focus the audience's attention on the wall. These are the only two sections of the book that contain no similes; the poet uses more direct description to make the wall a focusing element. Then the final appearance of Hector, enhanced by the implied comparisons to the unsuccessful Asios and Sarpedon, completes the general direction of the narrative as he easily achieves what they have only attempted.

Hector is introduced grandly in book 12. He was last mentioned in the middle of book 11 (537–42), where his success was sufficiently great that he seems to require no further introduction. Book 12 has its own design, though, and Homer introduces Hector as he would present a hero entering his aristeia.[8] Hector immediately receives two juxtaposed similes,[9] both of which are traditionally associated with the most powerful heroic fighting—wind and lions (40 and 41). The whirlwind simile is short and in itself would be insufficient to elevate Hector, but it introduces the topic that is used again at 11.297 describing Hector's increased authority when Agamemnon is forced to leave the battle.[10] The lion simile, however, presents at length one of the strongest lions of the simileme:[11] a lion or boar confronts hunters and dogs that attack and finally kill him. They form themselves into a defensive force that is like a fortification or wall (*pyrgedon*)—thus tying this simile closely to the central object in the narrative.[12] Even though the lion is stated to be alone confronting a dangerous group armed with javelins, he never gives way; rather, they back off whenever he charges. In selecting from among alternative elements in the simileme, the poet stresses bravery and might. Other lions may be more bloodthirsty or crudely vicious; this lion shows sheer valor.[13]

Hector's forceful introduction by juxtaposed similes is translated into action as he becomes more assertive in leading his troops. First, Polydamas advises Hector on battle strategy: let the troops leave their horses, cross over the wall, and fight the Achaeans by the ships. Hector accepts this advice, and the other Trojans follow him. Then there is a catalogue listing the five companies and their commanders; the largest and bravest contingent is commanded by Hector.[14] Such a catalogue has introduced the aristeiai of other warriors.[15]

In section 3 (108–94) Asios ignores the plan of Polydamas and Hector to advance on foot, choosing instead to attack the wall from his chariot. Homer immediately begins to build a poetic structure of rising resistance: Asios is a fool and will not return to Troy (113–15). As he charges the gate defended by the two Lapith spearmen Leontius and Polypoetes, his foolishness is illustrated in two complementary ways: his misjudgment of the Greeks' inherent strength and his attempt to shift blame to Zeus. Asios himself and his troops receive no simile at all, while Leonteus and Polypoetes are described by a simile structure that recalls the earlier introduction of Hector (40 and 41). Again there is a double simile (short + long) in which Leonteus is compared to Ares and then the two Lapiths are likened to oak trees that stand firm before the constant wind and rain (130 and 132). Immediately thereafter, even though the rest of the Greeks flee before Asios' attack, these two stand before the gate like wild boars that fight to the death (146).[16] All three similes describing the Greek resisters are taken from similemes that customarily describe strong warriors.[17] In addition, even Asios acknowledges Greek strength, describing the defenders with a traditional warrior simile: as wasps or bees who defend their young from hunters (167).[18] In exasperation he attempts to reproach Zeus: "Father Zeus, now even you are totally a lover of lies" (164–65) — another misjudgment. He cannot understand that the force of Zeus and other gods is strongly behind Hector and supports only those Greeks who are participants in his plans.

The only simile in this section that does not stress the might of the Greeks describes the weapons that fly from the hands of both sides like snowflakes (156). The presence of such an even-handed simile underlines the balanced quality of the battle. All five similes in this section emphasize the stalemate between Greek and Trojan warriors.

The next division of the poem (195–289) presents a general description of the battle as the Greeks continue to resist the Trojan attack even as the pressure increases. The evenness of the battle is emphasized by the only simile in this section, a second simile of snowflakes, likening the weapons that fly from both sides to a blanketing blizzard sent by Zeus. The name of Zeus adds a foreboding quality to this summarizing simile, since Zeus is the only god active in book 12.[19] At the opening of this section Zeus sends a sign — an eagle clutching a snake that escapes by biting the eagle's neck; the eagle flies away with a cry of pain (200–207). Polydamas interprets this omen in a reasonable way: the Trojans are vulnerable, even though they seem powerful at the moment. Hector, however, rejects these words and drives his men firmly forward, trusting in Zeus' earlier promises.[20] Then Zeus strengthens Hector by raising a wind from Mt. Ida that blows dust in the eyes of the Achaeans and makes the defense of the wall all the more difficult (252–55). At this point the second snow simile recalls the previous failed attack of Asios (278, cf. 156); it is longer and more complex, just as the battle scene is more elaborately described.[21] The threat is greater, the opponents are more powerful, and the support of Zeus is evident; correspondingly, in the simile the snow is steady and relentless, it covers the whole scene, and Zeus is twice cited as the cause of the storm.[22] Even though the battle remains balanced, the temporary advantage that Zeus has granted to Hector becomes increasingly clear as he enters the action more decisively.

In the fifth section Sarpedon leads the Trojan advance (290–412). He is the third warrior introduced with a pair of traditional warlike similes (293 + 299, cf. 40 + 41 and 130 + 132).[23] The first briefly compares Sarpedon to a lion among cattle; the second continues this subject in an extended simile of a hungering lion that attacks the herdsmen and dogs and will fight on until he kills or is killed.[24] Yet the surrounding battle is presented as continuing in balance,[25] and each side receives a short simile; the Trojans charge like a dark whirlwind, and Ajax slays his enemy, who falls like a diver (375 and 385).[26] At the climax of this scene Sarpedon grasps a chunk of wall and it gives way, but Ajax and Teucer are able to fend off his attack.[27]

The final scene centering on Hector presents a different kind of battle. At this point nontraditional similes enter book 12 for the first time. The evenness of the conflict is described by two similes that have no parallel in Homeric poetry and are drawn from country life; whatever the source, the similes are not the lion, boar, god, or wind similes that have proven to be well suited to the battlefield.[28] In the first, two men with measuring sticks quarrel about the placement of boundary stones; in the second, a woman weighs wool on her scale (421 and 433).[29]

This radical shift in subjects echoes other indications that the nature of the battle has changed. Zeus has repeatedly entered the battle to show his underlying favor for the Greeks through omens, natural occurrences, or direct inspiration—all revealing the weakness in the Trojans' situation. When Hector makes his move to break through the wall, even his victorious entry is qualified by the statement that the battle remained balanced until Zeus gave him glory (436–38). A few lines later, Zeus directly aids him in picking up a large stone—a point emphasized by another nontraditional simile:

> As when a shepherd easily carries a ram's fleece,
> picking it up with one hand, and slight is the weight burdening him.
>
> (12.451–52)[30]

When Hector enters the city, his face is like the swift night (463). No one is able to explain adequately what this simile means, but it may be a traditional simile with connotations of an alarming and powerful attack, thus presenting Hector as stronger than expected and sufficient to surpass the earlier Trojan initiatives.[31]

It is now clear that while Hector may be the hero of book 12, his successes all depend on the goodwill and power of Zeus;[32] the driving force of this book and those surrounding it is the plan of Zeus as he fulfills Achilles'/Thetis' petitions in book 1. Zeus announced the enforcement of his plan in book 8, pressed it in book 11, and brings the plan close to fulfillment when Hector breaks open the gates in book 12. The extent of Zeus' control is clear in books 13–15, where the course of battle is reversed both through the vigorous actions of men and through Poseidon's interventions once Zeus has averted his eyes from the Trojan plain. In book 12 Hector is his army's leader; his advice is sound at the beginning of the book and is accepted by his troops even after he ignores the omen of the eagle and the snake. He is presented as a strategist who guides his troops well, an ability underlined by the negative experience of Asios, who in refusing to heed Hector's instructions accomplished little. In addition, he has skilled and valuable allies, exemplified by Sarpedon. Yet though the victory won by the Trojans in book 12 is presented as the culminating event of a carefully structured narrative, it is in fact a fragile achievement. Actions fulfilled only by a divine force are inherently futile and entice Hector to pursue honor blindly. He does not perceive his success as due to Zeus' manipulation of warriors—and he easily dismisses the clear omen of the eagle and the snake.

Somewhere in Homer's presentation of the Trojans' attack their fighting becomes surreal. While it is difficult to define the exact point at which this happens, the switch from traditional similes customarily used in war scenes to nontraditional, more peaceful topics accentuates the brittle quality of the victory: two men who squabble over boundary markers, a poor woman who balances scales by carefully adjusting the weights as she weighs her wool, and the ram's fleece easily lifted by the shepherd. In the final section of this book (413–71) similes reduce the effort and striving of the warriors to an almost absurd level.[33]

Yet none of this is intended to criticize Hector; rather, it shows the heroic code's distorting effect on humans. Sarpedon appropriately highlights this code in his classic statement to Glaucus at 310–28, and even though it strongly motivates human achievement throughout book 12, the narrative provides no critical perspective on the actions it promotes or on the human lives it puts at risk.

Given that each incident in this book seems to have its place in a well-structured and economical mosaic, emphasis through the careful placement of similes is also a significant element in the total design. Three heroes, Hector, Asios, and Sarpedon, successively enter the narrative. In each case the poet uses the same simile pattern, a short simile followed immediately by an extended one; and in each case he uses a simileme that the tradition has previously suggested for such a scene. A hero's entrance into the narrative can be a moment for a simile, but the balanced patterning of the similes in each of these three introductions invites the audience to evaluate these incidents as parallel scenes in a developing structure. Significantly, the poet does not give Asios any similes; although in form he is introducing the short-then-long pattern that will favor the Trojans, the first pair of similes strongly emphasizes the book's theme and structure in calling attention to the initial strength of the Greeks.

In addition, the poet presents a view of the general battle at several places, yet at only four junctures does he use a simile (156, 278, 421, and 433). Because an extended simile strongly draws the audience's attention to a particular passage, it is important that the poet stress only those moments where this general view enhances his theme. At 156 the extended simile of snowflakes emphasizes the balanced battle between the two sides to show that Asios' attack has little effect and to motivate his futile prayer to Zeus; then the related simile at 278 stresses the evenness of the battle resulting from Zeus' temporary support for the Trojans — an emphasis that prepares the audience for the Trojan victories led by Sarpedon and Hector. At the end of the next episode the battle is presented as equal through two similes (421 and 433 — men quarreling over boundary stones and the woman weighing wool) to set the scene for the reentrance of Hector as Zeus' champion. In each of these four pivotal passages the poet uses a simile at a traditional location, but he chooses a nontraditional topic for a warlike context — a choice emphasizing the unreal quality of human victories largely attributable to Zeus.

The wind is the most prominent continuing subject in book 12. Zeus raises a wind to blow the dust from the mountains that blinds the Greeks,[34] and the wind is the most frequent subject in similes. Hector enters the book like a whirlwind; Leonteus and Polypoetes stand firmly like oaks against the wind; the wind drives the snowflakes in a blizzard; in the next simile, when the battle is balanced, the wind is lulled by Zeus as he sheds snow on earth and sea; and the Trojan army attacks like a whirlwind (40, 132, 156, 278, and 375). Generally the wind, often stirred by Zeus, is the topic that favors the Trojans as they move successfully against the Greeks—continuing even into book 13, where their advance is accompanied by a simile of flame or a wind (39).

At a few places it seems clear that the poet has rejected the tradition's strong suggestion of a simile. The Greek wall does not receive a simile in either the opening or closing sections of the book; such indirect emphasis would divert the audience from the restricted importance of the object. It is only a marker on the battlefield; there is little point in stressing any other element concerning the wall than its transience, and this is best done by telling its history.

It would have been customary for Homer to use a simile in the catalogue of Trojans that begins at line 88, but at this point he is not stressing the overwhelming mass of the army or the quality of any individual fighter.[35] He is interested in presenting Hector as a leader of the Trojan army and the first among competent warriors; therefore none of these supporters of Hector receives a simile.

When Hector breaks through the wall at the end of the book, the poet does use the "like the swift night" simile to emphasize this culminating act, but at the same time he stresses Zeus' gift of strength (450). Likewise, tradition would have suggested the use of a simile for emphasis at line 397, where Sarpedon actually removes a segment of the wall. But because the section concerning Sarpedon is a preliminary stage in the larger narrative movement that builds toward Hector bursting open Troy's gates, Sarpedon's act is described without elaboration. Then, appropriately, Hector's achievement receives two similes.

The similes of book 12 continually reinforce the book's basic structure, yet the most striking feature of this book's similes is the sudden shift in tone in section 6, the breaching of the wall. At this point the poet is at his most creative in manipulating the expectations of his audience. The direction in the narrative, in the development of three repeated attack scenes as well as in the placement and patterning of the similes, has led the audience to anticipate the success of Hector and the collapse of the Greek defenses; Homer, however, uses his audience's knowledge of traditional forms to present Hector's brilliant triumph as a diminished achievement for Zeus' puppet.

ILIAD, BOOK 5: THE USE OF PARALLEL SIMILEMES
TO CREATE A UNIFIED THEME[36]

It is more difficult to discuss the similes' design in book 5 than in book 12 because in the former there is no clearly stated, single focusing element like the Greek wall. Diomedes is the main character in book 5, but he was introduced in book 4 and continues to play a major role at the beginning of book 6.[37] In addition, there are signs within book 5 that the theme is broader than this one hero; the narrative moves in several different directions and appears to be as much about gods as it is about men.[38] Book 5 falls easily into four basic units, each one centered on one or two major figures:

1. 1–165: Diomedes enters three times, slaying groups of Trojans
2. 166–459:[39] the action focuses on Aeneas and Aphrodite, both wounded by Diomedes
3. 460–710: Ares reenters and rallies the Trojans
4. 711–909: Ares continues his support of the Trojans, but Athena and Hera encourage Diomedes to wound him

This outline reveals that the tight focus of the initial section is then scattered as the narrative concentrates on several gods and their participation in battle. Diomedes plays the main role for only 165 lines before Aeneas enters, bringing along the problems caused by the presence of a divine mother ill suited to the battlefield — and from that point the spotlight moves between Diomedes and the inevitable complications that arise when gods mingle closely in mortal warfare.

Within the shifting mix of characters and subjects, the distribution of similes both throughout the book and in each of the four sections provides guidance in identifying the theme. Section one contains four long similes, while section 2, longer in terms of lines, contains only three part-line similes. Both long and short similes are spread widely throughout section 3, and in the final section reporting the battle between Diomedes and Ares, similes cluster: three following line 770 and two after line 860. The final two sections concern the interrelationship of gods and men on the battlefield. Such an uneven distribution of similes suggests that the poet is not employing them to emphasize the linear development of a single action; rather, similes are placed to reinforce the complex narrative centered on situations and issues that develop around the actions and reactions of a series of characters.

Diomedes, usually regarded as a model hero, is indisputably the major human actor in this first aristeia of the *Iliad*.[40] The Homeric audience has heard enough war narratives to have a full awareness of this form and to be aware of its possibilities and variations. Book 5 appropriately reports the mighty acts and achievements of this one hero, accompanied by long lists of enemies wounded or slain. Yet it is not necessary to regard this aristeia as a prototype for others in the *Iliad*, or even the norm, simply because this is the first. To be sure, the more intensely focused aristeiai of Agamemnon, Patroclus, and Achilles are derived from the same basic structure, but Diomedes' appearance in book 5 is as much a creative use of the aristeia form as the later examples.

One of the strangest features of Diomedes' aristeia is its ineffectuality.[41] Diomedes enters book 5 as one of the most vigorous and valorous of the Greeks:

> Then to Tydeus' son, Diomedes, did Pallas Athena
> give power and courage that among all
> he might be preeminent and win excellent honor.
>
> (1–3)

Diomedes' subsequent entrance is preceded by a list of specific Greek heroes who slay individual Trojans (37–83), with the result that Diomedes is presented as only one warrior on a list of several equals. At the close of book 5 not much has been accomplished,[42] and book 6 even begins with a general line stressing the evenness of battle between the Trojans and Greeks.[43] In addition, during book 5 no major hero is killed, and the only injuries to such heroes are rapidly healed by the intervention of favoring gods; Diomedes, struck with a spear, is regenerated quickly by Athena, and his victim Aeneas is immediately healed by divine aid and sent back to the battle with no serious deficiencies. Indeed, one of the notable motifs within this book is the instant healing of severe wounds in both gods and men; Diomedes, Aeneas, Aphrodite, and Ares all are wounded and emerge unblemished. Of course, Diomedes slays a series of less significant warriors, but for all his effort he accomplishes little in terms of disabling the enemy or reversing the tide of battle. Even though he twice ignores the dividing line between god and mortal by stabbing Aphrodite and Ares, the gods only grumble; no vengeance is taken.[44]

The broad narrative is structured around two parallel episodes: the woundings of Aphrodite and Ares. Diomedes becomes so involved in the individual squabbles and personal concerns of these major divinities that he is occasionally eclipsed. At line 127 Athena tells Diomedes that she has removed the mist from his eyes so that he may distinguish god from man and orders him to fight only Aphrodite among the gods.[45] The rivalry between Athena and Aphrodite arising from the judgment of Paris is a presupposition throughout the poem.[46] Still, it is surprising that Diomedes never raises the slightest objection to her command—especially since the gods are unanimous in their verdict after the event: Dione calls Diomedes foolish for not realizing how dangerous it is for a man to fight an immortal (403ff.),[47] and Apollo is explicit:

> Reflect now, son of Tydeus, and relent! Do not hope to think
> as the gods do since never is the race of the immortal gods
> like that of men who go about on the earth.
>
> (440–42)

Yet later, when Athena commands Diomedes to wound Ares, he strikes without further question (825f.). Only in book 6 does he seem to react to these strange events in insisting that he will not fight Glaucus if he is a god because such activity is risky (6.128–41). This scenario of unreasonable and inconsistent commands may make some sense in terms of the individual animosities of the Greek gods, but it should confuse Diomedes.[48] Heroes may be hesitant in calculating the most honorable course in the midst of battle, but no one, Greek or Trojan, is foolish enough to ignore or to attack a god, especially when he is given exceptional power to identify them.[49]

These two features of book 5, the ineffectiveness of Diomedes and his repeated attacks on gods, seem purposely developed structural units rather than a series of his battle scenes. There is no doubt that Diomedes is presented as a major warrior and an appropriate member of the inner council of the Greeks; but he is only one of the *Iliad*'s many models for a heroic fighter. He always acts effectively in response to the commands given by those who have authority. When Agamemnon delivers a stinging rebuke to Diomedes in the *Epipolesis*,[50] telling him that he is not equal to his father, Tydeus, as a warrior (4.364ff.), the king is immediately challenged by Sthenelus. Diomedes warns Sthenelus to endure such criticism in silence, respecting the position and rank of Agamemnon. Two strong imperatives control Diomedes in this scene: his desire to measure his performance by his father's success and the necessity of honoring a man of higher rank. The reverence for his forebears extends even to his moment of reconciliation with Glaucus in book 6, when he acknowledges a special relationship of guest-friendship between their fathers.

It is equally a part of Diomedes' normal behavior that he should follow a god's commands. There is no questioning of such orders; they are to be obeyed with no calculation of the costs or contradictions involved. In fact, Diomedes never challenges these commands or even reflects on the results. He is a routine man accepting orders on the battlefield and executing them well. But as there is no questioning, so also there is no potential for moral greatness. Never a perverse or evil hero, Diomedes is not criticized for his unhesitating performance of the ritual of warfare, yet he is presented as a limited hero, since all motivating forces are external and dependent upon the thinking of those who outrank him. The gold of Troy may finally be worthless and the leadership of Agamemnon inadequate, but still Diomedes will follow his king's commands and seek the destruction of Troy because these are the codes and policies of those in authority.

The Diomedes of book 5 is only one of a series of portraits in books 2 through 8 that provide contrasting heroic models to Achilles. Homer presented the causes of Achilles' original rebellion in book 1, and he will explore these reasons more deeply in Achilles' responses to the ambassadors in book 9. Between these two books there is a series of vignettes focusing on Agamemnon, Menelaus, Paris, Diomedes, Hector, Ajax, and Odysseus. In these books Diomedes and Ajax are the models of a high type of heroism in service to the Greek cause; as a result, Achilles finds Ajax's humane proposition for serving the Greeks even at the cost of one's own anger the hardest to reject in the Embassy Scene, and Homer appropriately frames this scene with Diomedes' speeches of uncomplicated, naive, even rash daring.

The placement and development of book 5's similes support this interpretation. In section 1 (1–165) Diomedes begins his aristeia gloriously, as the personification of traditional heroism; he is introduced in a series of three separate entrances, each carefully scaled to enhance his stature as a warrior. When he first appears, Athena has given him courage and might and kindles a flame from his armor. Such a fiery entrance is given to few warriors, and to accompany this entrance the book's first simile describes the star at harvest time that shines the brightest of all other stars (5).[51] Then Diomedes kills one of two brothers, while the other is snatched away by Hephaestus; he captures their horses and has them led back to the ships.[52] At this point Athena persuades Ares, always a supporter of the Trojans, to sit apart from battle as a series of Greek heroes kills individual Trojans (29–36 + 37–83).[53] When Diomedes enters the narrative for the second time at line 84, the poet lists him with other Greek champions in the forefront of the battle; he is described by a simile of a roaring river that sweeps away embankments, vineyards, and farms (86–92).[54] Then he is wounded, healed immediately, and sent back to fight by Athena; at line 133 he enters battle for the third time, accompanied by the simile of a lion who slaughters sheep in the farmyard. He alone slays a long list of opponents. Here the elements of the first scene that illustrated his dominant position among the other Greeks are heightened. He kills a series of paired brothers[55]—culminating with two sons of Priam—and caps the list by taking their horses; his success is summarized in a second simile of a bloodthirsty lion (161).[56]

Even the gods' movements in these three incidents are designed to provide less aid as the hero moves increasingly on his own. First, Athena glorifies Diomedes and then supports the Greek cause by leading Ares from the battlefield. After he is healed, Athena returns him to battle with a lightened step and a clearer vision. In the last scene he emerges as the preeminent Greek warrior on his own, neither requiring nor receiving help from the gods.

Four similes closely accompany this structure, marking each entrance of Diomedes and closing the scene.[57] The subject matter of these similes becomes more warlike as Diomedes moves from being the wearer of the shining helmet to the able fighter killing a series of men. In the first scene, the gleam from his armor is compared to a beautiful star that offers no threat (5); it is an image of pure brilliance. The second simile (87) describes a river swollen by Zeus' rain to full spate as it destroys orchards and farms. The third (136) centers on a lion that has been wounded[58] and escapes from the fold after slaughtering unprotected sheep, while the fourth (161) describes a lion that attacks cattle in the open pasture and breaks the necks of his unsuspecting prey.[59] In each case Diomedes is portrayed as an increasingly threatening and dangerous force.

In the next section (166–459), where the focus moves to Aeneas, there are only three similes, all short and two repeated. At 299 Aeneas stands over the fallen Pandarus "like a lion confident in his strength."[60] At 438 Diomedes charges against Apollo "like a god," and Apollo uses this same simile at 459 in reporting Diomedes' attack to Ares. Even though each of these similes is short, they all support the thematic organization of book 5. The lion emerged as Diomedes' simile in his triple introduction, and now Aeneas receives the same comparison in coming forward as a warrior of equal ability; appropriately, Diomedes will not vanquish Aeneas but will only wound him momentarily. The comparison of a warrior to a god is traditional,[61] but in the context of book 5 this simile has an ironic significance, since Diomedes acts as a god's equal in presuming to attack Apollo. He may think that he is only pursuing his enemy Aeneas, who is being shielded by Apollo and, in addition, is following divine orders in attacking Aphrodite, but Apollo's rebuke of Diomedes repeats the simile to mark his undue arrogance.[62]

There is no other scene in the *Iliad* or the *Odyssey* where a man so easily crosses the line between mortal and divine, even to the point of inflicting a wound upon a goddess—an unusual action that could well attract a simile. The scene, however, is presented as a direct report of the event followed by reactions, thus highlighting the complications that arise when men interact too closely with gods; in such a straightforward style it would be distracting to introduce long similes as poetic embellishments. The parallel closing scene of book 5 is different: Athena, Hera, and Ares provide all motivation and act in the foreground using Diomedes as their agent. The same actions are augmented by several long similes in order to end the book with a display of the gods' power and dominance over men (770, 778, 782, 860, 864, 884, and 902).

In the third section of this book (460–710) Ares rallies the Trojans. Sarpedon, in rebuking Hector for the lackluster performance of his troops, uses two short similes comparing the Greeks to lions who terrify dogs and the Trojans to fish who die caught in a net (476 and 487). Again, though the similes are short, the Greeks are presented as the stronger force in the similes as well as in their resistance (541–89). The reentrance of Ares (590–95), however, leads to a series of scenes that reverse the relative strength of the two armies:[63] Hector rallies the Trojans; Aeneas, healed by Apollo, is returned to battle; Ares pulls a veil of night over the battle to aid the Trojan troops; Hector leads, with Ares and Enyo guiding him as Diomedes gives way; Hector and Ajax both kill enemy warriors but Ajax is unable to strip the armor from his victim and must fall back; in single combat Tlepolemus, a Greek, is killed while Sarpedon is saved; and the section concludes with a list of those Greeks slain by Hector and Ares.

Similes closely accompany this movement. At first the Greeks hold their ground, their heads and shoulders growing white from clouds of dust just as piles of chaff in the blowing wind grow white around the threshing floor (499). The scene is a peaceful harvest time in the country — a significant lessening of the warlike tone in the earlier similes describing the Greeks, especially Diomedes. At 522 the Greeks are as unmoving as mists on the mountain tops.[64] Wind is often used as a subject to describe an attacking warrior, but in this simile it is specifically stated that the winds are asleep;[65] the traditional topic is drained of its normal strength to show that the force of the Greeks is blunted when the Trojan army is driven by Ares. In addition, when Aeneas kills two Greeks, the emphasis is thrown on them by the simile of slain lions — and then by a second simile in which they are compared to fir trees (554 and 560). Lions are not only a traditional object of comparison for the attacking warrior but have also been impressively applied to Diomedes in this book — yet here the lions die;[66] fir trees traditionally describe warriors who lie dead.[67] When the poet describes Diomedes watching Hector surge across the battlefield like a rushing river (597), he has again chosen the subject of an earlier simile, the one at 87 describing the entrance of Diomedes.[68] Now roles are reversed as Diomedes stands on the bank quailing before the river. Prior to the entrance of Ares, Diomedes fought like a lion and a god, but as soon as the Greeks are halted, the winds sleep, the lions die, the tree similes connote death, and a simile subject that has described the strength of Diomedes, the river torrent, illustrates the limitations of the Greek effort.[69]

The last section of the book (711–909) is a much-elaborated doublet of Diomedes' spirited attack on Aphrodite (310–61). The hero himself fades into the background, and the motivation shifts to the divine level as both Hera and Athena worry over the weakened Greek initiative. Appropriately, all similes with the exception of two short ones call attention to gods. These two short similes are both familiar from previous usage: the Greeks are again like lions or boars in their strength as they rally around Diomedes, who is supported by Hera and Athena, and Ares charges that Diomedes in attacking him is equal to a god — again the formulaic short simile that has such ironic resonances in this book (782 and 884).

The remaining similes, all of which are extended, focus on the gods' actions. At 770 and 778 the ease of Hera and Athena's journey to the battlefield is underlined. The simile at 770 stresses the power of the divine horses, who are able to leap as far as a man can see;[70] 778 shows the goddesses entering the battle as timorous doves.[71] Both similes accentuate the differences of scale between men and gods, and this unbridgeable dichotomy becomes the dominant theme of the final section. In three further similes the mortal perspective on divine action is either specifically mentioned or implied. Ares cries as loudly as nine or ten thousand warriors in battle (860),[72] and Diomedes sees him rise as a dark whirlwind (864).[73] At the end of the book there is one additional divine cure, when Ares is healed as rapidly as a man curdles milk (902).

Though Diomedes' major action — attacking a god — is repeated, the effect of the passage is far different: Diomedes, earlier called foolish for wounding a goddess, still obeys Athena without question when she tells him to attack Ares. In the first incident the action at least seemed to develop from the hero's normal instincts: Diomedes confronted Aeneas, they cast weapons at each other, Aeneas was wounded, and Diomedes pursued his advantage. Aeneas' mother picked her son up and tried to shield him, but Diomedes kept pursuing his victim; and, of course, he was specifically told by Athena to strike Aphrodite alone of the gods. The second incident, Diomedes' attack on Ares, leaves the hero in the background. The motivation is provided by Hera and Athena, who are disturbed that the Greek attack has been stalled. When Hera takes the shape of Stentor, she provides the impetus for Diomedes' attack and Athena drives his chariot. Hera's Stentor disguise is effective for the rest of the Greeks; Diomedes, however, states that he recognizes her because he retains the special vision given by Athena early in the book (815–24). As a result, the usual understandable heroic motivations are not driving this action; gods direct it. Their predominance is marked by several signs of the disparities between gods and mortals: the axle of the chariot groans beneath the weight of Athena, and the extended similes focus on the smallness of men compared to the massive scale of gods' actions — the far-leaping horses and the god who cries as loudly as a whole army.[74]

Book 5 is rightly regarded as Diomedes' aristeia. He does gain glory, as Athena intended — she gave him might and courage so that he could be preeminent among all and earn renown — but he remains a mechanical hero within a hollow and ineffective aristeia. The last incidents of the book focus on Ares — the rapid healing of his wound, Hebe's bathing of him, and his restoration to divine favor. The final lines bring appropriate closure to a book that seems to be centered on the unpredictable and meddlesome actions of the Olympians in entering mortals' campaigns:

> They then returned back to the house of great Zeus,
> Argive Hera and Alalcomenean Athena,
> after stopping the killing of man-slaying Ares.
>
> (907–9)

The divine action ends, but the situation of the human warriors has changed little from the beginning of the book. Book 6 opens with another list of valorous Greek warriors, among whom is Diomedes, but his special opportunity for honor has now passed (6.5–71).[75]

The similes in this book do not provide a new dimension to interpretation by offering a series of ironic analogies as they do in book 2. There Homer's similes revealed the thinness of the appearance that sought to cover the reality; here the subject of interest is the heroic code. Throughout book 5 the poet mixes mortal and divine directly in order to test the heroic code's effectiveness in a world where dominating divinities interrupt human calculations and expectations easily and often. Overall, the book moves from man to god. In the opening sections, gods progressively withdraw, leaving the spotlight to Diomedes. Once Diomedes is established in a preeminent position and pushes through the barrier separating men and gods, the gods are brought back into the story; and in the final section the gods take almost total control of the action as they manipulate mortals for their own pleasures. The similes in book 5 appear in predictable or traditional places and for the most part contain the normal topics used to describe actions on the battlefield. As each is developed and placed into the sequence of similes, it responds closely to the design of the book. Thus the initial four similes (in section 1) are taken from traditional similemes, but they describe the entering warrior in increasingly bloody terms. Then similes virtually disappear in section 2 as the poet directly presents the confrontation of men with gods; in section 3, similes that were introduced earlier are now inverted to show the relative loss of the Greeks' strength as Ares rallies the Trojans. Finally, while the last section contains only one short simile describing men, six extended similes focusing on divine actions enhance the magnitude of the gods as they intermingle in human events. The major repeated pattern of book 5 is the wounding of a god, and it is within this repeated scene that gods apply special rules yet become angry when men do their will. Diomedes, however, never shows the independence to raise a protest. He is in every way the normal warrior, and his easy acquiescence to authority provides a striking comparison to Achilles' questioning and probing of the heroic code.

There are a few junctures in book 5 where the tradition suggested a simile but Homer chose an alternate means of developing his story. Following line 10 Diomedes wounds two warriors and takes their horses; because this configuration of two warriors despoiled of their horses is repeated twice later in the book, one might expect a simile for variety.[76] Yet the poet is seeking to show the development of Diomedes' war strength rather than his list of prizes. A simile to vary the scenes would blur the effect of this repeated motif with no gain to the direction of the narrative.[77]

At line 35 Athena leads Ares from the battlefield. It would be possible to include a simile describing this divine action, but instead the poet immediately turns to a list of Greeks who slay Trojans, culminating in the reentrance of Diomedes. The effect is clear and complementary to the design of the book. In this section the poet focuses attention on the actions of men; later, when it suits his theme, similes will call attention to the actions of divinities.

Homer, though sparing in the use of similes in the first three sections, has placed them precisely to focus on Diomedes' advances. At lines 43–83 one might expect a simile for variety in the list of the Greek victors, but this list of killings leads to the reentrance of Diomedes in a more focused way by not calling attention to itself. It would also be in accordance with tradition to describe the quickness of the divine cure at 121 with a simile. Once again, however, the role of the gods attracts less attention because Homer is working to enhance Diomedes' third entrance at line 133. He postpones a simile until 161, where it calls attention to Diomedes' slaying of the last two victims, thus emphasizing the final stage of the hero's development.

At line 512 Apollo sends Aeneas, now completely cured, back to the battlefield. A simile might be expected to accompany this miraculous cure, but Homer clearly states in lines 516–17 that the Trojans asked no questions because they had no time. This section presents the tense equality of battle—the fact that the Trojans have blunted the Greek attack—and the similes at lines 499 and 522 stress that fact. Similarly, at line 592, when Homer presents Ares and Enyo leading the Trojans across the battlefield, the tradition suggests a simile to accompany divine action, but the simile is placed a few lines later, where it describes the dismayed reaction of Diomedes to the resurgent strength of the Trojans.

Similes to Delineate a Narrative Theme · 111

In each of these passages the poet has avoided elaborating random incidents in order to keep the emphasis on his larger theme. Similes tend to retard action and to invite reflection as the audience relates experiences from two different areas in order to achieve a unified understanding of an event. Thus a poet concerned with the pace and consistent direction of his narrative must learn to evaluate carefully the suggestions of the tradition. If he does not choose subject and placement well, his narrative may be logical in its chronology and the superficial cause-and-effect relationships yet fail to develop a dominant theme. The aristeia of Diomedes could easily become a listing of incidents, but Homer, controlling his material, has effectively improvised within the aristeia form in order to expose the empty soul of his traditional warrior.

Book 5 is a long book, with many actions shifting between heaven and earth, but that fragile mixing of unmixable locales and characters is precisely the theme of this narrative. By repeating similemes from section to section, by choosing to develop each simileme in order to follow the narrative's theme, and by repeating the events for which varied similes are created, Homer makes effective use of the simile form in organizing this long but tightly structured book.

ODYSSEY, BOOK 22:
SIMILES TO INTERPRET TYPICAL ACTIONS[78]

Book 22 is easily regarded as the *Odyssey*'s most Iliadic book, since it presents a continuous series of battles fought by armed warriors contending for a prize. Yet there are significant differences that raise this book above the level of conventional battle narrative and mold it into one of the culminating acts toward which the second half of the poem has been building. The battle between Odysseus and the suitors has been anticipated since the beginning of the poem and became inevitable at the moment when Odysseus landed on Ithaca. As a result, the theme of hostility between those who seek the return of Odysseus and those who oppose it constantly underlies the structures of books 13 through 21, leading to the moment when Penelope arranges a symbolic contest of strength. Significantly, this competition is centered around a weapon, the king's bow, thus prefiguring the open battle between Odysseus and the suitors.[79]

In the contest the suitors are too weak to string the bow. Telemachus almost does, but only Odysseus completes the task—an action that underlines the strength he brings to the battle and foreshadows the actual defeat of the suitors in book 22. Odysseus' power rests on several bases. Of course, the tradition includes him among the major Greek warriors, but there are deeper strengths on which Odysseus will draw in recapturing his palace. He has rallied a group of loyal allies, all of whom have been keenly affronted by the behavior of the suitors. In his stay with Eumaeus, Odysseus discovered a loyal servant of his family, a thankful man who appreciated his upbringing at the hands of Anticlea as well as an honorable person who fled from the palace to seek a decent life in the countryside. Obviously, Telemachus and Penelope remain loyal to the missing king; but there are also others such as Eurycleia, Philoitius, Phemius, and Medon, who are identified as stalwarts even though they have assisted the suitors.[80] Throughout the last half of the *Odyssey* Homer presents a group of civilized men and women who wish to live a life drastically opposed to the paralysis, cynicism, and purposelessness characteristic of the suitors. These are characters who show pity for unfortunates, sympathy for suffering humans, understanding and kindliness to those in need — but, above all, a desire for just punishment for unacceptable actions. Their code is probably best presented in the scenes with Eumaeus in the countryside, but is also exemplified by Odysseus' warning to Amphinomus (18.125–50), in his gentle treatment of Penelope during their nighttime meeting, in his thoughts when he lies alone at night in book 20, and in his words restraining Eurycleia from gloating over the fallen suitors at 22.411–18. The simple and unrehearsed bonding of civilized men is the real strength that will return Odysseus to his throne as the welcome king of Ithaca.

In addition, Athena's support has been constant since the meeting on Olympus reported in books 1 and 5.[81] After Odysseus' arrival on Ithaca in book 13 she advised him to use guile and then disguised him as a beggar, in book 16 she reunited father and son, and in book 21 she lighted the way for them as they removed the weapons from the great hall. This support is clearly continued in book 22.

Opposed to Odysseus are the suitors who are not sufficiently united in pursuing a common cause to be effective conspirators. In their numbers they may seem to possess power, but in fact they are 108 individuals competing against each other for a single prize; Odysseus easily maneuvers them into open hostility at the end of book 18. There are continual disagreements among suitors about the appropriateness of their behavior — most strikingly in Amphinomus' objection to their plan to kill Telemachus and the anonymous negative

Similes to Delineate a Narrative Theme

comment about the propriety of Antinous' attack on the old beggar (*Ody.* 16.400–405 and 18.401–4). Thus the basic contest pits the strength of Odysseus and his few associates, civilized humans who wish to live in a community sharing a basic sense of cooperative virtues, against the weakness of the numerous suitors, hopelessly isolated and divided individuals who employ every conceivable means to debase and corrupt others.

Book 22 comprises six units that portray the relentless momentum toward Odysseus' victory from his first seemingly accidental shot through the full purgation of his halls:

1. 1–78: the killing of Antinous, which triggers cowardly bargaining as Eurymachus instantly abandons his colleague. The focused skill of Odysseus is directly contrasted to the inept intrigues of the suitors in the opening section.
2. 79–100: the first two killings by Odysseus and Telemachus
3. 101–204:[82] the arming scenes: Odysseus and his colleagues arm, as Eumaeus denies the suitors access to armor and punishes Melantheus for supplying it.
4. 205–309: Athena encourages Odysseus and finally sends the suitors fleeing in panic from the hall.
5. 310–89: Odysseus acts as the just king, killing the guilty and sparing the innocent as he triumphs in the battle.
6. 390–501: Odysseus completes his work of punishing the adherents of the suitors and cleansing his halls.[83]

This developing structure is strongly supported by the similes that fall at the conclusions of the fourth, fifth, and sixth sections. Since only one simile describing men's activities does not fall in such a position (402), it seems that the poet has carefully placed his similes to enhance major moments of victory as Odysseus moves from being the lonely warrior in a room of hostile men to the returning king welcomed by his subjects.

There are no similes in the first three sections. Two similes in section 4 stress the overwhelming strength of the small group of loyal conspirators against the muscle-bound weaklings who are their opponents.[84] The first (299) describes the suitors as a herd of cattle fleeing in panic from a stinging gadfly, and the second (302) presents them as small birds slain by vultures as men rejoice in the chase.[85] Both are developed from a traditional simileme. Insects have elsewhere described the ferocity of warriors,[86] and Odysseus and his allies are likened to powerful vultures, a precedented choice for a warrior within the bird simileme.[87] But in each of book 22's similes there is a mildly joyful tone. One small insect replaces the usual swarm of wasps or bees, and neither the gadfly nor the cattle are defending their home or young against attack. These cattle run aimlessly before the gadfly, having an infinity of time before them because it is springtime, "when the days are long";[88] the vultures chasing small birds bring men joy. Homer chooses elements from the simileme that reflect peaceful life in the countryside and tempers the effect of a list of slain suitors by juxtaposing the two similes.[89]

At the end of the fifth section (310–89), after Odysseus takes the life of Leiodes but spares Phemius and Medon, he finds all the suitors fallen in blood and dust like fish on the beach (384). Fish are traditionally used to describe warriors who have been killed, but these fish have been drawn up onto the beach in a net and lie completely helpless.[90] Similarly, the suitors, who appeared so strong, have been proven weak when confronted by the community of men organized by Odysseus. Even though the scene in the hall is a gory one, the simile itself is once again designed to show the normal pursuit of day-to-day business on the seacoast. The sun's heat and the lack of water kill the fish naturally; likewise, Odysseus' desire to regain his own throne is the understandable pursuit of a reasonable man whose strength catches the suitors totally by surprise.

The final section (390–501) begins with a lion simile, the only simile in the book to present the strength of Odysseus in terms typical of a Homeric warrior (402). Significantly, the battle has already been won when this simile is used. While Odysseus fought, no matter how bloody the battle in the narrative, the stages in the fighting were paralleled by images that presented nature at its most peaceful. Though the lion simileme was available as an appropriate subject for Odysseus throughout book 22, it is only at the moment of Odysseus' triumph that Homer draws on this simileme to present the warrior's true strength:

> spattered with blood and gore like a lion
> who comes after feeding on an ox of the farmyard;
> for his entire breast and his cheeks on both sides
> are bloody, and he is a fearful sight
>
> (402–5)

Such delayed use of a topic freighted with traditional meaning allows the poet to incorporate both Odysseus' strength in executing his enemies and his mercy toward the innocent in his role as Ithaca's returning king. He uses the lion as an appropriate image for Odysseus' performance and superficial appearance, but he immediately limits its cruder connotations by applying it to the now peaceable and just king, who prohibits Eurycleia from vaunting over the slain men and directs her attention to the continuing task of separating the guilty from the innocent.[91] Then, in punishing the women, Telemachus hangs them like thrushes or doves who fall into a snare, a simile from the world where man hunts small helpless animals as a normal pursuit involving no risk or danger to the hunter (468).[92]

The similes of book 22, with the exception of the bloody lion, fall at the end of sections as summarizing images. Each stage of the battle is filled with bloodshed, yet the effect of such warfare is mitigated by the choice of lyrical, peaceful, normalizing similes from day-to-day life. It is important that the battle Odysseus fights presents him as a strong warrior, for he was; it is equally important, however, that this battle not appear to be a contest for plunder and spoil. The king struggles to regain his rightful place and to reestablish a community of men who feel a strong common bond. Although taken from different similemes (insect, bird, fish, and lion), the similes are organized to reinforce the coherent design supporting the book's theme: both the violence of the battle and the peace of the simile world characterize the new Ithaca that will arise directly from the deaths inflicted by Odysseus.[93]

Homer's control in designing these similes is further evident in the several places where he chose to omit a simile. At line 1 there is an obvious occasion for a simile when Odysseus suddenly reveals himself before the suitors as the returned king, but such a simile would be more appropriate for a single hero entering a full-fledged aristeia emphasizing battle strength.[94]

The language of the second and third killings, those of Eurymachus and Amphinomus, is reminiscent of the *Iliad*, and the addition of a simile here, as often in the *Iliad*, would provide variety for either one of these individual slayings (79–98).[95] However, at this point Odysseus is presented as seeking a communal goal with the aid of Telemachus rather than personal honor through heroic fighting. Homer therefore uses these two suitors to present a single moment of battle as he begins to develop his theme, the united power of Odysseus and his allies. For the same reason there is a short list of killings by Odysseus and the others at 283–85, a technique familiar from the *Iliad*, but there is no simile to emphasize this joint activity.

At 297 Athena displays her aegis, sending the suitors racing through the halls in panic; in a brief summary Homer reports the groaning as Odysseus' comrades slaughter the remaining suitors and the floor runs with blood (308–9). The lack of a simile describing Athena's divine action raises the question whether the goddess actually does anything in the course of this battle to help Odysseus.[96] First, she appears in the disguise of Mentor and encourages Odysseus by comparing his present strength to that which he had at Troy; Homer says expressly at this point that she was testing the might and strength of Odysseus and his son (236–40). Then, when the suitors throw their spears, Athena renders them ineffectual (256); yet at 260 Odysseus and his comrades are stated to have successfully evaded the spears. Since the previous books have not presented even one scene of suitors drilling with spears in the recent months of high living at Odysseus' palace, there is no sign that anything unusual or unexpected has occurred. At 272ff. Athena again scatters their spears harmlessly throughout the hall; there seems to be no break in the chain of human activity that justifies the suspicion of divine interference.[97] After each of these actions Odysseus and his associates slay a series of enemies, until even the oxherd Philoitius is able to boast over the fallen Ctesippus (287–91). It is no wonder that the remaining suitors are panic-stricken. Their retreat did not require Athena to raise her aegis; Homer used the goddess as poetic shorthand to present an action that would involve complicated factual justification and psychological motivation if told realistically.[98] Although Athena is present during the scene, Odysseus and his colleagues are responsible for winning the battle, and appropriately Homer did not use a simile to call attention to this unnecessary divine action.

Finally, at 495–501 it would be possible for similes to describe the emotions of the loyal women as they welcome Odysseus back or his joy at being safely home among his people.[99] However, the act of judging the guilty and the innocent as well as the cleansing of the palace is more important to the poet. Thus the simile is placed to call attention to the punishment that Odysseus metes out to the disloyal servants (468ff.).

Book 22 presents an Odyssean battle. Though a warrior, Odysseus is not an Iliadic seeker of honor; he is dedicated to creating a new Ithaca where men may live within an organized and civilized society. The spotlight continually falls on him as he kills a few in order that many may live happily. The similes are an effective device by which Homer repeatedly undercuts any idea that this battle is being fought for heroic glory. Similes from the world of normal, often lyrical, nature consistently present an Odysseus who fights battles that

Similes to Delineate a Narrative Theme · 117

are compared to peaceful images. At no place is this design clearer than in the delayed appearance of the simile that the audience of the *Iliad* would expect: the bloody lion. Only when Odysseus has won and his restraint has been shown is he displayed as the powerful warrior he has been from the beginning of the book.

ODYSSEY, BOOK 5: THEMATIC SIMILES[100]

Book 5 is framed to present a crucial week in the life of Odysseus.[101] In the first line Dawn rises from her bed; in the final lines Homer brings closure:

> Upon his eyes
> did Athena shed sleep so that it would quickly
> free him from toilsome weariness, veiling his eyelids.
>
> (491–93)

During this time Odysseus confirms his desire to leave the comfortable island of Calypso and seek a world of death, sickness, weakness, and compromise — a flawed world dominated by powerful and often vindictive divinities. This choice may seem strange, perhaps even wrongheaded, yet the rest of the *Odyssey* demonstrates that this dangerous world outside the sheltered island is an arena where a man of determination and skill can welcome challenge and strive for achievement. Such a choice is worthy of the epic's hero, a man who embraces the chance to flee anonymity. The *Odyssey* initially focuses on the end of Odysseus' wanderings, because the choice on Calypso's island is pivotal in his career. During ten years of wandering he has learned what this choice should be. On the verge of returning to Ithaca he undergoes two final temptations, Calypso and Nausicaa; both times he affirms his plan to return home.[102] Book 5 is built on two themes: Odysseus' resolve and the support for his actions through divine mechanisms — Calypso's island, the world of the storm, and the plan of Zeus.[103]

Homer is careful to assure his audience that those elements in the story that threaten Odysseus offer no real danger. At the outset of book 5 Zeus declares that Odysseus is fated to see his friends and to return to his palace on Ithaca (41–42).[104] He also receives the aid of Ino, who protects him as he heads for the Phaeacian shore, and Athena smooths his way while he is involved in the storm:

But Athena, the daughter of Zeus, thought of another plan.
She checked the paths of the other winds;
she ordered them to stop and be lulled to sleep.
She roused the swift North Wind and broke the waves before him
until Zeus-born Odysseus arrived among the Phaeacians,
the lovers of oars, after escaping death and destruction.

(382–87)

Yet though Odysseus is shielded during the storm, he has no means of knowing it.[105] Hermes had informed Calypso that the hero is fated to return to Ithaca, but she did not report these words to him and even attempted to sow suspicion by saying:

If only you knew in your heart how many sorrows
you are fated to fulfill before you come to your native land,
then remaining here with me you would guard this house
and be immortal

(206–9)

Odysseus is compelled to build his own raft, an act implying that he must earn his way home relying on his own wits. When he is caught in the storm, he almost despairs, envying those who died a normal warrior's death at Troy and even suspecting that the aid offered by Ino is an untrustworthy snare (299–312 and 356–64). The skin is scraped from his hands as he struggles to reach the shore. Once he escapes from the sea, he still must devise ways to protect himself, since he has lost his raft and equipment, even his clothes. In the course of the storm he confronts death and suffering and learns to work with nature and respect it. He ends the book with an awareness of the tenuous and fragile quality of life in the chancy world that he has chosen:

Woe is me, what am I to suffer? What now at long last will happen to me?
If I spend this weary night at the river,
then together the evil frost and the fresh dew
will overcome me when I have gasped out my life from weakness;
the cold breeze blows up from the river in the early morning.
But if I climb up the slopes to the dark wood
and lie down in the dense thicket — if cold

> and exhaustion leave me, and sweet sleep comes upon me,
> still I am afraid that I will be prey and booty for wild beasts.
>
> (465–73)

The experience of the storm is sufficiently intense to rouse his sense of purpose and to energize the abilities that Odysseus will need to survive on Ithaca, where equally hostile forces will turn their destructive power against him. His enduring, indomitable spirit remains a constant element in the epic from book 5 through his final reinstatement in Ithaca. He begins the book yearning to escape the dominating nymph Calypso and ends it having passed through a series of tests, still clinging to life, yet not for a minute renouncing the crucial choice that is the fixed point from which all the later episodes of the epic arise.

The background to this book is a rapidly changing unpredictable element: the world of nature. Calypso's island is a paradise, filled with a variety of trees and flowers, birds and fountains, odors and music.[106] Opposed to this lovely area where nature freely pours forth her gifts is the sea, where nature threatens to overwhelm puny, terrified mortals. Calypso provides Odysseus with food and welcomes him to her bed each night; the storm offers him no shelter and so strips him of protection that he fears being eaten by wandering animals. The nymph offers him immortality, while the natural world offers death. In choosing between Calypso and Penelope, Odysseus consciously makes a choice worthy of a hero:

> My queenly goddess, do not be angry with me for this.
> I myself know it all — that wise Penelope
> is far less than you in beauty and bearing,
> for she is a mortal while you are immortal and ageless.
> But what I want and yearn for during all my days
> is to go home and to see the day of my return.
>
> (215–20)

Book 5 is designed to highlight the hero's choice between two alternatives: the effortless life of anonymity in the service of a preponderant goddess versus the risky world of challenge, danger, and individual achievement. Appropriately, the book is split between Calypso's island and the open sea as the hero seeks to move from one to the other. The narrative falls into three sections:

1. 1–42: The conference on Olympus
2. 43–282: Odysseus on Ogygia
3. 283–493: Odysseus and the storm
    a. 283–353: He abandons the raft (Poseidon and Ino)
    b. 354–87: He escapes from the storm (Poseidon and Athena)
    c. 388–457: He finds refuge from the sea
    d. 458–93: He finds refuge from nature[107]

Because the narrative's structure is so clearly marked by contrasting locations and a series of coordinated scenes, similes are not needed to organize a chain of incidents. Rather, book 5 contains more similes than any other book in the *Odyssey* because—though used in a wide variety of situations—they are tightly focused on the theme of the book, the hero's choice.

Divinities play a major role in surrounding Odysseus with sufficient protection to effect his final escape from Poseidon. Appropriately, book 5 opens with a divine council in which a plan to return Odysseus to Ithaca is sanctioned by the words of Zeus himself, and it closes with Athena's care for the exhausted hero. The poet sets this narrative in motion by sending Hermes to Calypso. It is traditional for a simile to appear in connection with the journey of a god to the world of men and equally normal for a god to be described by the bird simileme. In this case the passage of Hermes from Olympus to earth is given special prominence when the poet juxtaposes three traditional means of presenting such a journey. First Hermes is given sandals in typological preparation lines for gods:

> [He/she spoke and] immediately bound beautiful sandals upon his feet,
> immortal and golden, which bore him over the sea
> and the endless stretches of earth with the streaming wind.
> (*Iliad* 24.340–42; *Ody.* 1.96–98, 5.44–46)

Then there is a brief listing of the god's itinerary, a customary device for describing such journeys. Finally, there is the extended simile of a bird skimming the sea looking for food (51). This is a peaceful scene in which Homer avoids the element of attack that is part of the bird simileme in order to echo the life in Calypso's paradise. Every feature in the presentation of the god's entrance is traditional, but the significance of this journey in inaugurating the action of the poem is emphasized by the multiplication of standard devices.[108]

Not all immortals receive such treatment, even though they appear constantly throughout this book. Ino, who lends Odysseus her veil and watches over him throughout the storm, receives two short bird similes (337 and 353). Athena and Poseidon, as the opposed divinities, receive no similes at all; Calypso is presented directly in actions and words. The tutelary divinity of the Phaeacian stream that graciously receives Odysseus from the sea is unnamed and in spite of this crucial assistance is not further highlighted. Similes are not employed to emphasize the continuing role of the gods in this book; they focus only on moments when Odysseus is divinely aided in pursuing his wish to be free from Calypso.

Similes also describe the world of the storm that Odysseus has so willingly chosen. When Poseidon sees Odysseus on the raft, he realizes that this is the last moment to assert his will if he is going to continue torturing his victim. Since he knows that Odysseus is fated to escape from his power once he reaches Phaeacia, he has every reason to make this storm violent:

> He spoke and gathered the clouds, and he shook the sea
> taking up his trident in his hands. He raised up the blasts
> of all the winds and covered the earth and sea
> with clouds. Night fell from the heavens.
> The East Wind, the South Wind, and the West Wind blowing ill
> all clashed together with the North Wind born in the bright upper air
>   as he rolled a great wave before him.
>
> (291–96)

Odysseus fears this severe storm, yet the audience knows that he is in no real danger. Similes enforce the impression of his protected existence. Two similes, both from the wind simileme, describe the storm itself. Though such similes could be forceful depictions of the large-scale destruction resulting from a violent storm, the wind similes in this book are gentle. In the first the wind blows thistle clumps across a plain;[109] in the second the wind only scatters a heap of dry straw (328 and 368).[110] To describe one of the most powerful sea storms in this storm-filled epic, these two similes present the wind expending itself on trivial and useless objects in scenes from a farmer's daily life; no one is hurt or threatened.[111] Likewise, in this narrative the wind, though threatening to Odysseus, has no fatal force and will merely blow and scatter his raft harmlessly. Odysseus himself is described by two similes that minimize his plight. He rides on a plank from the ruined raft like a man who rides a horse (371), and the flesh ripped from his hands on Phaeacia's rocks is likened to pebbles that an octopus carries away in its suckers when it is pulled from its lair (432).[112] In the first, Odysseus is compared to a man who is not threatened or out of control; in the second, there is no blood, pain or destruction—just a minor disruption in the life of the octopus who is free to return to his dwelling.

All these more peaceful similes accompany potentially dangerous narrative situations; only the similes reveal that all is under the control of the gods who guide and protect the hero. The remaining similes focus on the human theme, Odysseus' choice. The keynote to his introduction is struck almost immediately: Athena praises the kingship of Odysseus, comparing him to a father at the moment he is yearning for his wife and family (12). This is not the first time that this simile has occurred in the *Odyssey*; when Telemachus earlier spoke to the assembly, he reminded them that Odysseus was gentle like a father, and Mentor also speaks of Odysseus' kingship and includes the same simile (*Ody.* 2.47 and *Ody.* 2.230–34). Throughout the poem, similes of family relationship cluster about Odysseus, Telemachus, and Penelope as they struggle to return to the peaceful existence that they enjoyed before the family was split by the Trojan War.[113]

An extended simile at 394 continues this pattern; Odysseus first glimpses Phaeacia, the land that offers salvation from the storm and will complete his return to Ithaca:

> as when a father's life appears welcome to his children
> after he has lain in sickness suffering strong pains,
> wasting away for a long time, and a hateful demon vexes him,
> but then the gods free him from evil and he welcomes it,
> so did land and woods seem welcome to Odysseus
>
> (394–98)

Odysseus' joy is like the joy of the children who have been expecting the death of their father—perhaps the ruination of the family. They have watched him suffer for a long time as his life is being eaten away; Odysseus too has been watching his life erode as he sits on the beach weeping in desire for his home even though he is surrounded by an island paradise. His despair at the prospect of an anonymous death by drowning is the culmination of his fears— the final inglorious, unheroic end of a life that once held promise. The simile suggests that Calypso's island has been the land of death; the sea is the place where death is only threatened; the land of Phaeacia, with its prospect of return to Ithaca, is the gift of life. If the simile had stated that Odysseus welcomed this land as much as the father welcomed the return of good health, it would have been intelligible but would have failed to emphasize the perspective of the children who have watched a life decline and draw near its end.[114] That external and objective view is the position of Odysseus in book 5; he is the man who can see his own life as an observer and choose from among the paths open to him. And, of course, starting in the proem and continuing throughout the rest of the *Odyssey*, Odysseus will be presented as the man who seeks to serve not only himself but also his family, wife, son, and father—and, as Mentor's and Athena's use of the father simile implies, his subjects, who are his figurative children.[115]

This theme of renewed life is echoed in the final simile of the book, that of the lonely farmer who buries a surviving ember that can be rekindled (488). Fire is a traditional topic for a warrior, but just as Odysseus feels small and threatened by overwhelming forces, so also the fire is diminished in size— though not in potential.[116]

In these last two similes, the recovering father and the preserved fire, there are implicit values that provide additional meaning on several different levels; the audience is informed through similes, among other devices, that Odysseus even at his lowest moment is the potential father to his family and subjects, he is returning to life, and he will once again be the inspiriting force that will effectively ignite his people to reestablish a community on Ithaca.[117] Although he seems aware only of the need to save himself by escaping the storm, there is a broader sense of salvation for a wider group, which will depend on the continuing role of gods as the family's protectors all the way to the end of the *Odyssey*. In addition, there is a metaphorical perspective in which Odysseus is escaping from a living death on Calypso's island and returning to the fullness of life in a human community as an effective hero. At the end of book 5 he is largely unaware of these second two levels of meaning, but the placement, subjects, and extensions of the similes at 5.394 and 488 point to actions that have larger dimensions than the single victim's experience of the actual storm.

The most revealing simile in this book falls at the moment when Odysseus is forced to use his vaunted intelligence to earn his independence, the moment when he begins to build his raft:

> as broad as the curve of a freight ship's hull
> laid out by a man well skilled in carpentry
>
> (249–50)

In the narrative this action is important because it allows Odysseus to leave Calypso's island by means of his own ingenuity as a man "well-skilled in carpentry";[118] his voyage is in every way the result of his own initiative and actions. Throughout the *Odyssey* the hero attracts craftsman similes. At the beginning of book 9 (3–13) he contrasts himself to a minstrel; later in the same book he is compared to a man who bores a ship timber and a smith who tempers an ax head (384 and 391). The images of the craftsman put the hero in a proper perspective. As a craftsman lays out a design and then brings it into actuality, so also Odysseus has a driving desire to return to home and family, and in retrospect he will be seen to have taken the initial step in achieving this goal by choosing to flee Calypso. His conduct from this point on—his employment of tact and discretion among the Phaeacians, his use of disguise and cleverness on Ithaca, even his final self-control before a resistant Penelope—all are signs that Odysseus is careful in planning his moves and competent in their execution.[119]

The building of the raft is a simple activity charged with meaning by its placement at the crucial beginning point of the return story. Book 5 is Homer's introduction of his hero both as he is and as he will be when all the forces involved in his complex life permit him to achieve his chosen goal. The events of the immediate narrative have a focused meaning for him because his view, as that of any mortal, is limited; but the poet has a broader perspective and is able to present his hero caught up in larger events. This wider view is made clear in a variety of ways, including the divine council, divine messengers, and gods and goddesses accompanying the hero, but also the similes. The fear and despair of the moment are real to Odysseus, and in fact they are vivid individual markers of the kind of life that he has chosen to embrace. In this book the hero needs divine protection; but on his arrival on Ithaca he will be left largely dependent on his wits to reestablish himself. He receives help mostly in the form of encouragement and a disguise from Athena (book 13). In book 22 he will stand on his own, with no more divine help than is given to most other Homeric heroes. The similes throughout book 5 reveal a variety of broader perspectives that will be crucial in Odysseus' successful return to his throne. Similes carry the theme. While the narrative follows the quick shifts and risks of Odysseus' continuing adventures, the similes, drawn from home, farm, and countryside, consistently focus attention on solidly developing forces that at the moment are unclear to the hero — the benign reality of his threatening experiences and the full potential of his significant choice.

CONCLUSION

The books discussed in this chapter are complex; each moves through a series of episodes, shifts the focus between various locations, and involves many characters.[120] Yet the firm hand of the poet is constantly evident in the development of a major theme that shapes and unites events, scenes, and characters. This control is at its clearest in book 12 of the *Iliad*, where the Greek wall provides a physical focus for the book; once this focus is established, the narrative is built in episodes centered on a series of three Trojan heroes whose achievement increases from Asios to Sarpedon to Hector. Yet at the same time the Trojan dependence on Zeus also increases, a discordant note that is ominous for the future defense of the city. The similes reflect these mutually reinforcing elements of the narrative so closely that even though their omission would not leave unbridgeable gaps, the contrasts between the characters and their actions would not stand out so clearly.

The subject of book 5 is ostensibly the aristeia of Diomedes, but the theme is the ambiguous situation of mortals in a world dominated by divine forces. Achilles occupies the same world of cause and effect and will fight the last single combat in the *Iliad*; he provides such an obvious contrast to Diomedes that his later aristeia threatens to reduce book 5 to the status of a mere precursor to the major action. Yet book 5 has its own contribution to make within the first half of the *Iliad*. The audience should not focus on Diomedes' individual actions so intently that they are unaware of complications that result from the mixing of human motivation and divine initiatives. The similes, consistently highlighting the book's theme, are constant supporters of this theme.

The promise inherent in Odysseus' choice to leave Calypso is realized as Odysseus returns to his family, his house, and his community as king. He must scheme, struggle, and finally fight for this position, but Homer makes the battles in book 22 of the *Odyssey* the means of expressing the communàl achievement when a man with a just cause gathers irresistible resources against inherently weak competitors. The similes, accompanying the final steps in this theme, are important factors in defining this victory.

In book 5 of the *Odyssey* Odysseus chooses to leave Ogygia—a choice sufficiently great to make him an epic hero. This book introduces the story of Odysseus at an advanced stage; later he will backtrack to tell the Phaeacians his story from the day he left Troy. Such a pattern, however, is characteristic of Homeric narrative: the opposites between which the hero will choose are presented first (books 5 and 6–8), and only then is the preparation for the decision reported (books 9–12). Thus it is typical that book 5 develops extreme positions between which Odysseus must choose.[121] Similes are especially effective in maintaining a focus on the divine protection of the hero as he shapes his own life rather than slumbering in isolation on Calypso's island.

In each of these books the themes are carried principally through the narrative; never does the simile control the direction of the story. Yet the similes are a wonderfully subtle and flexible device to enhance and bring into focus the essential features of that narrative. Two examples of comparative passages make the simile's contribution clear. First, there are two scenes in book 12 of the *Iliad* where heroes pick up stones to hurl at the enemy; Ajax bashes in the head of Epicles and Hector dashes down the gates in the Greek wall:

> First, then Telamonian Ajax slew a man,
> the comrade of Sarpedon, the great-hearted Epicles,
> striking him with a huge, jagged stone,
> which lay inside the wall near the battlement on top of the others.
>   Not easily
> would a man, such as men are now—
> even a very young man—hold it with both hands.
> But he raised it high and cast it forward,
> and it crushed his four-horned helmet and shattered all the bones
>   within his head.
>   (12.378–85)

> Hector snatched up and carried a stone, which stood
> in front of the gates, thick at the bottom
> and sharp at the top. The two best men of the people,
> such as men are now, would not easily have heaved it upon a wagon
> from the ground. But he by himself handled it easily;
> the son of crooked-counseling Cronus made it light for him.

Just as when a shepherd easily carries a ram's fleece,
picking it up with one hand, and its mass weighs him down little,
so Hector lifting the stone bore it straight against the doors....

(12.445–53)

Since the stone of Ajax is meant to seem heavy and destructive, the poet describes its size, its shape, its position, and the inability of any living man to pick it up. When it strikes its target it is only to be expected that it instantly kills a man; realism pervades this small scene. Hector's stone is so much heavier that it would require two men to lift, and it is large enough to have different shapes on top and bottom; yet Hector, though no stronger than Ajax, easily lifts it. Without the simile of the shepherd juggling the fleece, this heavy stone would still be light for Hector, since he is bolstered by Zeus' aid; but because of the simile Hector's act seems eerie and surreal. In a literal sense the simile is an extraneous repetition of action already in the narrative; but in terms of the poetic effect the simile makes Zeus' aid a tangible force in Hector's success.

Second, there are comparable scenes where a hero is saved and brought back into the narrative. First, the miraculous return of Aeneas in *Iliad* 5:

[Apollo] himself sent Aeneas forth from his rich shrine
and cast power into the breast of the shepherd of the people.
Aeneas stood in the midst of his companions, and they rejoiced
as they saw him alive, moving fearlessly,
and of sound strength. But they asked him nothing
for their other toils did not let them....

(5.512–17)

Aeneas' cure is presented as simple, and his men quickly turn back to the business of fighting. Since one of the principal characteristics of Diomedes' aristeia is its ineffectuality, this instant cure of the only wounded hero seems appropriate. Compare Apollo's healing of Hector in book 15:

Thus speaking he breathed great might into the shepherd of the people.
Just as when a stalled horse, fed on barley at his manger,
breaks his halter and runs galloping over the plain.
He is used to bathing in the beautiful river—
a proud stallion. He holds his head high and his mane
streams over his shoulders; confident in his glorious strength,

his knees bear him swiftly to his haunts and the pasture land of the
   other horses.
In this way Hector moved his feet and knees nimbly,
driving on his charioteers after he heard the voice of the god,
just as when dogs and country men
press on a horned stag or a wild goat,
but a steep rock and a shady grove
save him and it is not fated for them to find him.
Yet at their shouting a bearded lion appears
in the road and instantly turns all of them back even though they
   are eager;
so the Greeks for a while followed after in a throng
jabbing with their swords and sharpened spears,
but when they saw Hector moving throughout the ranks of his men,
they grew frightened. . . .

                                                                (15.262–80)

Both horse and lion similes are suited to a hero who has just been healed by Apollo. Hector is not only spirited in his return to the field, but so powerful in his attack that he will drive the Greeks back to their ships; and yet in this controlled battle every success of Hector is far more a show of spirit than of real strength. For Hector this return to battle is really the chance to earn his death, a fact which has already been made clear in Zeus' prophecy at the opening of the book (15.54–77). Thus the horse is harmless but filled with spirit, pride, and confidence;[122] and the lion turns the hunters from their mission, but he neither kills anyone nor gains any meat himself. With such similes as support, Hector does not measure up to Aeneas as a warrior.

Aeneas is presented as an effective and vigorous fighter in his own right, a strong leader and defender of his troops. Homer's audience not only knows the simile subjects available to describe effective fighters but also is familiar enough with the horse and lion similemes to appreciate the poet's choice of elements from the similemes for emphasizing Hector's weakness.

The technique of contrasting parallel passages — one with similes and the other without — reveals the real power of this traditional device in supporting the narrative. The similes at 12.451, 15.263, and 15.271 are so well designed to underline the themes developing in the surrounding narrative that they become clear guideposts to the poet's broader concerns.

CHAPTER FIVE

Problem Books

There remain several books of the *Iliad* where major difficulties in interpretation persist—especially in regard to structure. Among these are books 13, 16, and 17—long narratives suited to this study because they are rich in similes. Book 13 is a famous frustration; it has so many diverse scenes and different characters that its action seems to drift. It is easy to say that book 17 presents the fight over Patroclus' body, in which Achilles' armor passes to Hector, yet it seems to be composed of many scenes that do not appear to be tightly organized. Book 16 is one of the most important books in the development of the larger narrative because here Achilles tries to save both his honor and his humanity; only later does he find that one must be sacrificed, although he cannot accept the loss of either. While critics have a relatively easy time of defining Achilles' dilemma, there must be more on the poet's mind in extending the narration of Patroclus' fighting and death to such a length.

I will argue in this chapter that the close relationship between narrative and similes found elsewhere in Homeric epic offers significant clues to the structuring and interpretation of these problematic books. It remains the guiding principle of this study that similes support narrative strategies; they do not create the design. But if there is a perceptible pattern in the placement, the choice of subject matter, and the extension of the similes, then it is probable that this plan reflects elements in the narrative that are crucial to each book's theme.

ILIAD, BOOK 13:
THE ORDERING OF CONSCIOUS CHAOS[1]

In his introduction to book 13 Leaf concisely presents the kind of criticism that is typical of this part of the *Iliad*:[2]

> With this book begins a great retardation in the story of the *Iliad* in its present form. From the beginning of 13 till we come again to the story of the

Menis near the end of 15, the action does not advance; every step gained by either side is exactly counterbalanced by a corresponding success of the other, so that things are brought back just to the point at which we start. From time to time the story becomes confused, and then again flows on clearly for a while. In order to disentangle the original elements we must be guided by these passages of clear narrative, regarding the intervals of confusion as the joints by which they have been patched together.

The most devoted Unitarian must admit that Leaf has identified some distressing features about the composition of book 13. Yet even he cannot ignore the larger structure: this book is part of a unit that begins in book 13 and does not conclude until the end of book 15.[3] The double themes that run through these three books, the divine deception of Zeus and the successful fighting of the Greeks, are woven together to create a meaningful narrative; some critics, however, contend that this weaving is not well handled, especially in this introductory book.[4]

In determining the structure of book 13 the assumption that the three books (13–15) have been planned as a unit is of prime importance. At the end of book 12 the Trojans crossed over the wall, poured through the open gates, and drove the Greeks back to their ships. Poseidon enters at the beginning of book 13, once Zeus has turned his eyes away from the battle, and encourages the Greeks to strengthen their resistance. The situation of the Greek warriors is sufficiently fragile that several wounded Greek leaders, concerned for their men, come out to the battle lines at the beginning of book 14. As Hera enlists other gods to aid in distracting Zeus, the Greeks press their attack, even wounding Hector. They then consolidate their resurgence to the point where Homer presents a list of Trojan warriors despoiled by Greek heroes as the final unit of book 14. In book 15, when Zeus awakens to find his plan gone awry, he sets about repairing the reversals inflicted on the Trojans. This book concludes when events are returned to the situation at the end of book 12, where the Trojans were driving the Greeks back to their ships. In this way it is possible to find a basic internal direction in books 13–15 that is bracketed by the unchanged narrative situation.[5]

Book 13 begins with the arming of Poseidon and his journey to Troy, a scene that emphasizes his strength and his dominance over the creatures of the deep and the sea itself; yet as this powerful god begins to manage the battle, all sense of order is lost, and the narrative rapidly degenerates into a series of vignettes involving a medley of characters.[6] These scenes are largely constructed on the basis of repeated typological descriptions of a warrior's slaying; as a result there is a diverse mix of styles and variations. Yet few of these units cause or even affect ensuing events, there is little predictable development in the narrative, and the battle has no decisive momentum. This lack of organization is so striking that it is worthwhile to consider at the outset whether it might be purposeful—in other words, whether the chaos so evident to the audience can also be found among the characters.

There are, in fact, numerous signs that the very theme of book 13 is cross-purposes, disappointed expectations, frustration, and confusion. At the opening of the book Zeus is confident that no other divinity will offer aid to the warriors on the battlefield, although his plan has been repeatedly violated since his threatening "Golden Chain" speech at the beginning of book 8. In that book Hera and Aphrodite attempted to enter the battle but were forcibly stopped by Zeus' threats. Critics have usually concluded that this show of force presents Zeus enforcing his plan; but it is equally true that the immediate violation of his command by two powerful goddesses reveals a deep-seated, incorrigible resistance in the other gods. In book 10 (if that book is part of the *Iliad*) Athena appears to help the Greeks; but in books 11 and 12 the gods completely abstain from participating in the battle. Once again their absence is testimony to the power of Zeus, yet it is also easy to believe that sufficient pressure has been building among the normally independent and ubiquitous gods that the audience is not surprised when Poseidon appears at the first sign of relaxed vigilance.

When book 13 opens with the clear assertion that Zeus believed none of the immortals would descend to Troy, the groundwork has been laid for the major theme of the resulting three-book interlude—the contest of wills between Zeus and the other gods. This theme culminates in the resentful speech of Poseidon against Zeus in book 15:

> [Zeus], though great, speaks arrogantly
> if he seeks to hold me by force when I am unwilling and he is an equal.
> For we were born three brothers from Cronus and Rhea—
> Zeus, and I, and third was Hades, who rules over the dead.
> The universe has been divided in three ways—each of us took a share.
> When the lots were cast, I received the gray sea
> to live in forever; Hades received the misty darkness;

> Zeus received the broad heaven among the upper air and the clouds.
> Earth and the peaks of Olympus were common among all of us.
> Therefore I will not at all walk in accordance with the will of Zeus —
> strong though he is let him sit calmly in his third share....
>
> (15.185–95)

From the conscious and obvious undermining of Zeus' plan by Poseidon arises a series of confusions and reversals throughout book 13, of which the most serious is Hector's failure to control the battle. He appears only at the start of the book, leading the Trojans toward the Greek ships and later confronting Teucer, Amphimachus, and Ajax (39–42 and 169–205). In addition to these brief appearances, Hector is mentioned by Poseidon and several of the Greeks as the leader of the opposition. Otherwise he is absent from the actual fighting until the final scenes, where it is made clear that he is unaware how badly the battle has been going for the Trojans; the confusion so characteristic of this book has infected even the Trojan leader himself:

> Hector, dear to Zeus, had not heard nor had he known at all
> that his people were being slain by the Greeks on the left side
> of the camp. Soon there would have been victory for the Greeks,
> so greatly was the Holder and Shaker of the earth
> urging on the Greeks and himself aiding them from his own strength.
>
> (13.674–78)

In book 14 the Greeks remain uncertain about the direction of events until Hector is struck, and they begin to despoil a large number of slain Trojan warriors.

Book 13 seems to lack direction. Yet on the assumption that such confusion is the beginning of a purposeful design, it is possible to divide the book into two large sections:

1. Lines 1–360: This part of the book is dominated by the conflicting plans of Zeus and Poseidon. The narrative opens with this opposition stated directly, and this section concludes with a summary scene of balanced divine conflict ending with the image of the cord: "The two pulled tight the rope of violent strife and equal war, a cord which could not be broken nor undone, a thing which loosed the knees of many men" (358–60). Poseidon has strongly influenced the battlefield situation by persuading several Greek warriors to renew their fighting; the long speeches of mutual encouragement between

Idomeneus and Meriones serve as a precursor of the second, less divinely motivated section.

2. Lines 361–837: After the presentation of opposed divine purposes Poseidon abruptly disappears from the narrative, and there is scant mention of his influence at any point. Battles seem to be won appropriately by the Greeks, and thus there appears to be little need for his intervention as long as Zeus directs his attention elsewhere. The strength of the opposing warriors becomes the dominant force guiding the battle.

Within this basic two-part division it is possible to identify discrete units that further define the structure of the book:[7]

SECTION 1

1. 1–135: Poseidon encourages the Greeks
2. 136–55: The Trojans and Hector fight around the ships
3. 156–68: The introduction of Meriones and Deiphobus
4. 169–205: Battle vignette where the Greeks win
5. 206–344: Idomeneus and Meriones encourage each other and enter battle
6. 345–60: Recapitulation of conflicting divine purposes

SECTION 2

7. 361–539: The "aristeia" of Idomeneus
8. 540–672: Random battles, with successes on both sides
9. 673–837: Consolidation of positions, focusing on Hector and Ajax

This scheme does not precisely identify episodes that are being developed within a tightly structured narrative; rather, this list is composed of several passages linked by conscious foreshadowing and recall. Meriones and Deiphobus are briefly introduced in unit 3 in a small vignette that seems inconsequential but leads causally to the later scene (unit 5) where Meriones, while fetching another spear, meets Idomeneus—who then has a major role in unit 7. Deiphobus appears often in the second half of the book. In the same disjointed way, Poseidon paralyzes Alcathous and guards Antilochus (434–36 and 554–55). Since these are the only references to the god in the second part and both are without later consequence, they seem to exist only to bind this section to the first part of the book, where Poseidon played the dominant role. Thus even though the two halves differ in their emphasis on divine and human protagonists, the poet makes a specific effort to link them in order to parallel the direction in which men move in the second half of the book to that established by the god in the first half.[8]

There are twenty-five similes in book 13, distributed evenly between the two major sections. But none occur in the two smaller units: the brief encounter between Meriones and Deiphobus in unit 3 (156–68) and the short recapitulation of the divine purposes in unit 6 (345–60).

Four similes are placed in the first unit, which recounts Poseidon's encouragement of the Greeks (1–135). These similes emphasize the relative strength of the two opposing forces. The Trojans fight like a fire or a wind; immediately after this Poseidon describes Hector fighting like a fire (39 and 53).[9] Later, as the god encourages Teucer and his comrades, he uses a negative simile: the Trojans are no longer like panic-driven does before jackals, leopards, and wolves (101). Traditional similemes lie behind each of these passages: fire, wind, and wolves are familiar subjects in descriptions of strong warriors and thus provide a highly favorable assessment of the Trojans at the opening of the book;[10] the use of does elsewhere to depict ineffectual warriors is equally traditional.[11] The Greeks, who are hard pressed, receive no similes, and as the sole source of Greek resistance at this point, Poseidon is given a simile that is customarily reserved for a victorious warrior: he is like a hawk chasing a smaller bird (62).[12] At the opening of book 13, similes support the ongoing narrative under the guidance of Zeus' plan: the Trojans are fighting well, and they are given comparisons used for other successful warriors; the Greeks, who depend on the support of Poseidon to regain their standing, receive no similes.

The short unit that follows (136–55) highlights Hector as the leader of the successful Trojans. The only simile in this passage compares Hector in his impressive attack to a boulder driven by a rampaging river that rolls down a hill, devastating trees in its course until it stops on the plain (137). Yet even at this early point in the book there is a weakening in the force of Hector: once likened to a river in full spate (5.597), Hector is now a rock driven by Zeus' rain.[13]

In unit 4 (169–205) the Greeks first show the effect of Poseidon's encouragement. This unit is organized around a complex vignette that shows only a slight connection to the surrounding narrative. Teucer kills Imbrius; Hector aims at Teucer but instead strikes a lesser Greek, Amphimachus. As Hector goes to despoil Amphimachus, he is stopped by Ajax. The Greeks then pick up both corpses; they strip the armor from the fallen Trojan and mutilate his body. Since the previous scene between Meriones and Deiphobus contains no act or character to motivate this vignette, it is appropriately introduced by a formula of general fighting: "The others fought on and an inextinguishable cry arose" (169). The scene is indirectly linked to the following unit, since Poseidon's anger at the death of his grandson, Amphimachus, impels him to encourage Idomeneus; yet the importance of this connection is minimal. Idomeneus does not need this extra motivation; he and Meriones would have had the same spirited conversation without Poseidon.

This independent passage, though based upon a typical scene, is placed to emphasize the initial resistance of the Greeks.[14] Appropriately, the similes underline this point: Imbrius falls like a tree that is cut down and spreads its young leaves to the ground (178). The Greeks need a notable kill to begin their resurgence, and Imbrius is ideal—he is young, has married Priam's daughter, and dwells in the palace as though he were the king's own son. The simile does not specify who does the cutting or what the instrument is, other than bronze. The extended description identifies the tree as ash (implying mortality and destruction);[15] it places the tree on the summit of a high mountain, thus visible from all sides (appropriate because the victim is a son of Priam and this killing is notable as the beginning of the Greek counterattack), and it conveys the sense of waste or loss by means of the tender leafage strewn on the ground (suitable for the death of a young warrior). These extending components have been selected from the tree simileme (tree type, location, usage)[16] and arranged to emphasize the significance of the action for both sides. Imbrius as a member of Priam's family is given sufficient weight by the simile to cause Hector's anger.[17]

But Hector, who materializes out of nowhere to avenge this killing and claim the body, is disappointed in both desires. He fails to kill Teucer and is unable to retrieve either the body of Imbrius or that of the Greek whom he does slay, even though Hector has been presented as powerful both in the narrative and in similes earlier in the book (53 and 137). As he is repulsed, a simile compares the Trojans to hounds from whom a goat is snatched by two lions (198). A confrontation between lions and hounds often occurs in the simile world, but usually there is a contest. Here there is none; the hounds lose the meat, and the lions have no trouble carrying it off.[18] The Greeks are even able to decapitate Imbrius and further insult the Trojans by rolling his head before Hector's feet "like a ball" (204).[19] Thus the details of the type scene that are insulting to Hector—the killing of the first Trojan in the book, the snatching of both corpses, and the stripping and dishonoring of the fallen Trojan—are strongly reinforced by similes.

In the fifth unit, where Idomeneus and Meriones encourage each other (206–344), the narrative continues to provide an upbeat tone for the Greeks. This section begins with Poseidon in the guise of Thoas challenging Idomeneus to make good on all the Greek threats and boasts of the past. Idomeneus arms and then meets Meriones as he fetches another spear to replace the one he lost in unit 3. They encourage one another in a set of responding speeches; then they return to the battlefield, and general conflict is joined.

The similes reinforce the theme of directionlessness in the clash of forces; in effect, the similes remain one of the strongest uniting threads in the book, a strong clue that the poet did have a constant purpose in forming this collection of seemingly independent units. As Idomeneus emerges fully armed, he gleams like lightning brandished by Zeus from Olympus (242).[20] This lightning is specifically stated to be a sign to mortals—and, indeed, the whole first section of book 13 is a sign that strength is returning to the Greeks, slowly but perceptibly. Though Poseidon has not produced a miracle by his sudden appearance on the battlefield, he has worked effectively in disguise as a motivator. When Idomeneus finishes describing the cowardly warrior, he urges Meriones to battle by telling him that they should not continue to prattle like children but should hasten to join the fighting—a negative comparison to be corrected in the following lines (292). When the two warriors do enter the battle, they are compared to Ares and Phobos, gods who turn the enemy to flight when they give glory to one side (298).[21] The comparison of warriors to gods is traditional, but the naming of these specific gods and the poet's choices in extending the simile demonstrate Poseidon's effectiveness.[22] When Idomeneus appears, the Trojans see him like a flame (330), the same phrase that was used twice at the beginning of the book to describe the Trojans and Hector (39 and 53). Since fire is a traditional subject for a powerful warrior, the occurrence of this short comparison implies the presence of fresh strength in the Greeks, but of greater significance is the transfer of this subject from the Trojans to the newly roused Greeks.

When the two armies, both presented as vigorous and strong, begin to battle in the last scene in unit 5, the collision should be violent. The poet chooses a simileme that has traditionally described such clashes—wind: gusts of shrill winds blow over the roads, raising up a large cloud of dust (334). This subject may be traditional, but its extension is not. Though the men on both

Problem Books · 137

sides are showing predictable power and are not controlled by divine force, the poet weakens this simile to indicate that the results of the fighting are momentary. Often the winds blow over waves, raising a destructive surf, or rush through forests, shattering the limbs of trees. Here there is only dust; tomorrow there will be no sign that anything unusual has happened.[23] Up to this point similes have been traditional in subject matter and placement and have been extended by elements that are appropriate in content and tone to the surrounding narrative. In this final simile of book 13's first half, located just before the concluding passage on divine purposes, the poet has chosen to stress the lack of achievement. In book 8 Zeus took charge of the battle, and he will reassert his power when he awakens in book 15, but the battle that is joined at this moment in book 13 is a deviation from that surrounding context. Zeus has turned his attention away from the battlefield, and Poseidon has been effectively rallying the Greeks. The similes so far in the book have reflected the competitors' natural strengths, but the final simile of gusting winds emphasizes the transitory nature of any advance.

The next unit (345–60) closes the first of the two major sections and from its opening words is clearly a recapitulation of the activity on the battlefield from the divine perspective:

> Two powerful sons of Cronus, hearts divided against each other,
> were bringing bitter agonies on the fighting warriors.
> Zeus willed the victory for the Trojans and Hector,
> glorifying swift-footed Achilles, yet not utterly
> did he wish the Achaean people to be destroyed before Ilion.
> . . . .
> Therefore Poseidon avoided giving aid openly,
> and secretly did he encourage them throughout the army, in the likeness
>   of a man. . . .
>
> (13.345–49 and 356–57)

The specific reference to Zeus' plan to honor Achilles relates the action in this book directly to his promise to Thetis in book 1, his commands to the Olympians in book 8, and his pledge to Hector in book 11. Though Poseidon's actions are outside this plan, the threats of Zeus in his "Golden Chain" speech (8.5–25) are not unknown to him, for he is careful to move only when he can escape notice and generally in disguise. There are only two brief mentions of Poseidon's activity in the remaining scenes of book 13—yet the continuing divine drama in the deception of Zeus in book 14 and his angry awakening in book 15 reveal the covert forces that are opposing him. Thus this recapitulation combines the two sides of the divine activity that has been developing over several books and that remains active in the present situation.[24]

Now the second half of the book begins (361). The focus shifts almost totally to the actions of men. Appropriately, the initial motivating force for unit 7, the parallel to Poseidon in the opening unit, is Idomeneus, who encourages the Greeks as he rushes against the enemy; the book ends with an exchange of challenges between Hector and Ajax, corresponding to the statement of conflicting divine purposes. Yet even in this last scene an eagle appears, an omen interpreted as favorable by the Greeks (821–23); thus the divine element never completely disappears, even though the narrative is focused on the actions and responses of men.

Unit 7 (361–539) is a sprawling construction that does not seem to be designed as a typical aristeia but contains enough elements of the form that it is impossible to deny it the title.[25] The spotlight does indisputably fall on Idomeneus for a series of killings. In addition, there is growing strength in Idomeneus' achievements: he first kills a Trojan, then so threatens Deiphobus that he must seek Aeneas, and finally becomes the new center of the battle. Within the action Idomeneus is described by a series of similes that are traditional and appropriate for an aristeia.

Other elements, however, seem to be missing or replaced by substitutes. First, there is no proper introduction of the hero, but it is possible to see his introduction split from the immediate context and included in Poseidon's earlier encouragement, the hero's previous arming with a simile, and his speech to Meriones about the brave and cowardly warrior—all in unit 5 (206–94). But, of greater significance, Idomeneus is not the carrier of the action; the narrative is constructed from the individual actions of many heroes: in order of appearance, Idomeneus, Antilochos, Deiphobus, Aeneas, Meriones, Menelaus, Paris, Hector, Polydamas, and again Hector. Finally, this aristeia has no conclusion; the hero reaches his point of maximum achievement and cannot sustain the role. He fades away and is never mentioned again. It seems probable that in this book of purposeful confusion the poet has brought together many elements of the aristeia form and then consciously diffused them, thus raising questions as to what is happening for an audience familiar with traditional forms.

Similes provide important clues to the poet's larger design. The first grouping of events in this unit describes two killings by Idomeneus and one by Antilochus, with a response by the Trojan Deiphobus (361–423).[26] Idomeneus opens his aristeia by killing Othryoneus and boasting about the promise that the young Trojan made to Priam when he married his daughter. Asios comes to avenge his fallen comrade but is also slain by Idomeneus; he falls like a tree cut by shipwrights to be a ship's timber (389). This is the second tree simile of the book, and it reflects the earlier scene from the first half where Teucer brought the first Trojan down like a solitary tree on a mountaintop (178). In that simile the tree's location and its destruction were important to the scene; here different elements are chosen from the simileme to emphasize those who cut down the tree and their purpose. Since Idomeneus is the hero of the aristeia, it is appropriate to emphasize that understandable human intentions are motivating the scene. He is also momentarily the parallel figure to Poseidon in section 1, the active instigator of the greater design, whereas Teucer in the first unit is only the initiator of a battle that was principally carried on through the direct planning and participation of Poseidon.[27] The repetition of subject in a parallel location responds to the development from the first section as men now take direction of events.[28]

The remainder of this section contains the killing of Asios' charioteer and the taking of his horses, followed by Deiphobus' vain effort to kill Idomeneus. Deiphobus strikes down Hypsenor and boasts over his body as Idomeneus did over the body of Othryoneus, but the parallel ends when the Greeks carry off their comrade. The two scenes are shaped to enhance the victory of the Greek hero.

The second vignette (424–67) again pits Idomeneus against Deiphobus. This passage is introduced as an independent event in the aristeia, not directly caused by the previous action and only in the most superficial way triggering the next scene, where Deiphobus sends Aeneas to take his place. Idomeneus kills Alcathous and gloats over him in answer to the preceding boast of Deiphobus. Briefly, divine purpose and human motivation are specifically united in the language of the narrative when the poet reports that Poseidon had cast a spell over the eyes of Alcathous, paralyzing his limbs. The simile describing the fallen warrior is a double simile of a stele[29] or a tree (437), a conscious echo emphasizing the continuing strength of Idomeneus (cf. 389); in addition, Deiphobus refuses the direct challenge and chooses to seek the aid of Aeneas. These two vignettes (361–423 and 424–67) are a doublet, closely linked by theme, responses of characters, and simile topic even though the actions described are typological and not joined as cause and effect.[30]

In the third vignette (468–95) the quality of the challengers is elevated — a usual development in an aristeia. The opposing hero now is Aeneas. Homer gives Idomeneus two juxtaposed complementary similes: he is not a pampered child, but a boar confronting dogs and men (470 and 471);[31] still, however, he calls to his friends asking for aid because he recognizes the Trojan's prowess. Aeneas summons his companions to join him, a scene that the poet describes with a simile of sheep following after the ram — a view that delights the shepherd (492).[32] The contrast is between the boar and the ram (or the shepherd).[33] The boar is described in full fury, his back bristling and his eyes filled with fire — one of the strongest examples taken from the lion/boar simileme.[34] The ram leads the flock to water and the shepherd rejoices — a scene of day-to-day country life with little danger, threat, or extraordinary achievement. In this third segment, similes build Idomeneus' strength.

As the battle re-forms over the body of Alcathous, Idomeneus and Aeneas are spotlighted for a fourth vignette (496–539):

> Two men, warriors above all,
> Aeneas and Idomeneus, the equals of Ares,
> yearned to cut each other's flesh with the cruel bronze.
>
> (499–501)

Despite this specific pairing of the two heroes, the episode is constructed in two parts focusing again on Idomeneus and Deiphobus as contrasting warriors. Aeneas does cast his spear at Idomeneus, who avoids it — and that is Aeneas' last appearance in this scene. Idomeneus kills Oenomaus but is unable to despoil him. Deiphobus tries to wound Idomeneus but hits Ascalaphus, whose helmet he takes before he is wounded by Meriones and carried from the field. This is the end of the aristeia of Idomeneus, who receives no further mention in this book; almost imperceptibly the impetus in the battle passes to his comrade Meriones. The curt postponement of Aeneas' appearance is calculated. He is held aside only for the moment in order to begin the next series of random battles.

Once Idomeneus has disappeared, Meriones inherits his role as opponent to Deiphobus. This shift is marked when Meriones receives the only simile in this vignette, a comparison to a vulture (531). This is a short simile, yet traditional for a fighting warrior; in addition, it recalls the earlier simile of a predatory hawk, used of Poseidon when he was the Greeks' only force of resistance (62).³⁵ The god's driving power has now passed from the hero of a quasi-aristeia to one of his comrades—a second shift reinforcing the effectiveness of Poseidon in transferring his desires to the Greek army.

The eighth unit (540–672) presents confusion at its height, a series of mutual woundings with a slight edge gained by the Greeks. Although Hector had assumed that the successes of the previous book were continuing, at the end of this unit the poet states openly that he has little knowledge of the course of the battle and that the Trojan attack has been blunted by a fairly broad group of Greek warriors. The change from the first lines of the book is remarkable. The plan of Zeus has been neutralized; in the next book it will be decisively reversed. With the passing of the immediate danger there is a less desperate quality to the Greeks' fighting; the similes follow this movement. Now they do not occur in wounding scenes emphasizing the victorious fighting of one warrior or accompanying major shifts in the strength of one side or another; rather, in this unit the similes fall at places unrelated to the direction of the war, and their subjects cast a more peaceful tone over the battlefield. Poseidon renders the spear cast by Adamas harmless, and the simile at 564 stresses the action of a god in human affairs rather than the killing of a warrior. The subject of this simile is unusual: the spear is like a charred stake. Perhaps in the background is the fire simileme, with its description of a massive fire, a subject that often accompanies the fighting of warriors; here the fire is over.³⁶ This effect is continued a few lines later, when the death agony of this same warrior is described by a normal scene of country life; he is compared to a bull bound and dragged by herdsmen (571).³⁷ When Helenus shoots an arrow at Menelaus, it jumps off his breastplate:

> as when black beans or chickpeas jump
> from a broad winnowing fan on the wide threshing floor
> when the wind is shrill and the winnower is strong
>
> (588–90)

An equally incongruous subject occurs in the wounding of Harpalion, who stretches out on the ground like a worm (654).³⁸

In this unit there is an abrupt change from earlier simile subjects. Rather than stressing the predominance of the Greeks, the similes now focus on moments like the intervention of the god in a battle or the arrow that is turned aside; even when the similes describe the death of a Trojan, the tone is softened as both sides now fight a more normal and balanced series of contests in which there is no overwhelming victory for either.

This same tone continues into the final unit (673–837), which is both an extension of the narrative development in unit 8 and a conclusion to the second half of book 13 — thus a parallel to the summary of opposed divine purposes at the end of section 1 (345–60). Finally, the situation on the battlefield becomes clear to the competing armies and their leaders, Hector and Ajax. After the series of confusing individual and independent vignettes, the opposing leaders appraise their present positions. This unit begins with a general line describing the armies fighting like fire (673), thus repeating the simileme used to describe the fighting of the Trojans in the first simile of the book (39); now, however, the two sides are equally matched. The reference to the beginning of the book is reinforced when the next simile repeats the second comparison in the book, where Poseidon describes Hector fighting like a fire (688, cf. 53); now this simile occurs in a passage where the poet has made it clear that Hector confronts a changed situation because of the resurgence of the Greeks.

But as the desperation of the Greeks fades, a simile provides a cooler and more peaceful tone as an introduction to the evaluation of stabilized positions: the Ajaxes are presented as two yoked oxen toiling to plow a field (703).[39] Likewise, when Hector goes to reconnoiter, he receives the simile of the "snowy mountain" — scarcely typical for a warrior (754).[40]

Hector now learns from Paris about the losses that have occurred in the course of book 13, gathers the survivors, and leads them to reestablish his lines. Again the battle grows fierce as the Trojans try to recoup their losses — and appropriately, the similes turn warlike again. The Trojans are compared to storm winds that join with the thunder of Zeus to whip up the sea, and Hector is compared to man-slaughtering Ares (795 and 802).[41] The final moment of this book is the shouting match of challenges between Ajax and Hector. Ajax steadies the Greeks and assures Hector that it will not be long before he will be praying to his patron Zeus for help. He even inserts a familiar simile, telling Hector that he will soon yearn for horses swifter than falcons to carry him back to the safety of his city (819).[42] This last simile of the book ironically echoes the simile used in the first unit to describe Poseidon:

> he rose like a swift-winged hawk
> which soars above a steep and lofty crag

> and rushes to chase another bird across the plain;
> thus did Poseidon, the shaker of the earth, race away from them. . . .
>
> (62–65)

As the reappearance of Hector at 674 injects a reference to the plan of Zeus into the final scene (*diiphilos*), so also this simile brings a memory of the opposing plan of Poseidon. These reminders of the two contending gods are reinforced by the sudden appearance of an eagle (821ff.), and in the final line of the book the sound of both sides rises high up to the clear light of Zeus.

Book 13 begins with a moment of clarity as the Trojans seem about to overwhelm the Greek ships; it also ends on a note of clarity as the Greeks and the Trojans join in battle on an equal footing. Between these two points, much is confusion. The plan of Zeus is reversed. The Greeks score victories on the field here and there. One Greek hero has a quasi-aristeia, and the leader of the Trojans loses track of what is happening to his troops. Because this book is the introduction to the larger narrative of books 13 through 15, it presents a gradual improvement in Greek fortunes, even though this movement is often so imperceptible that it is difficult to see how and where it is happening. There are guideposts in the book revealing the developing theme to the audience, but even the participants are little aware of an orderly direction.

A strong sign of this purposeful design is the conscious repetition of the same simileme in contrasting narrative units. The clearest example is the balance of battle in the book's first and last units. Echoing similemes pinpoint the contrasting features precisely in order to give the audience no chance to be unaware of the increasing success of the Greek army. In the final unit the need for Hector as the Trojan leader is emphasized when the fire simile is repeated from the first unit (688, cf. 39 and 53); the Trojans' attempt to regain their position in the battle is supported by a wind simile (795), which is echoed from the earlier simile at line 39. Hector's role as inspirer of the Trojans against the efforts of Poseidon is accentuated by the simile comparing him to Ares (802)—a simile borrowed from the earlier description of Meriones at 298 in order to emphasize the current equality of the Trojans and Greeks. Then the final simile of the book, that of hawks, recalls the movement of Poseidon in the first unit (819, cf. 62).

Even though the subject matter of the similes throughout the book is bewilderingly varied, their placement is often seen as merely typical, and one longer simile is repeated from another book.[43] Nonetheless, the poet's active choice of the scenes to emphasize with similes, of the narrative patterns to highlight with similes, of extended similes and those left short, and his selection from among alternatives as he extends certain similes are all part of a larger plan providing a firm foundation for the strong Greek attack in the coming book.

ILIAD, BOOK 17: SIMILES AS GUIDES THROUGH A SERIES OF TYPE SCENES

In book 17 there are clear signs that Hector's promised day of glory is about to end; he has performed his role in the plan of Zeus, and his effectiveness begins to fade as the Greeks rally. The book introduces this change by centering its theme on the human responses to Patroclus' death.[44] The absence of Achilles, the need to inform him, and the necessity of adapting to the new situation are major undercurrents throughout the narrative. The most important Greek warriors must fight doggedly to protect Patroclus' body and its armor, since Hector threatens to gain control of both. The narrative shifts focus between the opposing forces as they contend for the prize. The Greeks lose control of the body long enough for Hector to take the armor of Achilles; yet by the end of the book they have organized their defense and are able to pull the body free and carry it toward the Greek camp. The Trojans experience the opposite fortune; they start out victoriously:

> When Hector had stripped Patroclus of his glorious armor,
> he sought to drag him away to cut his head from his shoulders with
>   a sharp sword,
> and haul away the corpse to give to Trojan dogs.
>
> (125–27)

This is Hector's most triumphant moment in the book. From this point he loses power until the body finally slips from his control and the Greeks begin to carry it to Achilles.

Book 17 contains a large number of similes (twenty-six) — indeed, some of the most striking in the Homeric poems. In addition, since only two are short, the poet seems to have chosen to develop similes as meaningful support for the narrative. This book is not much admired; many critics are scornful of its endless battles as dilatory and meandering.[45] The deeper problem is that few agree on its theme. Once again it is important to place this book within a larger structure: with the death of Patroclus and the awful burden of responsibility that descends on Achilles, the *Iliad* turns to his death-centered rededication. Only such total blindness to human suffering can permit him to rise to his final magnanimous act in allowing the funeral of Hector.

The book is divided into six units, five of which are organized around a repeated basic scene: defense by the Greek(s), rebuke of the Trojan, and the frustration of the Trojan advance.[46] Crucial to the Greek defense, which solidifies at the end of each of the first five units, is Telamonian Ajax or the Ajaxes.

1. 1–131: Menelaus protects Patroclus' body; Apollo rebukes Hector; Hector drives Menelaus away from the body; Ajax drives Hector back.
2. 132–318: Ajax protects Patroclus' body; Glaucus rebukes Hector; the Trojan advance drives Ajax to seek aid; Ajax firms up the Greek lines and strips two Trojan bodies of their armor.
3. 319–65: Greeks threaten; Apollo rebukes Aeneas; Aeneas attacks; Ajax stops the Trojan advance.
4. 366–542: The battle is balanced; Achilles' horses are given strength by Zeus; Hector encourages Aeneas to take the horses; the Ajaxes advance and the Trojans retreat as Automedon strips the body of his enemy.[47]
5. 543–714: Menelaus slays a Trojan encouraged by Athena; Apollo rebukes Hector;[48] the Trojans attack and have success with the aid of Zeus; the Ajaxes and Meriones guard the body of Patroclus while Menelaus withdraws to give news to Achilles and then returns.
6. 715–61: The corpse is taken away by the Greeks.[49]

The book is structured as a series of initiatives by Hector/Aeneas that are blocked each time by the opposition of Ajax, who finally manages to pull the body free from the Trojans. Within this repeated structure a series of Greek heroes draws the spotlight, each for a brief moment while the design of the similes emphasizes the temporary effectiveness of these characters in their individual scenes. Even more importantly, these similes reinforce the clear indications in the narrative that the Greeks are gaining power through the course of book 17 while Hector loses both strength and divine favor. This shift in force from the Zeus-supported Trojans to the Greeks, driven by thoughts of their obligation to Achilles, provides an effective introduction to the final books of the *Iliad*, the aristeia of Achilles.

In the first unit (1–131) Menelaus stands alone over the body but is able to withstand Hector only when Ajax arrives to support him. This unit contains seven similes, two of which are short. Menelaus stands over Patroclus' body like a mother cow over her calf (4); he is by no means a weak warrior, but throughout book 17 his performance emblemizes the Greeks' inability to gain possession of the body on their own. Here he attracts one of the strangest similes accompanying a warrior in the *Iliad*, yet the unwarlike tone of this simile is echoed throughout the first unit:[50]

He protected him as a mother cow bawling over her calf—
her first born, for she has not before experienced birth

(17.4–5)

The second line stresses the inexperience of the cow; perhaps Menelaus is chosen as the initial defender of the body because of his relative ineffectiveness as a warrior. Even though he fights well and is appropriately described in the other similes by topics customary for a warrior, the opponents in these similes are chosen to present uneven battles among adversaries of different strengths. Menelaus calls Euphorbus unequal to a leopard, a lion, or a boar (20),[51] thus denying him the most traditional and heroic comparisons for warriors. Homer continues the description of ill-matched forces in the next simile, where Menelaus is likened to a whirlwind that lays low an olive sapling (53). The whirlwind is the proper description for a strong warrior, but in other wind similes the opposing force is a whole forest or a giant, firmly rooted tree;[52] here the wind wins a meager victory over a young, weak plant. This effect is immediately reinforced when Menelaus is described as a mountain-reared lion who devours an undefended heifer and scares off men and hounds (61). At 109, when Menelaus confronts Hector, these dogs and men reappear to drive the lion off. In other words, in these early similes Homer has undercut Menelaus' warlike acts by choosing such weak opponents that these similes fall short of being strong examples within their families. As a result, the narrative presents the Greeks as comparatively weak so that they can be made to grow stronger during the course of the book. There are only two other similes: Hector and Ajax, the two rival champions of the book, receive traditional short similes that introduce them as stronger central figures for the more serious battle in the next unit (88 and 128).[53]

The second section (132–318) is a variation of the first; its participants and the terms of the battle are raised to a higher level.[54] The defeat of the Trojans is more decisive, and the Greeks capture and despoil the two fallen bodies. Initially Hector is able to strip the armor of Patroclus, but he cannot get control of his body. Glaucus' rebuke is harsher than Apollo's in unit 1, suggesting Hector's cowardice and adding a threat to withdraw the Lycians as allies. As Hector puts on Achilles' armor, Zeus appears in this book for the first time, criticizing his arrogance in stripping the armor from Patroclus and underlining the temporary quality of his previous success.

The contrast between the two sections is initially signaled in the opening lines in a simile (132ff.): in the first unit Menelaus stood over the body of Patroclus like a mother cow over her calf (4); here Ajax takes the same position and is compared to a mother animal over its young, but this time the subject is a strong lion glorying in his strength.[55] Both the quality of the warrior and the strengthening of the simile are reinforced when Ajax rallies the Greeks like a boar who scatters opposing hounds and hunters (281);[56] earlier Menelaus was like a lion who retreated before hounds and men (109). There are only two other similes in this unit. Meriones is compared to man-slaughtering Ares as he comes to help the Greeks (259). This introduction is short, but strong, since it uses the god who exemplifies war; this provides a proper introduction for Meriones, who will stand with the Ajaxes when they are finally able to snatch away Patroclus' body.[57] The second describes the shouting of the Trojans, who advance noisily like a wave (263).[58] This is a customary simile subject for an advancing army, but there are more potent elements available in the simileme; here the wave only makes noise. This section is clearly based on the same type scene as the first, and modifications to the similes demonstrate the conscious parallelism.

The third unit (319–65) combines the previously developed motifs into an unadorned, direct presentation of narrative action. It is quite short and contains no similes. Apollo encourages Aeneas, as he did Hector in the first unit. Then there is a short battle sequence: Trojan wounds Greek; Greek wounds Trojan; Trojan tries to wound Greek but is stopped when Ajax encourages the Greeks to stand firm. The first lines of this section summarize the situation:

> Then the Trojans would again have retreated to Ilion
> overwhelmed by their cowardice before the Achaeans, beloved of Ares,
> and the Argives would have taken honor even above Zeus' allotment
> for their power and strength. . . .
>
> (319–22)

The weakness brought into the earlier narrative by Menelaus is simply no longer present, even though Zeus still helps the Trojans. The last time the Greeks showed such strength was in books 13–15, when Zeus' aid to the Trojans disappeared and Poseidon assisted the Greeks.

At this point it is clear how tightly the first three units are constructed around a repeated series of typological actions. In the first two units the similes underline the increasing success of the Greeks. The scene with Menelaus could well have contained both the despoiling of Patroclus' armor and the dragging of his body, but when Ajax—a stronger warrior—appeared, the poet repeated the first action with heightened intensity; Greek warriors more powerful than Menelaus beat Hector at his own game, stripping the armor from Trojan victims. In the third unit the strength of the Greeks is confirmed in a scene centering on Ajax and Aeneas, Hector's surrogate.

In the fourth unit (366–542) Hector not only fails to take the horses of Achilles but also loses one of his men, whose body is stripped by Automedon. The Ajaxes are again the protectors of the Greeks; significantly, though, Zeus aids Achilles' horses in escaping capture—a further sign of the impending limitation of Hector's power.[59] The key elements in this scene are the full establishment of balanced battle after the introductory section, the active involvement of Zeus on the side of the Greeks, and finally the victory of a Greek from the camp of Achilles. These three moments receive similes.

The evenness of the battle is presented in the first two similes. The first is short and traditional: like a fire (366). This simile occurs often in descriptions of real warfare, and there is no doubt that both sides are eager to gain control of Patroclus' body—so eager that a darkness shrouds their area of the battlefield.

The Achilles theme is sounded when the poet states that neither Thrasymedes nor Antilochus knew that Patroclus had been killed; at the end of the book Antilochus will be approached by Menelaus to carry news of Patroclus' death to Achilles. Once again the poet stresses the evenness of the battle in a strikingly peaceful simile (389) that in tone is reminiscent of the countryside scene opening book 17, where Menelaus is compared to a mother cow (4). Such a reflection signals that this unit of balanced battle opens a new phase in the book's action.[60] The simile describes men stretching a bull's hide to cure it as an image of the equal striving on both sides. The combination of the Achilles theme and the balance of battle is underlined once again by the immediate mention of Achilles' continuing ignorance of his comrade's death, as well as the balanced speeches of both Greeks and Trojans to their fellow soldiers (412–22). This sense of arrested motion is reinforced by the image of the charioteer whipping horses who refuse to move; a simile describes them as standing fixed like a pillar over the tomb of a dead man or woman (434).[61] Of course, it is appropriate to book 17's position as the introduction to the final quarter of the *Iliad* that the horses of Achilles are stricken with sorrow for the fallen Patroclus.

At this point the irreversible movement toward the death of Hector in book 22 begins. Zeus, pitying the horses, tells them that Hector will never drive their chariot and that he will have glory for only this one day. Automedon, Achilles' charioteer, is now presented as a Greek champion, driving the horses through the Trojans like a vulture swooping on geese (460).[62] When he finds Alcimedon to share the chariot, he immediately attracts Hector's attention. Automedon prays to Zeus, is filled with strength, and slays Aretus, a lesser Trojan, just as a man kills an ox (520). When the Ajaxes bring aid to Automedon, he is able to despoil the body and climb into his chariot like a lion that has devoured a bull (542).[63]

Although Homer had been careful to reestablish a balance in the fighting at the beginning of unit 4, this battle now goes badly for the Trojans, a trend reinforced by the similes. Zeus sides with the Greeks, especially those who are directly associated with Achilles, and the section ends when Automedon kills and strips the body of a Trojan in the very presence of Hector. The increasing effectiveness of the Greeks is emphasized by the scaled intensity of the similes. At the start there is the countryside scene of men stretching the bull's hide, but then in each of the final three similes the Greek is identified with the dominant force: a vulture over geese, a man killing an ox, and a lion devouring a bull. In the last simile the Trojans are not even given the honor of being included as one of the customary worthy opponents of the lion, nor are there the familiar men and dogs. The lion simply devours the bull and all mention of opposition is deleted. On this note the unit ends.

The movement toward Achilles continues in the repeated structure in the fifth unit (543–714), the final struggle for Patroclus' body.[64] The scene begins as usual with a statement that the battle was drawn taut over his corpse. Almost immediately Athena appears to aid the Greeks, described in a half-simile/half-description as a rainbow that Zeus has placed in heaven to be the harbinger of a dire event for men (547).[65] Thus the poet stresses not only the harshness of battle for both Greeks and Trojans but also the continuing involvement of divine forces as Hector fruitlessly exhausts the remaining time left in his day of prominence. Athena gives strength to Menelaus, the warrior with whom the book began. As if to recall his earlier stand over Patroclus' body, Homer uses another strangely unwarlike simile: a fly keeps bothering a man (570).[66] Yet in spite of this unpromising beginning Menelaus will be the hero in this unit, and his similes increase in strength as he retreats like a lion giving way slowly before dogs and men — and then looks for Antilochus with the eyes of an eagle seeking and killing his victim (657 and 674).[67] He tells Antilochus morosely that the battle is being won by the Trojans and that a god is rolling destruction upon the Greeks; then he informs him that Patroclus is dead, that Hector has taken his armor, and that they are in need of Achilles to save the body.

In unit 6 (715–61) the battle is renewed, with strong fighting on either side. In both units 5 and 6 speakers are discouraged, and yet each is so involved in his own scene that he appears unaware of the irresistible direction in events, and mixed signals are sent at the end of the book. Because Menelaus fears that Achilles will not enter the battle even now, he urges Ajax to take Patroclus' body and to organize a retreat, but both words and actions presage the reentrance of Achilles. Hector's last charge is the most spirited and successful in book 17; yet the opposing power of the Ajaxes is great, a messenger is on his way to Achilles, and the Greeks are able to gain possession of the body. In support of these narrative elements Homer provides a cluster of similes. The Trojans are likened to a destructive fire and to hawks bearing death to smaller birds (737 and 755).[68] The Greeks, in contrast, are described with weakened forms of each simileme; the Ajaxes are like a wounded boar that manages to defend himself although he is unable to attack and also like a wooded ridge that holds back a river (725 and 747).[69] In both comparisons the item describing the Greeks is solid but nonaggressive: the boar and the dam stand firm, and the object parallel to the Trojans keeps attacking. Even those who are dragging the body are described as mules that struggle steadily to pull a large timber down a rugged path (742). The very ending lines of the book point to the hard battle to come:

Beneath the press of Aeneas and Hector the youths of Achaea,
shrieking cries of doom, fled and forgot their fighting.
Many beautiful weapons fell around and about the trench
as the Greeks fled. There was no rest from war.

(758–61)

Yet despite of the appearance of a closely balanced battle, the narrative has begun to move forcefully in a single direction; the second line of book 18 reports Antilochus' arrival at the tent of Achilles. From this point on there is no release for Hector, who continues to fight bravely even though he is facing an invincible enemy.

Book 17 has presented the Achaeans growing stronger, and Hector still strong but unable to break their line; the similes have been carefully crafted to reinforce this impression, and they carry significant weight in organizing the series of repeated typological actions from which this book is built. In units 1, 2, 4, and 5 the similes serve to highlight the dominant hero: in order, Menelaus, Ajax, Automedon, and Menelaus. Although Ajax is the protective agent who continually holds the Trojans away from the body, the action in each unit centers on a single hero, and the similes mark that hero as the central character. In addition, in these units the hero who has been introduced with weak similes for a warrior is likened to a lion or a boar at the end of the scene; in this way the poet constructs a repeated pattern of traditional simile subjects that emphasizes the growing strength of the Greeks and the developing weakness of the Trojans. Throughout the Greeks are often described in similes where they are paralleled to forces that so drastically outweigh the strength of their opponents that there is virtually no contest: a whirlwind against an olive shoot, lions against heifers and bulls, a man against an ox, vultures against geese, and eagles against hares. There are only three similes for Trojans prior to unit 6 (versus thirteen for the Greeks), and they are by comparison less focused on battle ability, in one case stressing the noise that the Trojans make rather than their strength.

There also seems to be careful coordination in the use of similes in order to invite comparison to earlier scenes. For example, Menelaus is weaker than Ajax and incapable of fending off Hector's attack by himself. When he stands over Patroclus' body, he is described as a cow over her calf (4), but Ajax in the same posture is described as a lioness over her young (133). Similarly, at the ends of these two units Menelaus retreats like a lion before dogs and men, while Ajax in the parallel position advances like a boar scattering dogs and men (109 versus 281). When Menelaus kills his opponent in the first unit, the Greeks are beginning to show strength and he is described by a simile of a lion who has killed a heifer (61); Automedon has the power of Zeus behind him and is far enough along in the development of Greek power in the fourth unit that Homer presents him as a lion having killed a bull (542).

Only in the final unit does the poet change this pattern. When the Greeks acknowledge that they must fight hard to protect Menelaus and Meriones as they carry the body away, equivalent numbers of similes appear for Greeks and Trojans, and their subjects become suitable in topic and extension for warriors. As was shown in regard to the cluster of similes preceding the Catalogue in book 2, the full series of closing similes in this book carefully reflects the developments in the narrative.[70] Together the four similes of destructive nature (725, 737, 747, and 755) focus on the clash of opposing forces and tend to give a momentary and fragile advantage to the Trojans; the one simile of nature at peace describes Menelaus and Meriones. Through such consistency the cluster of five similes in forty-six lines provides an impressive poetic background drawn from a wide variety of similemes to summarize memorably the situation prior to Achilles' reentrance into battle.

Several of the topics seem to evolve through the book or at least are incorporated into the sixth unit, where subjects that have described the Greeks are applied to the Trojans. These similes momentarily prop up the Trojans, though they are really on the verge of destroying themselves by arousing Achilles. Automedon is a vulture swooping on geese (460), and Menelaus, an eagle killing a hare (674). The Trojans receive an equally strong simile when they close the book: they are compared to hawks bringing death to starlings and daws (755). The same direction is clear in lion similes: Menelaus and Ajax are both described as successful lions (61, 133, and 281), but at the end of the book Menelaus is like a lion who is driven away by dogs and men (657, cf. 61) and the twin Ajaxes are like a wounded boar (728). Thus, striking sets of parallels throughout the book show that later similes are orchestrated to produce responsive variations on earlier comparisons. With such an intense clustering of similes the poet expects his audience to recall this moment when he returns to it in book 18.

There this design continues the scene that closed book 17. The similes are drawn from the same families: Hector is like a fire, just as the Trojans were earlier (18.154; cf. 17.736); at 18.161 Hector has become a lion, the constant simile of the Greeks in book 17, but he is now a lion who fights so strongly that he cannot be driven off by shepherds. But as soon as Achilles lends his support to the rescue of Patroclus, he attracts the fire image— indeed, the strongest fire simile in books 17 and 18: a gleam rises from his head as it would from a fire which rages through a city that summons its allies for help (18.207; cf. 17.737). Not only has this subject rallied the Greek forces throughout book 17, but the simile in book 18 prefigures the downfall of Troy.[71]

The final test of the care with which Homer has placed and developed his similes in book 17 is the identification of places where the tradition would have suggested a simile yet Homer has chosen alternatives. The most obvious location for similes in the book would be as marks for the entrance of a warrior. This main warrior in the series of scenes that make up book 17 is Ajax, who shores up the Greek lines in each of the six units of the book. The narrative, however, is not about Ajax but about the series of Greek successes that ensure the capture and protection of Patroclus' body. As a result, while Ajax does receive some similes, they are constructed to emphasize his role within the individual scene. When he first enters the narrative to stop Hector from mutilating the body of Patroclus, he is introduced with a short simile. Menelaus, however, is the principal figure in the first unit, and his actions of defense and retreat appropriately receive four of the seven similes, all extended. When Ajax becomes the main character in the second unit, he receives a long simile to describe his position over the body; this simile also emphasizes the parallel to the earlier actions of Menelaus. As Ajax strengthens the lines and motivates a successful resistance, he is also described by a long simile. Yet, though he benefits the Greek cause throughout the rest of the book, no simile calls attention to him until the final unit, where both Ajaxes are described as part of the retreat. Clearly book 17 is not designed to be the aristeia of Ajax; it is the introduction to the coming aristeia of Achilles, and all individual scenes in this book lead to this missing hero who is about to return to lead the Greeks against Troy.

Hector keeps entering the battle, at first victorious, but increasingly unsuccessful. His diminishing strength might be expected to attract similes, but Homer has not chosen this method of highlighting Hector — a lack that may be especially noticeable when Hector puts on the armor of Patroclus. However, similes are at best only an indirect means of drawing attention to the single event. Hector's increasing weakness is brought forcefully into focus by his repeated setbacks as well as the ominous words of Zeus on seeing Hector in Achilles' armor, his promise to the horses that he will never let Hector capture them, his change of heart when he sends Athena to encourage the Greeks, and his lifting of the darkness over the battle scene in response to Ajax's prayer. Hector receives only two of the large number of similes in this book even though his declining fortune is one of the book's major themes.

When he first enters, he is described by a short, traditional simile; when he is last seen fighting the Ajaxes for the control of the body, he and Aeneas share a simile (88 and 755). But that is all. It seems to have been important to Homer that Hector's performance and limitations be portrayed directly rather than by comparisons—probably to prepare for the rapidly approaching confrontation of two very different champions in book 22.

And, of course, many other heroes enter the battle for their brief moment in this book. Because each of these warriors is prominent in his small unit of the poem, each individual could have received a simile on entering or even similes for variation within the repeated basic type scene, but the poet remains firmly focused on the development of the greater themes and ignores these smaller opportunities in order to concentrate on the series of Greek victories.

There are a number of divine entrances to the battlefield. Three times Apollo tries to aid the Trojans by adopting a mortal disguise, but this intervention never receives a simile. Only the mission of Athena is described with an extended simile (547)—appropriately, because the narrative states directly that the mind of Zeus shifts toward the Greeks at this moment.

Numerous other customary opportunities for similes are passed over. There is much emotion in this book, especially Menelaus wondering whether he should stand against the advancing Hector, Glaucus rebuking Hector, Hector boasting to the Trojans and promising them half of the spoils if they will take the body of Patroclus, a series of encouragers trying to rouse the troops on both sides, Automedon in frustration lashing the horses who refuse to move, and Antilochus reacting to the news that Patroclus has been slain. Yet these are only minor elements in the development of the major two-sided, mutually reinforcing theme that provides the dominant design of the narrative in book 17: the increasing power of the Greeks and the corresponding weakness of the Trojans. Both narrative and similes focus steadily on this design.

ILIAD, BOOK 16: SIMILES FOR COMPLEXITY

Book 16 of the *Iliad* is best described as a house of mirrors: actions often have a double image, but one image is the reverse of the other; nothing is quite what it appears, and characters discover the truth only when it is too late.[72] Each main character proposes a solution to the critical problems on the battlefield, only to discover that his scheme was impossible from the beginning.

Patroclus enters battle with the intent of saving the Greeks, but that goal is unreachable; Achilles prays for Patroclus' success and safety but is instantly denied; Achilles wants to make the Trojans think that he has returned to the battle, but they are not fooled. Although Sarpedon is slain by Patroclus and the Greeks strip him of his armor, he receives a triumphant, miraculous burial; as the Trojans retreat, Patroclus hopes to take the city of Troy but is killed. The poet is telling a story filled with illusions.

The action of the book is built upon the misconceived stratagem of Achilles. Since book 11 he has observed the battlefield with concern and careful attention. Although he removed himself from the army awaiting rewards from Agamemnon, he is unable to ignore the Greek defeat. At this point the ominous theme of the misguided plan is heard for the first time. Achilles, seeing a chariot go by carrying one of the wounded, calls to Patroclus:

> Immediately he called to his comrade Patroclus,
> summoning him from beside the ship. Hearing he came from the tent
> like the god Ares, and this indeed was the beginning of evil for him.
> (11.602–4)

Two conflicting forces begin to rend the soul of Achilles: his desire for uncompromised heroic glory stands firmly opposed to his need to aid comrades who are dying on the battlefield. Achilles, frustrated in his isolation, sends Patroclus to get information about the situation of the Greeks, an act that reveals the separation of his more humane Patroclean half from the Achillean part.[73] Patroclus, though he realizes that he must support Achilles' strategy for maximizing personal honor, hears Nestor's gloomy list of Greek casualties and takes time to help the wounded Eurypylus. When he returns to the Myrmidon camp at the beginning of book 16, he is overwhelmed by his awareness of human suffering — a very different reaction from the strained and stoic insularity of Achilles. As a result, once Patroclus reinforces feelings that had already been awakened in Achilles, the hero is driven to satisfy his opposed yearnings through a stratagem. This scheme originates in Nestor's suggestion that Patroclus enter the battle wearing Achilles' armor.[74]

The disguise is futile; the initial success of the plan seems due far more to Patroclus' prowess as a warrior than to any deception.[75] In addition, the device is flawed. It is difficult to see how Patroclus can win a meaningful respite for the Greeks when he is ordered to advance only to a vaguely specified limit and then to return to the ships. One must wonder why the Trojans will not simply sweep back to regain the area they have been forced to abandon, in which case there will have been no solution and the problem will return to haunt Achilles the next day. If this plan does work, it is uncertain how Patroclus will manage to avoid attracting the glory of the exploit to himself, thus lessening the honor of Achilles — even though Achilles has expressly crafted the plan to protect his own honor. Thus there is a fatal uncertainty in determining that point on the battlefield at which Patroclus will have offered relief to the Trojans but will not yet have begun to take honor from Achilles. Achilles is explicit about this in giving his friend orders:

> Once you have driven them from the ships, come back again.
> If the loud-thundering husband of Hera allows you to win glory,
> do not seek to fight against the war-loving Trojans
> without me. You will deprive me of honor.
> And do not, exulting in war and slaughter
> as you kill Trojans, lead on toward Troy.
>
> (87–92)

The last sentence contains the major problem. In the heat of the battle, Patroclus — with the aid of Zeus — ignores this limit (16.684–91); one must question whether any warrior in the confusion of battle could identify such an imaginary point.

Given the misguided plan and conflicting motives, the main characters in book 16 base their hopes, actions, and words on a construct that is at best chancy, and at worst, unworkable. The poet uses numerous techniques to keep his audience clearly informed of the forces operating in the narrative — the intentions of Zeus are directly reported,[76] characters often bluntly criticize the projections of other characters,[77] and normally effective items in the narrative are found to have a limited usefulness.[78]

The book falls into four units:[79]

1. 1–256: The devising of Achilles' plan and preparation for its execution
2. 257–418: The initial success of Patroclus[80]
3. 419–683: The death of Sarpedon
4. 684–876: The death of Patroclus

In a book where foreshadowing is so crucial, it is not unexpected that these units are not sharply discrete; rather, each leads easily to the next. Events that seem to be moving toward a brilliant conclusion for Patroclus inexorably guide him to death — as foretold in book 11. Achilles' plan and its preparation lead directly to the success of Patroclus; his achievement is emblematized in the death of Sarpedon — but such victories lure Patroclus into overextending his aristeia.[81] Similes play a major role in foreshadowing what is going to happen, despite the best hopes of the participants. In fact, several repeated simile subjects are woven into events in order to provide foreshadowing in a narrative that seems contradictory or confused.[82]

The first unit (1–256) opens with a surprise: Patroclus returns to camp weeping so openly that Achilles seeks an explanation. The surprising quality of this opening scene is most strikingly conveyed through the similes. First, Patroclus sheds tears like a mountain spring pouring water down a cliff (3–4) and Achilles compares him to:

> a little girl
> who runs alongside her mother and asks to be picked up;
> she clutches at her cloak and pulls her back even though she is in a rush,
> and the child weeping looks up at her until she is picked up.
>
> (7–10)

The second simile is unusual for a warrior in any case,[83] but even the first is strange for this setting because the break from the customary tone of the battlefield is so strong. The first line of the book is "The others were fighting around the well-benched ship . . ." This is what Achilles has prayed for since book 9; the fighting has now surrounded the Greeks, his comrades are being slain, and the Trojans are about to set fire to the ships.[84] Achilles expects to be vindicated by this bloody, highly public demonstration that the Greeks cannot succeed or even endure without him. Yet at this supposedly victorious moment, Patroclus returns to Achilles deeply distraught — a surprise emphasized by the unexpectedly peaceful pair of similes.

The dark-watering spring appeared before at the beginning of book 9, where the situation of the Greeks was sufficiently desperate for Agamemnon to send an embassy to Achilles. In book 16, when the situation of the Greeks is far worse, Homer repeats the simile to introduce a second moment when Achilles receives urgent appeals to save the Greek army,[85] and then he immediately reinforces its peaceful tone in the simile of the little girl.[86]

There is a truth contained in these two early nonviolent similes. Patroclus fights bravely but is not adequate for the role that Achilles has devised; Patroclus cannot lift the Pelian ash spear, he is limited when the mortal trace horse Pedasus is harnessed to his team of divine horses,[87] and — most notably — Zeus denies Achilles' prayer for his safe return.[88] It is thus appropriate that Patroclus receives unwarlike similes at the beginning of the book. With equal accuracy the two other extended similes in this first unit describe the Myrmidons as warriors. They arm like ravenous wolves who have devoured a stag and now vomit up blood while lapping water from a spring (156),[89] and they stand in close formation like a wall that a man builds to shield himself from the winds (212). Throughout the *Iliad* the Myrmidons are presented as a strong fighting force, and these similes reinforce that characterization.[90] The conscious contrast in tone between these sets of similes, peaceful versus warlike, is emphasized by the wolves' befouling of the "dark spring" (160), recalling the first simile describing Patroclus (3).

The single short simile in the catalogue of Myrmidon leaders echoes the contrast between warriors and children (192), but there seems no intent to belittle the ability of Eudorus. Such a simile provides variation in several catalogues.[91]

The second unit of book 16 (257–418) begins with the initial charge of Patroclus and the Myrmidons against the Trojans — an unqualified success for the Greeks and hopeful evidence that the device of Achilles is working. The narrative is shaped by progressive stages of the Trojan withdrawal. First, the Myrmidons advance and engage; when the Trojans see Patroclus, they are shaken and fall back. He kills Pyraichmes and puts out the fire on the Greek ships; this leads to a full-scale Trojan retreat. Then there is a list of killings by individual Myrmidons, testifying to Patroclus' success in rallying the Greeks.

At the end of the unit (380–418) the focus narrows to the flight of Hector and the victories of Patroclus. Given that Hector has been viewed as the proper opponent for Achilles from the moment in book 1 when Achilles insisted that only his strength defended the Greeks (1.240–44), the immediate pairing with Hector raises Patroclus' status. In addition, at the end of this section Hector flees as Patroclus seeks to trap the Trojans in a flanking action, penning many of them back against the ships; appropriately, the final lines list Trojans killed by Patroclus (415–18).[92] The movement of the unit is carefully constructed: Patroclus emerges from the camp, kills a single Trojan, and extinguishes the fire on the ships; the Greeks advance; Patroclus pursues them and slaughters a series of enemy warriors. In this victorious charge Patroclus maintains both aims of Achilles' self-contradictory plan: respite for the Greeks and preservation of Hector as Achilles' special adversary. Yet Patroclus yearns for battle, and Hector's flight is a significant mark of Patroclus' success — thus an unavoidably appealing temptation. Here the two warriors only cross paths, but the conclusion of the book, fatal for Patroclus and the cause of shattering remorse for Achilles, comes into view.

During the second unit, however, the audience is not encouraged to devote its attention to such deep strands in the narrative. The story focuses on the glorious advance of Patroclus and the Myrmidons, and the similes for the most part support this theme. Achilles' troops stream forth from the ships like wrathful wasps defending their young against a traveler who unwillingly arouses them (259),[93] and later they are likened to wolves setting upon defenseless lambs or kids scattered through the witlessness of their shepherd (352). The first simile is the strongest simile derived from the insect simileme: the wasps, incited prior to the arrival of their victim, are ready to defend their homes and families.[94] The wolves in the second simile are murderous and ravening, and there is also an unavoidable allusion to the earlier simile from unit 1 (156), the strongest of its category. Both similes powerfully support Homer's characterization of the Myrmidons as tough and able warriors. Yet at the same time the opponents are weak: the anonymous and unsuspecting traveler and helpless sheep and goats. In each simile their ignorance of danger emphasizes the Trojans' resourcelessness before the fury of the Myrmidon attack.

Three other similes in this unit, however, are ambivalent; they not only emphasize the success of the Greek effort but also reveal the events of this book as inextricable parts of the plan of Zeus. At 297 the Greeks' sense of relief is compared to the clearing of a stormy sky.[95] Not only is their relief ample and welcome; it is also a complete and almost miraculous change from their previous situation. No wonder: the change is caused by Zeus, who controls the storm. Similarly, at 364 the Trojan withdrawal from the Greek ships sounds like the coming storm when Zeus sends a whirlwind.[96] The most complicated of these weather similes describes the roar of Hector's horses as they retreat (384): a storm pours down rain until rivers flood and torrents ruin the fields of men;[97] Zeus has caused this storm because he is angry at men who give false judgments with no fear of the gods' vengeance.[98] False judgments could include: Patroclus pursuing Hector, Achilles' proper enemy, thus entering upon the beginning stages of the confrontation which will destroy him; the folly of Achilles' device; the futility of Achilles' insistence on honor — but, most significantly, the unintended completion of Zeus' plan.

The final simile of this unit (406) solidifies the impression of Patroclus' dominance. He kills two Trojans whose deaths are described individually and then massacres a list of opponents. The second individual killed is Thestor, who cowers in his chariot; Patroclus reaches over the chariot rim to spear him and lift him out of the chariot:

> just as when a man
> sitting on a jutting rock draws a sacred fish
> from sea to shore with a line and gleaming bronze hook
>
> (406–8)

This simile makes the deed look easy. Given that fish similes have been used frequently enough in the Homeric poems to be regarded as derived from a separate simileme, they do have varied tones that can be established. Usually they picture the situation of helpless victims, the strongest of which shows a gluttonous dolphin pursuing smaller fish (21.22).[99] Book 16 has the only fish simile that presents a lyrical scene; it is the gentlest of its family and the one least focused on the death of the fish. On the surface the simile does make Patroclus' action seem effortless, just as the narrative does, with its unelaborated listing of the slain; but this is the only simile in unit 2 that is a small, peaceful country scene, not involved with large-scale weather events, swarms of angry insects, or vicious animals. In addition, it is the only simile in this unit that describes the fighting of Patroclus, thus the third simile in the book to describe Patroclus after the similes of the "dark-watering spring" and the little girl (3 and 7). These similes present Patroclus as less of a warrior than his comrades. Even though he slaughters many Trojans, his similes present the events as in a mirror where the images are major distortions of the crucial realities in the narrative. In this case, the audience realizes that the warrior receives a simile which could be honorific but which in its extension reflects both his inability to measure up to the Myrmidons and his limitations under Zeus' plan. The illusory image adds to the threatening atmosphere gathering around the unwitting Patroclus.

In addition, each simile in unit 2 is placed to mark progressive stages of the narrative. Immediately at the beginning of the unit (259) the simile of the wasps underlines the Myrmidons' ferocity and their effectiveness as a fighting force. In the next segment (268–305) the Greeks begin their attack by putting out the fire on the ships; the conclusion of the passage is marked by the simile of Zeus removing the dense cloud, accompanied by the statement that the Trojans were not yet driven back. Then (306–67) after a list of successful killings by the Greeks Hector realizes that the battle has turned decisively. Prior to this report stands the simile of the wolves (352) and the statement that the Trojans began to think of flight. The simile of Zeus' storm describing the noise of the Greeks attacking across the trench follows immediately (364). Thus this segment concludes with two similes: wolves for the Greeks and the gathering storm for the Trojans. The final part of this unit (367–418) narrows the focus to the two heroes: as Hector flees, his horses sound like the roar of a rushing river that destroys the works of men (384); Patroclus performs several easy killings, summed up in the simile of the peaceful fisherman (406) and a list of others killed.[100] Both similes undercut the heroes' motives and actions.

Unit 3 (419–683) continues the mirror design: the more the battle centers on Patroclus' success, the more the similes emphasize the role of Zeus. Homer intensifies the focus on Patroclus by highlighting Sarpedon as an equally matched opponent. As the two close in, they are compared to vultures screaming and clawing at each other (428);[101] this simile's subject and placement are traditional for warriors entering battle.[102] The emphasis on the two warriors is immediately reinforced as the narrative moves to Olympus for a dialogue between Zeus and Hera; though Zeus knows that it is fated for Sarpedon to be killed by Patroclus, he considers saving his life. Hera counsels him to consider the potential chaos that would erupt if all gods were to favor their offspring in this way, and Zeus limits himself to the provision of an honorable burial, shedding raindrops of blood on the ground to mark this honor. Sarpedon is thus targeted as Patroclus' assigned victim, and the two heroes join in a vignette built directly on the now closely linked themes of the book: the self-destructive triumph of Patroclus and the dominance of the plan of Zeus.

The battle between the two is briefly told. As Sarpedon falls he receives two similes: he is likened to a tree that men in the mountains fell to be a ship's timber and to a bull who is killed by a lion in the midst of the herd (482 and 487). The clear decline in Sarpedon's prospects is marked by the shift from the two evenly matched vultures to the fallen tree and the easily overpowered bull.[103] The first simile is a scene from daily life in which loss and destruction are combined with a sense of men's progress and purposefulness.[104] Patroclus parallels the shipbuilders who cut down a tree for a determined purpose; the simileme provides other means of felling trees that emphasize destruction and confusion such as wild windstorms or fire, but these are suppressed. The choice of this alternative adds a note of thoughtful planning that is appropriate to the calculations of Achilles and the controlling plan of Zeus. In contrast, the second simile, the lion, presents a scene of brutality in nature. The bull is in the midst of the herd; the elements of the protecting shepherd, men, dogs, and sheltering farmstead from the full simileme are passed over.[105] Every item in this simile emphasizes the lion as the disrupter of a peaceful and ordered herd, an animal who uses sheer force to destroy his enemy; there is even an added note of bloodiness when the bull dies caught in the jaws of the lion. This simile stresses raw instinct, not calculation; such natural enthusiasm will cause Patroclus to cross Achilles' invisible barrier on the battlefield and attack the walls of Troy.

Though Patroclus' attack results from a variety of motivations, several of which seem to run at cross-purposes, there is also a single fate driving him into the deadly position from which he will be unable to retreat. All of the naturalness and generosity, the tragic greatness, and the futile excesses of Achilles and Patroclus are intertwined in the small vignette centered on the battle with Sarpedon; the three similes (vultures, tree cutters, and lion) accompanying this scene focus directly on the warriors and reveal through resonances from the tradition the wide spectrum of counterforces active in the narrative.

In the remainder of unit 3 the killing of Sarpedon could lead directly to the anticipated confrontation between Patroclus and Hector. Patroclus is described by a simile appropriate to a warrior, a hawk pursuing daws and starlings (582).[106] Hector withdraws before his charge with a simile describing the length of a javelin throw and identifying it as an activity suited to either peace or war (589).[107] It might seem that the battle between Patroclus and Hector is imminent, but this expectation is rapidly dissipated by fights among other heroes with vaunts and boasts, slayings of minor warriors, and futilely cast weapons.

The scene ends in a general battle over Sarpedon's body, which cannot be recognized because of the weapons, blood, and dust covering it from head to toe (638–40). This confused battle is described by a second simile of woodcutters that injects another note of lyrical nature into a scene of brutal and gory fighting (633).[108] This time the following simile does not provide a contrast. It is common for warriors to be compared to insects — in more warlike contexts, bees or wasps.[109] Here the insects are flies, and this basic subject is extended by a series of details that make this scene the most peaceful and nonthreatening image drawn from the insect simileme: these flies only buzz as they circle a milk pail; the season is spring, when the milk is plentiful (641).[110] The simile presents a scene of nature at its day-to-day and most humdrum pace; there is no attack or destruction, no threat, no disruption of order. All is peace.

The development of the similes in unit 3 shows a clear pattern. Three similes (two of which are violent and warlike in tone) are placed at the beginning of the unit to characterize the two warriors as they confront each other (428, 482, and 487). Then in the middle there are two juxtaposed similes (one warlike, the other ambiguous) that focus on the actions of Hector and the Achilles-substitute (582 and 589). In the final lines there are two more similes that seem wildly incongruent with the bloody actions they are describing (633 and 641); but this tone is proper for a scene in which the human actions and motivations are increasingly undercut and rendered unnatural by the controlling plan of Zeus.

Patroclus strips Sarpedon of his armor—customarily the sign of one hero's domination over another and the mark of supreme honor, but once again the view is twofold. The divinely ordered, honorific burial of Sarpedon demonstrates the ineffectuality of Patroclus' wishes. He has earned honor in the battle, but Sarpedon is carried away for anointing and burial by two divinities. As this burial in his homeland among family and friends is awarded to the defeated Sarpedon, the self-infatuated Patroclus enters unit 4 undaunted on his mad course toward death. Achilles specifically ordered Patroclus not to attack Troy's walls because he feared that a god would confront him. Patroclus, however, has all the natural motivations of a warrior, and in addition, this unit (684–867) opens with an explicit statement that Zeus dominates the mind of Patroclus—driving him toward Troy:

> Patroclus shouting an order to his horses and to Automedon
> pursued the Trojans and the Lycians, and was blinded,
> a fool—if he had kept the word of the son of Peleus,
> he surely would have fled the evil fate of black death.
> But always the mind of Zeus is more powerful than that of men:
> it terrifies the brave man and easily takes away his victory
> whenever he is roused to fight.
>
> (16.684–91)[111]

The irony is deep when the first simile in this section equates Patroclus to a god (705); he is incited by Zeus and opposed by Apollo. He will need every bit of that godlike equivalency to save his life.

Of the seven similes in this final unit, three are short. This is striking in itself because throughout the first three units of book 16 Homer chooses extended similes solely to offer varied perspectives on the developing narrative—with one exception.[112] Similes still retain an important function in the final unit, but their role diminishes as facts limit characters from holding different views of the same action. The device of Achilles fails, the hope of Patroclus to be a light of salvation to the suffering Greeks is lost, and Hector's boasts are misguided. The death of Patroclus removes all ambiguity; clarity and direct expression replace the complexity of the previous units.

When Apollo rouses Hector to confront Patroclus, the audience should expect that the battle between the two champions is near—but, as usual in this book, expectations are stimulated only to be disappointed.[113] Hector encourages his charioteer, Cebriones, to drive him toward Patroclus, but Patroclus cuts the attack short by striking the charioteer with a stone. He falls "like a diver" (742), and Patroclus boasts over his body.[114] The simile is short but does recall the simile of the fisherman at 406, where the deadly action, the slaying of a charioteer, is made to seem simple and uncomplicated—even fun. Patroclus immediately picks up this tone by developing the subject of the simile in his boasting words:

> Behold! The man is nimble—see how easily he dives.
> If he were anywhere on the teeming sea,
> he would satisfy many by diving after oysters,
> leaping from his ship even if the sea were stormy—
> so easily now does he dive to the plain from behind his horses.
> Indeed there are divers among the Trojans.
>
> (745-49)

The mocking tone about another's death as well as the recall of the earlier simile seems inappropriate at the moment when Patroclus should most remember the warning of Achilles, the signs of his limited ability, and the danger to which he is exposing himself. But boasting is the prerogative of a warrior, and Patroclus is now one and will soon play the full role to its end.[115] In many ways Homer has structured the narrative to show that Patroclus grows to be a worthy opponent for Hector, not least of all in the next similes, where Patroclus is compared to a lion or boar risking its life.

The twenty-seven-line scene over the body of Cebriones contains three long similes that underline the complexities in the final contest. Patroclus rushes toward the body like a wounded lion whose strength has brought him to death (752).[116] The topic is traditional for the attacking warrior, but seldom is it extended to show the wounded lion destroying himself by his own lust for conflict.[117] Patroclus and Hector then join in battle like evenly matched lions contending over a slain stag; both lions hunger for the prize and are driven by thoughts of victory (756).[118] Again the items to be compared are carefully delineated. The fallen charioteer is a minor warrior—thus, a stag, not a match for the lions' strength. In this simile there is no foreshadowing as in the previous simile of the lion whose desire for battle will destroy it. Here the fight is between equal opponents—equal in the sense that both are deluded in their dreams of the eventual outcome. At this point the combat between the two champions is again avoided as the battle becomes general. The heroes and armies attack each other fiercely like two winds clashing in a mountain forest; this is a violent, noisy storm with rushing winds and shattering branches (765).[119] In fact, throughout this book the similes describing the activities of the armies—principally the Myrmidons but also the Trojans—present the strongest versions of their similemes: the Myrmidons are likened to wolves, a tightly built wall, wasps, and a storm sent by Zeus; the Trojan army shouts as loudly as the sound of a huge storm.

These three extended similes (752, 756, and 765) emphasize the fatally crippled nature of Patroclus' campaign, even though on the surface he appears irresistible; Hector and Patroclus are equally vulnerable—both pawns in the dominant plan of Zeus and in the uncompromising nature of the battle to which they have exposed themselves. There is little illusion in these similes. No longer are there comparisons to fishermen or divers; by the end of the book one of these champions will die, and the similes state the seriousness of the situation clearly even though the heroes remain oblivious to danger.

The death of Patroclus is meant to be an amazing event. Three agents are involved: first Apollo so dazes him that Euphorbus, a minor warrior, is able to spear him from behind. At the start of this passage Patroclus is portrayed as continuing on his victorious course by a repetition of the short formulaic simile "like a god" (786; cf. 707); this simile occurs at the moment when Patroclus attacks Troy's walls—ironically, the moment when Apollo strikes him. The irony is marked in the text:

But when he rushed forward for the fourth time like a god,
then did the end of life appear for you, Patroclus.

> For Phoebus confronted you in the strong conflict,
> a terrifying god. But Patroclus did not see him approaching through the turmoil.
>
> (16.786–89)

Hector then wounds Patroclus, who is compared to a boar overwhelmed by a lion as the two fight alone on a mountain peak (823). Again, these two animals are close to being equal in strength and are common alternatives in the simileme, but lions generally dominate other animals.[120] Boasting over the dying warrior, Hector imagines Achilles' original command:

> Do not return to the hollow ships, Patroclus master of the horses,
> until you have split the cloak of Hector, the slayer of men,
> about his chest and made it red with his blood.
>
> (839–41)

Again, delusion. Achilles specifically prohibited Patroclus to act as his replacement; in addition, it shows that Hector believes Patroclus to be equal to that role.[121] Both are untrue.

Only Patroclus in his final moments states the truth: Hector was not the person who slew him, nor could twenty Hectors have done it; Fate and Apollo among divine forces and Euphorbus were responsible for his death, with Hector as a poor third. Patroclus through his own desires and actions has caused his own death by overextending himself and not heeding the commands of Achilles; he was not qualified to take the city of Troy, and the gods themselves stood in his way. But then all of book 16 is filled with distorted views, and expectations have usually resulted in the reverse of projections. Thus the two heroes have fought as bold, valiant warriors; they have both shared in a simile of a lion fighting and finally overmastering a boar. But as closely matched combatants they are also parallel to one another in that both have been involved in a greater plan and have allowed themselves to be infatuated by motivations that prove self-destructive.

Hector offers proof of this self-imposed yet natural delusion in his final words:

> Patroclus, why do you prophesy sheer death for me?
> Who knows whether Achilles, the son of fair-haired Thetis,
> will not die first struck by my spear?
>
> (859–62)

Hector's last act in the book is his futile pursuit of Automedon, who escapes because he is driving immortal horses; even when Hector undertakes a task inherently impossible for any mortal, he does not correctly assess his ability.

The design of the similes in book 16 is difficult to define because they arise in a variety of situations and contain a bewildering profusion of subjects. In addition, though the narrative focuses principally on one hero, the structure of this book is not easy to outline because of the relentless forward motion of the action; each event leads directly to the next even though the results usually differ from the participants' expectations. There are no sharply discrete units within the book; rather, the action flows easily from unit to unit, expectations are created that are disappointed in both characters and audience, and no one is ever able to halt in mid-action to find a fresh starting point or to obtain a clear vision. The failure of Patroclus is, in fact, the result of the flawed plan of Achilles. The device with the exchanged armor does lead to the initial success of the Greeks and to the encouragement of Patroclus—both of which then convert his humanitarian motives for fighting into the pursuit of glory appropriate to a heroic warrior. Patroclus is never more himself than when he accepts the challenge offered by Sarpedon and later strips the fallen enemy's armor as his trophy. In attacking the walls of Troy he moves quickly and competently, seeking ultimate triumph. It is all understandable—and, at the same time, fatal in view of his limitations. As each unit moves to the next, it is impossible for the human participants to appreciate that the action is leading in directions that they may not want—because they all feel that everything is going well. Given that the narrative is seamless in terms of mortal causation and perceptions, the similes—especially their extensions—are a major device that Homer employs to mark meaningful stages in its development for the audience.

The book is closely focused on one main problem; the inherent inability of Patroclus to play his assigned role in Achilles' plan. Yet this is too simple a statement for a story that is so complex in its telling—and similes make their major contribution in providing significant enrichment. In general terms the characters in the book stake both their own lives and the lives of others on their judgments of events; yet the plan of Achilles collapses, Patroclus' natural desires seduce and mislead him even to his death, and the constructions and boasts of Hector are hopelessly wrong. Each crucial act in the book has dark implications that are seldom known to the participants until death finally compels them to accept the truth.

Thus book 16 is built on discrepancies between the surface appearance of events and their deeper meanings. The audience is made aware of the disparity between appearance and reality in the first lines of the book, where Achilles fails to understand Patroclus' tears. The principal means for indicating continuing misperceptions are the characters' own ill-judged or misconceived words, the poet's indication of the direction in which events are actually moving, scenes in which the will of Zeus becomes clear, direct comments on the wishes of characters, and similes.

Several further details show how carefully the poet has designed the similes of book 16 to support the major narrative themes, most notably the strongly contrasting tones between the individual similes. This book contains some of the most peaceful scenes of everyday life in the Homeric poems, along with several of the most violent images of nature as a destructive force.[122] The similes centered on the little girl, the fisherman, and the flies around the milk pail are extended by lines that remove any note of threat and create a picture of normal, day-to-day life (7, 406, and 641). In the last two the similemes are sufficiently traditional that there are parallels against which the audience can measure the individual simile (fish and insects).[123]

In addition, at least two themes developed within the similes show a unified conception at the base of the four units, thus enabling events from one unit to comment on parallel events. The "storm" theme is most notable because it is closely associated with the plan of Zeus. The Myrmidons initially close ranks as tightly as a wall intended to keep out the wind's might; in the next unit Zeus drives away the clouds and clears the sky as the Greeks beat back the Trojan threat; then Zeus brings on a storm as the Trojans flee back over the trench; and finally, in the strongest simile of the group, Hector's horses sound like a river swollen by the rains of Zeus as it destroys the works of men (212, 297, 364, and 384). As the strength of the storm and the detailing of its destructiveness are increased from the description of the shielding wall to the undermining of men's efforts, so also the rout of the Trojans spreads.

Similarly, the topic of the attacking lion is developed throughout the book as Patroclus draws nearer to his death. When he kills Sarpedon, he is compared to a lion crushing a bull in his jaws; then, as the expected battle with Hector approaches, Patroclus charges the fallen Cebriones like a wounded lion attacking a farmstead where he will die, fights Hector like a lion vying with another lion over a carcass, and then loses to Hector like a boar overwhelmed by a lion (487, 752, 756, and 823). The relative strength of simile opponents increases as the quality of the actual warriors becomes greater.[124] In the case of Hector and Patroclus the close parity between them is not only in their strength; they both will meet death by being pulled into a contest that is beyond their abilities—and neither realizes it.

Further, there are cross-references through similes. The most precise is that of the dark spring describing the tears of Patroclus in the first simile of the book; it is immediately associated with the humane instinct he displays in proposing to enter the battle on behalf of the Greeks. Appropriately, the first simile describing the Myrmidons as they prepare for battle has the wolves belch forth blood and gore into a "dark spring" (160–62). Already the humane motivation of Patroclus is being sullied by the warlike motivations of the community. The final simile of the book describes a lion overmastering a boar, both of whom are fighting for a spring (823); at this point Patroclus finally loses all connection with the spring.

Similarly, soldiers fighting in the midst of the battlefield are described as insects, angry wasps; when they are involved in the battle over Sarpedon's body, where Zeus has removed all opportunity of their success, they are also like flies buzzing harmlessly (259 and 641). Sarpedon is compared to a tree felled by shipwrights to be a ship's timber; later these woodcutters appear, but Homer omits the purpose for their work; at this moment Zeus makes Patroclus forget the stratagem of Achilles and turn toward the battlements of Troy in an impossible quest for glory (482 and 633).

Finally, the ambiguity and confusion prominent in this book are enhanced by the use of sequential similes. As Patroclus kills Sarpedon, he is compared in two juxtaposed similes to shipwrights and a bloodthirsty lion (482 and 487); the qualities of both are involved in this one action, but while Patroclus has been instructed to craft an artfully designed respite for the Greeks, he will soon recognize that only the forces emphasized by the second simile will determine the emerging action. When Cebriones is struck from his chariot and falls like a diver, Patroclus develops the simile into an arrogant vaunt trivializing his death but then is immediately likened to the wounded lion who will die (742 and 752). Together each pair of similes points to the hopeless situation of a fatally limited man enthusiastically pursuing a path that will lead to his death. Once again human plans are foiled as reality reverses the expected result.

CONCLUSION

Books 13, 17, and 16 are largely battle books. The quality of the fighting in these books varies widely, and each presents a gradual transition in the general situation on the battlefield. For comparison, book 2 is simple and direct—as might be expected when the armies have not yet come into conflict. Books 11 and 12 seem more clearly structured; book 11, focusing on the wall, and book 12, constructed from three movements, were each centered on a different hero. In contrast books 13, 17, and 16 are more difficult to understand because they show less organization on the battlefield and less clarity in describing the situations of the armies. In addition, each is often interpreted as an independent unit, with little attempt to place it into the larger framework.[125]

Each of these books, however, has a significant role to play in the broader development of the narrative. Books 13 and 17 are both introductory to major segments of the epic—books 13–15 contain the reversal of Zeus' plan, and books 17–18 show the consequences of Achilles' plan to send Patroclus.[126] Interpreting any introductory statement as though it must stand completely on its own can only lead to frustration. The characterizations, the phrasing, the settings, and the actions may be far more complex and suggestive in introductory parts than they are in the concluding units, where the artist draws his themes together into their most focused presentation. Book 16 offers similar problems if it is not treated as a pivotal book in a larger structure. It is the conclusion of a series of themes that began in book 1 and have been developed through the mutually supportive activities of Achilles and Thetis, Zeus and the other Olympians, and the Greek and Trojan heroes and armies; but it also leads directly to Achilles' forceful reentrance into battle, as well as his inevitable meeting with Hector. Thus each of these three books is designed as an important part of major structures within the epic.

Though the similes, as usual, play only a supportive role, they are numerous, they are crafted effectively and economically, and they are so closely coordinated with the narrative design in each book that they point clearly toward the larger structures to which they respond. Thus the proper understanding of the placement and design of the similes can offer clues to these structures. Their effectiveness in augmenting scenes that are important to the themes is especially clear when parallel passages include similes of a different quality in order to make a totally different contribution to the narrative.

The death of Sarpedon is a major moment in book 16. In this passage Patroclus performs as a warrior who seeks the honor that will come from slaying an important Trojan ally and at the same time advances his humane goals. Yet his expectations are fundamentally wrong. Sarpedon will obtain the major honor, and Patroclus' goal fades from his view precisely because he is so excellently victorious. He immediately forgets the order to avoid preserving Achilles' honor and moves blindly toward his death — all in the service of Zeus' plan.

The scene over Sarpedon is a realistic battle, but the addition of an incongruous simile moves the whole passage to a level that shows the misperceptions of Patroclus:

> From their bronze and oxhide and strongly made leather
> a din rose from the earth with its broad ways
> as they struck one another with swords and double-edged spears.
> Nor would a man, not even a clear observer, recognize
> the divine Sarpedon, since he was covered from head to toe
> with weapons and blood and dust.
> And they thronged around his body just as when flies
> buzz in the farmyard around the filled milk pails
> in the springtime when milk overflows the buckets.
> So did they throng around the body
>
> (16.635–44)

There are many comparisons of warriors fallen on the battlefield in the *Iliad*; as one among many, the scene surrounding the bloodthirsty killings of Agamemnon in book 11 will serve as a strong contrast:

> These he left behind, but he lunged in where the most warriors
> were being routed, as did the other well-greaved Achaeans.
> Foot soldiers killed foot soldiers who needed to flee,
> cavalry killed cavalry, from beneath them rose up from the plain
> the dust which the thundering hooves of the horses stirred up;
> they kept killing with their bronze weapons. And King Agamemnon,
> giving commands to the Argives, followed killing more.
> Just as when destructive fire falls on a dense forest,
> and the wind whirling carries it in every direction, and attacked by
>   the force

of the fire down to their very roots thickets fall;
so at the hands of Agamemnon, son of Atreus,
did the heads of the fleeing Trojans fall, and many lofty-necked horses
drew rattling chariots along the bridges of war—
empty—without their blameless charioteers. For they were lying on
    the ground
far dearer to the vultures than to their wives.
(11.148–62)

The surrounding scene of fallen and fighting men is similar in the two passages, but the addition of similes of opposed tone separates the meaning of the deaths and thus reinforces the themes. The peaceful simile in book 16 powerfully increases the complexity of a battlefield setting and helps to emphasize the competing forces that are at work in such an intricately designed book. The killings by Agamemnon are realistic in tone and effective in order to emphasize the onset of Zeus' plan when he is forced to leave the battle. In each example, design is paramount—and similes are significant tools used by the poet to construct a well-told tale.

CHAPTER SIX

The Creative Poet and the Co-creating Audience

> *Creativity and invention not surprisingly must be considered inherent properties of oral poetry itself.*
> NILS BERG AND DAG HAUG

> *Composition is neither oral nor written, it is mental.*
> MARTIN L. AND STEPHANIE WEST[1]

THE SIMILE WITHIN THE NARRATIVE

It is the prominence and expressiveness of the simile within Homeric epic that justifies its close study. Because the similes in the two Homeric epics occur in an easily identifiable form, are opened and closed by standard phrases, are composed of traditional language, and several times are repeated like type scenes, they seem closely related to the oral tradition's modes of composition. At the same time, they are not required by that tradition or by the demands of metrical form for the completion of any scene. In fact, various narrative passages are modeled on a single type scene that can be equally well sung with or without a simile. One of the finest examples of the distinctive emphasis and coloration an inserted simile can provide to a traditional scene is a portion of Achilles' arming scene at 19.369–80:

> First he placed the greaves around his shins,
> beautiful and fitted with silver pieces at the ankles.
> Second he put the breastplate around him,
> and about his shoulders he slung the bronze sword
> with its silver studs. Then he took up the shield,
> large and heavy; *it shone from afar like the moon —*
> *just as when from over the sea the light from a burning fire*
> *appears to sailors, a light which burns far off in the mountains*

> *on a lonely farmstead. Breezes sweep the sailors all unwilling*
> *over the teeming sea away from their friends —*
> *so from the beautiful well-crafted shield of Achilles*
> *a gleam rose to the heavens.*

The first five lines are repeated at the beginning of the three other parallel arming scenes of the *Iliad*. Each passage is modified in its own way, but only the description of Achilles' armor contains the extended fire simile, which is further reinforced by 381 and 398:[2]

> Lifting up the mighty helmet
> he placed it on his head, and *it shone like a star*

> And behind him came the armed Achilles,
> Shining in his armor *like the brilliant Hyperion*

In many ways the choice of these similes to enhance the arming scene is appropriate to the narrative setting. First, similes are constant additions to the fighting of Achilles in books 20–22. The whole aristeia of Achilles, from the description of his shield in book 18 to his final slaying of Hector, is enacted before the broad poetic background of an expository digression (the Shield of Achilles), varied landscapes, and physical settings — several developed through similes. Second, the aristeia contains ten fire similes; fire has been identified as Achilles' sign in these final battle scenes, and the poem will end only when the flames on Hector's funeral pyre die out.[3] Third, the added enhancement to the description of his armor is appropriate because it is his divine protection and makes him unconquerable. Achilles' aggressiveness is inhuman — literally nonhuman; only a warrior with divine armor and a protective team of gods could be so unbending and cold. At the point when he is about to plunge his spear into Hector — locating a weakness in his old armor and decisively slaying his former, more humane self — the image of fire is tellingly echoed:

> As a star goes among the stars in the darkness of the night,
> the evening star that is the most beautiful star in the heavens,
> so shone the point of the sharp spear which Achilles
> poised in his right hand thinking evil thoughts against Hector. . . .
>
> (22.317–20)

Finally, the content of the simile at 374 is appropriate to the moment. Achilles is compared to a distant fire marking the sailors' wide separation from their community. This is exactly Achilles' position at the end of book 19.[4]

The fire similes in Achilles' arming scene are hardly necessary for an audience's understanding of the basic action. They are, however, coordinated with the wider narrative strategy to portray the gory onslaught of Achilles as different from the actions of other heroes. This study has made clear the variables that the poet must consider in structuring the passage in book 19, including the decision to use a simile, the selection of a specific simileme, the extension or limitation of its length, and the appropriateness of certain standard motifs in the surrounding narrative.

One way to approach the creative moment that produces a simile is to fictionalize it. The basic outlines of the stories and their language are known to poet and audience; he continually draws upon this joint experience to recast each scene by shaping his own version of earlier tales. Today's critic can only try to enter a mind—not necessarily the poet's mind, but a mind that will deal with the full range of tradition and previous performances in order to give apt expression to a narrative moment.[5] The mind entered is probably ours, not his, but such an experiment will at least make clear the elements that must be balanced. In undertaking this heuristic exercise I will propose a possible program of thoughts that might have occurred to the poet as he composed three tree similes.

I. 13.178

In the first part of book 13 Poseidon spurs the Greeks to renew the assault that had been momentarily blunted by Zeus' sponsorship of the Trojans. The first killing by the resurgent Greeks is Teucer's slaying of Imbrius, a son-in-law of Priam, held in equal honor to the old king's sons:

> The son of Telamon struck him beneath his ear with the long spear,
> and pulled the spear out. Imbrius fell then like an ash tree
> that on the peak of a distant mountain, visible from all sides,
> is cut down with a bronze axe and drops its tender leaves to the ground.
> Thus he fell, and about him his armor decorated with bronze crashed.
>
> (13.177–81)

In designing this passage the fictional poet begins to think:
This is the first of a series of killings in the Greek resurgence. A simile will call attention to this moment. I have used similemes of lions, fires, winds and waves, and divinities to emphasize the attack of the warrior who kills his opponent and wins full honor. However, since this killer is being inspired and aided by Poseidon, I will stress the killed warrior to mark the fact of the resurgence; at the same time I avoid equating the killer to the great independent heroes who have succeeded on their own.[6]

To emphasize a single fallen warrior I have used similemes of trees and farm animals.[7] Farm animals often accompany rather weak warriors,[8] but I have presented Imbrius as equal in honor and strength to Priam's own sons, so here I will use the tree simileme.

Since this simile will mark an important introductory passage, it should be long. The full tree simileme includes such topics as the species of tree, the locale of the tree, the activity around the tree, the agent, the implement used, and the purpose of the action. Some of these elements necessarily involve further choices: for example, the agent must be human if an implement is to be introduced and if there is an intention cited. Conversely, if the agent is inanimate, there is no need to worry about the categories of agent or intent.

The surrounding passage calls for a single tree that is cut down by a specific individual, although I want the emphasis to be removed from the killer (the agent) and placed on the fallen warrior (tree). I will mention only the implement, passing over all description of the agent and his intention. I will make the only action within the simile the bringing of tender leafage to the ground; as a result, all purpose is suppressed (e.g., making a ship timber or chariot wheel) and the wastefulness of the event is stressed. I will use the ash tree as the species because of the overtones of mortality and destruction.[9]

Finally, since this simile will introduce a shifting of the balance of battle between Greeks and Trojans, I will introduce a phrase that makes the tree's function widely visible: it will stand on the peak of a mountain to be seen from all sides.

The audience that then hears the final version of the simile will understand from their knowledge of the simileme that I have suppressed the agent and the purpose of his action but have included the other items that are standard within the simileme. Each of this simile's components stresses the significance of Imbrius as a son of Priam, the importance of his slaying, and the waste in his individual death. He serves only as a marker in introducing a new direction in this battle as it begins to be controlled by Poseidon. Such a simile seems well designed to support the importance of the passage as well as the characters involved and the significance of their actions.

II. 13.389

Later in book 13 Idomeneus opens his aristeia by killing Othryoneus and boasting insultingly about the promise that the young Trojan made to Priam when he married his daughter. I have argued earlier that this action opens the second half of book 13.[10] Next Idomeneus slays Asios as he comes to avenge his fallen comrade:

> Idomeneus was too fast and struck him with his spear
> in the throat beneath the chin, and he drove the bronze straight through
> and he fell just as when an oak falls or a poplar
> or a tall pine, which shipbuilders in the mountains
> have cut with their newly sharpened axes to be a ship timber.
> Thus he lay stretched out before the horses and the chariot,
> moaning and grasping at the bloody dust.
> (13.389–93, 16.482–86)

The fictional poet begins to plan the simile:
Since this is the beginning of the second half of the book, I will mark it with an aristeia for Idomeneus, a major Greek hero, that will lead him into a confrontation with Aeneas; thereafter the scene will broaden to a wider general battle. Idomeneus replaces Poseidon as the initiator of the new design in this part of the narrative, as the pattern of the book moves from the activities inspired by god to those planned by men. Idomeneus will enter the battle killing a son-in-law of Priam and boasting over his body; Asios will come to avenge this Trojan's death, but Idomeneus will represent renewed Greek strength in killing him also. The assertiveness of Idomeneus' entrance will be heightened by his boast and then by the addition of a simile. Since I want to show that the Greeks are gaining strength in the course of this narrative, it is appropriate that the simile be long and focused on the killer in order to make the increase in Greek power unmistakable.

The earlier simile describing the first Greek to kill a Trojan was a tree simile (178). To stress the more forceful action of the Greeks, I will repeat the same topic, trusting that my audience will recall that weaker description. There is no need to specify the ash tree, with its overtones of mortality and death; any tree will do — oak, poplar, or pine.[11] In this simile shipwrights will use axes to cut down the tree to be a timber for their ship; thus there is a purposefulness to this action that suits the hero embarking on his aristeia — there is no sense of loss or waste in this scene.[12] The tree simileme contains alternate locations: a marsh, a mountain, or a vineyard slope. The marsh and the vineyard slope provide water and human cultivation for trees; the mountain suggests a tree that has grown independently and developed its own strength.[13] The location "in the mountains" will enhance the inherent might of the victim and emphasize the renewed aggressiveness of the Greek warriors.

The choice to use all the elements from the simileme will make clear to my audience the desire to highlight this turning point in the battle. This simile is one of the strongest versions of the simileme in that it uses a mountain-grown tree, hardened by nature and brought down by humans with a purpose. In addition, it provides a contrast to the occurrence of the same simileme only two hundred lines earlier in a simile that had more random motivation and emphasized the tree/the slain more than the agent (shipwright)/the slayer.

There is one additional fact to support this interpretation. This simile appears in the same form to describe the slaying of Sarpedon at 16.482, where Patroclus parallels the shipbuilders who cut down a tree for a determined purpose. This is a strong simile, appropriate to major events that result directly from the calculations of Achilles and the ongoing plan of Zeus. There is no intended cross-referencing; Homer used a simile that had worked before.

III. 5.560

In the second half of book 5 the Trojans are so successful that Hera and Athena decide to journey to the battlefield in support of the Greeks. At an early point in this resurgence Aeneas kills two Greeks — twin sons of a prominent family:

> like them two lions were reared in the mountain peaks
> by their mother in the thickets of the deep woods;
> the two of them snatching cattle and fat sheep
> bring chaos to men's farms until they
> are killed by the sharp bronze in the hands of men.
> Similarly the two warriors overwhelmed by the hands of Aeneas
> fall, like two lofty fir trees.
>
> (5.554–60)

The fictional poet thinks:
One Trojan kills two Greeks, but the one Trojan is the hero Aeneas. Aeneas needs no introduction, and in any case he is not going to play a great role in the ensuing narrative. The major point is that two Greeks were killed. Similemes applicable to attacking warriors involve lions, birds, and wolves, and of these, by far the best known are lions.[14] Lions are usually victorious, but there are several instances of lions being wounded or killed.[15] Since I want to hint at the weakness of the Greeks by emphasizing the strength of the Trojan, I will use the best-known simileme for attacking warriors and still have the lions die. As a result, an extended simile will be required to present both the valor of the lions and their death in the midst of a successful attack.

And to further describe the two slayings I will use the device of joined similes. Trees often appear in contexts where a warrior dies. Because I have already used one long simile, there is no need to draw out the tree simile; I need only mention fir trees to call to mind the full simileme and its usage.[16] Though I will suppress as unnecessary the topics of locale, action, agents/force, tools, and purpose, the message should be clear to my audience.

In the preceding chapters the simile has been shown to be as much a product of the poet's imagination as his presentation of character, setting, and plot. The decisions made by the poet in creating the similes are often familiar from his methods in designing the narrative. Since Homer's audience was sufficiently aware of the alternatives that the poet passed over as well as those that he chose, they could appreciate the values in the final version. As a result his audience heard each passage as the simultaneous product of negative choice (suppression) and positive addition. Once the complexity of this moment of co-creation by poet and audience is recognized, the artistry of the poet and the co-creating role of the audience are all the more remarkable.[17]

THE POET'S CHOICES IN FORMING
THE INDIVIDUAL SIMILE

The major assumption underlying this study can be stated quite simply: each individual simile—even the shortest—is the result of a complex process. The poet was primarily dedicated to expressing his theme clearly and forcefully, yet he always needed to construct his verses and scenes in a register, meter, and language familiar to his audience. At each step he was aware of the range of possibilities that the tradition offered to him as workable and feasible suggestions. Among such possibilities were similemes—typological scenes that had often been employed in customary locations or adapted to new situations.

The poet undoubtedly made the choices that produced the individual simile by a kind of instinct or knack; Homer probably never needed a checklist of alternatives. But the analysis of the elements that his mind had to process in creating a complex passage enables a critic to better understand the resulting simile. And this, in turn, provides a better appreciation of the creative moment.

If the *Iliad* and *Odyssey* are poetic wholes, then their unity is based on large concepts that were presented through a series of individual narrative units—for example, something like book-length segments. It is typical for such compositional units to convey their themes so independently that there arise factual contradictions and striking disjunctions between units, as well as radical shifts in tone. Thus it is not necessarily a decisive proof of multiple authors when Circe tells Odysseus that he must see Teiresias in the underworld in order to learn about his route home, even though Teiresias reveals little crucial information and Odysseus must return to Circe for guidance. Factually, of course, there is a contradiction between the two units, but the poet has stressed the necessity of his seeing Teiresias in order to introduce a major new theme: the presentation of life after death. Similarly, the poet can start the *Odyssey* twice, each time for a different purpose, with the repeated meeting on Olympus at the beginning of books 1 and 5.[18] The beginning of book 2 of the *Iliad* presents a restless Zeus who has completely changed from his final appearance at the end of book 1, and there is a shift in tone between the ordered heroic world of the games in book 23 and the continuing individual anguish of Achilles at the beginning of book 24. But all these "inconsistencies" in plot, motive, and tone are characteristic of paratactic composition, a customary

Homeric technique that develops themes by producing sequences of individual units with lessened concern for harmonizing the details. To make sense of the resulting passage, a critic must begin by understanding the theme of the poet in larger sections as well as analyzing how the individual units build to support the major conceptions underlying the full epic.[19] Even small features, usually concrete objects and physical actions, are presented one after another, a compositional method that leaves the audience to interpret these items as meaningful contributions to the evolving scene. Similes are almost ideal units for studying paratactic technique because they are so carefully bounded, often repeat phrases and lines, and are constructed to suit the surrounding scene. While simile subjects can be repeated to describe similar actions, there is no need to avoid variations in topics — often wild and seemingly unnatural — in the presentation and development of one unified action.

In the course of composing a narrative section the poet had to determine where he would include a simile; this is virtually the same as choosing to exclude a possible simile that he or others may have employed in parallel passages.[20] The striking effects achieved in scenes where the poet elects to include or suppress a simile are especially clear in comparisons of parallel scenes, such as repeated heroic slayings. Some heroes merely perform a list of indiscriminate killings. Others kill enemies in scenes that are significant for the plot as well as being carriers of themes, and these are often enhanced by the addition of similes — for example, the similes, both short and long, describing the series of Agamemnon's bloody slayings before he is wounded in book 11.[21]

Just as type scenes describing standard actions of arming, arriving, serving, and the like were familiar units for the poet, the tradition provided a variety of similemes that even included suggestions for extending each subject. The converse, of course, is also true: there are many imaginable directions that subjects do not take — probably because the simileme did not contain such suggestions. Lions do have a life in the wild where they are hunted by men and stalked by other beasts; alternatively, they attack farmyards and prey upon herds — and these scenes are the lion's only activities in the simileme. The lion is attacker or attacked, and nothing else. Similarly, trees either stand firm or are chopped down; they are not objects of beauty or bearers of fruit.

Most similemes seem to have been used often enough in specific contexts to have gained a kind of coding as appropriate subjects for certain types of scenes. For example, lions were consistently used to describe warriors and fawns to describe cowards. Given such connotative associations in the minds of both poet and audience, there were possibilities for employing similes in unexpected contexts in order to enrich and deepen a description. Penelope is compared to a lion because in her own way she is a steadfast "warrior" in support of the cause of the Odysseus (*Ody.* 4.791). Further, this coding could be used to provide differing degrees of support for the narrative scene. When a strong warrior is described through a simile of a strong lion, the agreement between the narrative and the simile is clear; but when a warrior is described as a woman having labor pains or a weeping girl, then there is such a clash of tones that the simile modifies the audience's impression of the warrior's strength (12.269 and 16.7). The choice of the proper simileme was not random or automatic; the poet chose a subject to suit the subtler qualities of the individual passage. The oral tradition contributed greatly to early Greek poetry by supplying sufficiently varied similemes to permit more complex, indirect descriptions of individual objects and actions.

After selecting the simileme, the poet needed to determine the length and density of similes he wanted for the passage. In some places the poet chose to mention only the subject in a half-line simile; in others he extended the same half-line simile by the addition of several other objects or actions until it presented a rather full picture. Whether he wanted to include a short simile bringing familiar values into his story or to stress a point by introducing an extended image, he could follow the tradition that offered him several scenes where the simile, either contracted or expanded, had worked well before. In book 2 of the *Iliad* the poet chose to include many different simile subjects placed at traditional junctures, but each of those junctures focused attention on the army — even the two short similes of children and flowers (2.468 and 872). In addition, the poet controlled the density of similes in the book, the massing of similes in summarizing a theme to close a section of narrative, and the possible accumulation of juxtaposed similes at important moments. The series of such similes just prior to the catalogue of ships in book 2 of the *Iliad* (455–83) summarizes the developing characterization of the army and its leaders, and in book 17 (725–59) the tense situation before the reentrance of Achilles is illustrated by a series of five similes. In contrast, in book 11 of the *Iliad* there are two clearly different sections — one with many similes and one with almost none (1–602 and 607–848). This shift in density aids an audience in perceiving the new direction in the narrative, as well as the changed setting and mode of presentation.

Similes cannot simply be regarded as impressionistic creations of an actual landscape developed by an individual poet; rather, they are rooted deeply in the resources provided by the traditional diction. The two epics even contain six repeated longer similes that do not seem to have been designed to provide long-range linkages between artfully echoing passages. On the contrary, at least four of these pairs appear to be repeated in a similar context because they were carried in the poet's mind as units that were suggested at parallel junctures in the narrative. Further, there is one quasi-repeated simile in which the opening two lines are sufficiently varied to give a qualitatively different cast to the final six lines (*Iliad* 11.548 and 17.657).[22] Yet both pairs of opening lines seem to be accepted alternate modes of introducing the repeated part of the simile; they contain formulaic phrases and are based on typological elements from the lion simileme. Given the reiterated scenarios within a subject family, the existence of duplicated similes, and the possibility of alternatives within repeated similes, a broad range of similemes seems to have existed in some prepared or traditional mode, ready to be shaped by the poet whenever he chose to augment his narrative with a longer simile.

The choice to extend a simile is equally well described as a process of deleting items from the full simileme or of adding lines to the simple short simile; there are clear parallels for expansion and compression in such type scenes as arrivals and departures, banquets, and arming sequences.[23] In adjusting similes to fit their surrounding contexts, the poet chose what to omit, what to include, and which alternatives to use from among elements of the simileme. The short half-line simile is best understood as the product of maximum deletion: the poet decided to omit all components except the simply stated object or action. Once the audience heard the words "like a fire" or "like the south wind," they would have in mind the customary extensions and tones of the full simileme, even though the poet blocked the individual simile's development.

After suppressing those features that he did not want in his simile, the poet organized the remaining elements into a coherent picture. If he chose to report that the tree falls and that there is an agent, then these two surviving facts must be brought into a single scenario that is intelligible to the audience and does not contradict the direction of events in the narrative. In most cases difficulties are obviated by choosing subjects that have worked well in similar contexts in the past. For example, the lion or wind/wave similemes include so many features relevant to aggressive battle scenes that the poet could choose or reject freely and still construct a scene that matches the details and the tone of a war narrative.

Once the poet had chosen to include a simile, had selected the appropriate subject, had deleted those features that did not suit the surrounding context, and had coordinated the remaining elements into a sensible scenario, he arrived at the moment to express the whole in words. Only at this point is he required to consider the types of phrasing available for expressing the components that he had chosen to retain; these phrases must both produce acceptable grammar and fit the hexameter line. The existence of repeated short similes, of repeated longer similes, and of repeated phrasing within similes from the same families testifies to the powerful influence of formulaic diction at this level of composition.[24]

The resulting individual simile, well expressed and seated inextricably as an integral part of its context, is the product of such series of complex choices by the individual poet. The tradition was always ready to offer suggestions — but these were only suggestions, not commands. Most of the poet's choices were neither ready-made texts nor results generated automatically by a rigid system of fixed formulaic expressions; yet because his audience expected the old stories to be told in the old way, he probably could never fail to hear the suggestions from the tradition. The presence of such voices from the past did not limit his thinking; on the contrary, the system of typological scenes and traditional phrases was flexible enough to permit a large degree of subtlety.

THE CREATIVE MOMENT: POET AND AUDIENCE

The analysis and coordination of choices in the previous section is so condensed and pointed that it runs the risk of being a deceptive tool for understanding the poet's methods of storytelling. Undoubtedly the process of creating this poetry was so spontaneous that no poet would have bothered to follow such a self-conscious list of decisions; more likely the choices that the poet confronted were largely unsorted yet deeply ingrained into his thinking and that of his audience. His audience knew his modes of composition so well that they could understand the significance of his choices and appreciate subtle variations. The moment of creation, if it can be imagined at all, was a hodgepodge of alternative suggestions — all bombarding the poet simultaneously. He knew, from being in control of his basic narrative themes, which options were irrelevant or inappropriate — but he also had an uncanny instinct for instantaneously finding verbal expressions that would reflect and refine the minute details of the immediate scene.

Homer may have gone through some forms of experimentation and rudimentary analysis of his technique in the early stages of his career as he learned what did and did not work. This process—especially the moments of awkwardness and failure—would have taught him well how to construct and adapt his language so that he did not have to work out basic solutions for each simile. In addition, there were many junctures where effective continuations of the narrative had been devised by earlier poets as they told their stories. As a result, confusing, ineffective, or wildly creative associations of context and simile probably did not easily become embedded in the inherited system: a rampaging warrior does not attack like a deer or a child, because these topics had been combined more comfortably with other contexts throughout previous years of usage. If a warrior was prepared to attack, the poet was well aware that the similemes of lion, fire, wave, or god had provided usable and adaptable comparisons to a variety of specific narrative situations. And his audience was prepared to appreciate the reinforcing qualities in the extended simile.

But there seem to be moments when the poet wanted to communicate something special for which he lacked examples of previous usage within the tradition. At these points he depended upon his audience to decode his uncustomary use of similes. It has been suggested that when Ajax is compared to both a lion and an ass (*Iliad* 11.548–62), the poet may be working to balance two traditional statements in order to present a complex situation. Each simile was good in itself, but alone neither was capable of expressing what the narrative called for.[25] Although the buzzing of flies around a milk pail in the springtime (*Iliad* 16.638) is a traditional subject, the use of this simile to describe the bloody and rugged battle over a fallen warrior illustrates the wide range of coloration and subtlety possible among the alternatives provided by the traditional diction.

This process of choosing from among suggestions offered by the tradition and of making innovative applications of traditional material is widely evident throughout the similes, but especially in the effective use of short comparisons and the clustering of similes. Once the short simile is defined as the result of maximum suppression, it is easy to appreciate the complexity that the poet can give to a scene by adding a formulaic half-line phrase. For example, in the course of the book 13 the Trojans have been deprived of their advantage in battle by Poseidon's efforts to restore Greek morale, and in response Hector makes a major effort in the final section to rally the Trojan forces (13.673–837). He receives several short similes that seem unrelated—fire, a mountain, Ares, and birds. Three of these subjects are traditionally associated with attacking warriors and were undoubtedly in the poet's mind when he made the decision to enhance his scene with a series of similes. In each case he chose to pass over the extending elements in the simileme in order to focus directly on Hector as a strong and active warrior, and he counted on the audience to supply the traditional connotations of each simile.

What is true of the smallest unit in the design of similes is also valid in the largest—namely, clusters of similes. As an example, the clustering of long similes at the end of book 17 is useful in fixing a scene in the audience's memory. At 17.720ff. a series of five extended similes emphasizes important moments in the complicated battle around Patroclus' body just before his death is reported to Achilles.

The contrasting designs of the similes at the ends of books 13 and 17 set before his audience two clearly different styles. While book 17 presents a broad scene to be retained in the audience's mind, book 13 ends with a series of short similes closing a book that does not have to be remembered immediately, since the action in book 14 moves to the divine level. In each case the poet confronts choices in dealing with the simileme; in each case he creates similes that aid the audience in following the overall design of the narrative.

The process of design in even the smallest, seemingly most formulaic similes is sufficiently complex that there is probably not a wide difference in nature between a long simile and a short one. Both extended and shortened similes result from one process and must be equally well fitted to the poet's theme; the length is determined by the effectiveness of the particular simile in its passage.[26]

When Homer chose to use devices and formulations developed in earlier performances by himself or others, the resultant similes might have been empty and cold repetitions of the tradition; but Homer's actual similes were shaped individually by the poet as he constructed each passage. The creative moment involving a choice from among variables offered by the tradition and their adaptation is dependent on a complex process that can never be adequately captured in an analytical model.

The simile provides a unique opportunity within the Homeric corpus to analyze a tradition-based unit that is spread widely throughout a variety of narrative situations, embodies the choices required in forming any Homeric verse, and allows consistencies in compositional methods to stand out clearly. By defining the various levels requiring decisions in the composition of the individual similes and by examining the variety of possible designs in each simileme, a critic can gain a greater awareness of the precision of the poet's focus at the moment when his choices coalesce into a Homeric line. All the devices of storytelling and all the forces within the tale are present as he develops his narrative — and all are combined in an instant by his remarkable mind and interpreted by his well-trained and responsive co-creating audience.

Understanding the broad dimensions of Homer's endless choice-making brings a critic closer to the creative moment. Even the shortest example of the most frequently used simileme, "like a lion," is not to be dismissed as mindless submission to a habitual reflex. The pervasive signs of the poet's supreme control and artistry offer testimony that he never surrendered his choice to the dictates of the tradition. The similes are unique pieces of evidence presented in a repeated, yet limited and definable form that allow critics to refine their insights into the dynamics of Homer's compositional methods. Through the ages Homer's similes remain exceptional in their complex and vibrant originality. The audiences of the Homeric poems heard few similes for the first time; they were usually rehearing similes composed of repeated motifs or phrases. And that is the kind of hearing the similes deserve for full appreciation. The more familiar they are, the more their suitability to their contexts stands clear — and even the most abbreviated examples take on an important role in conveying tone to a developing narrative. The similes cannot be extracted from their surrounding narratives without losing their power; likewise, passages deprived of their similes forfeit major dimensions of meaning. The closely woven unity of simile and narrative remains the sole carrier of the extra values that Homer put into these passages, and the re-creation of that unity required constant interpretation by the audience as they drew on the many rich skeins known to them from their lifelong participation in the old ways of singing.

CHARTS OF SIMILEMES: THE BASIC MOTIFS

These charts contain an analysis of each simileme with the basic subjects of Fire, Lion and Boar, God, Wind and Wave, Bird, Tree, and Insect. These are the most commonly used similemes and are arranged in the order of their number of occurrences in both the *Iliad* and the *Odyssey*.

The motifs or elements in each simileme are listed across the top of each chart. In each simile these motifs are usually nouns and verbs, but there are also some adjectives that are repeated.

These charts are meant to be minimal statements; in other words, one could say that "at least" these motifs are present in the simileme and could be chosen easily by the poet. There may be other elements that are common but are not represented in the similes that we have. They may also be of high importance in the simileme, but we are unable to see that.

Sometimes the numbers of objects in the narrative differ from those in the simile. I have listed these numbers by using *1* for a single object, *2* for dual objects, and *Pl* for more than two objects. When a simile contains two or more sections, I have divided its entry into parts: *a*, *b*, and so on.

1. FIRE SIMILES

Reference	Number	Source	Material	Locale	Effect	Witnesses	Time	Associated Divinity	Outside Force
Iliad									
1.104	2/2	Fire			Gleam				
2.455	1/1	Fire	Forest	Mountain	Gleam				
2.780	Pl/1	Fire	Land	Arimoi	Groan/destroy			Zeus	
4.75	1/1	Star			Omen	Sailors/army		Zeus	
5.5	1/1	Star			Gleam		Harvest		
6.295	1/1	Star							
6.401	1/1	Star							
6.513	1/1	Sun							
8.555	Pl/Pl	Stars		Heaven/around moon	Gleam	Shepherd	Windless moment		
10.154	1/1	Lightning						Zeus	
10.547	2/Pl	Sun rays							
11.62	1/1	Star		Clouds	Shines				
11.66	1/1	Lightning						Zeus	
11.155	1/1	Fire	Thicket	Forest	Destroy				Wind
11.596	Pl/1	Fire							
13.39	Pl/1	Fire							
13.53	1/1	Fire							
13.242	1/1	Lightning		Olympus	Omen			Zeus	
13.330	1/1	Fire							
13.673	Pl/1	Fire							
13.688	1/1	Fire							
14.185	1/1	Sun							
14.386	1/1	Lightning							

Reference	Number	Source	Material	Locale	Effect	Witnesses	Time	Associated Divinity	Outside Force
14.396	1/1	Fire	Glade	Mountain	Roar/destroy				
15.605	1/1	Fire	Forest/thicket	Mountain					
17.88	1/1	Fire							
17.366	Pl/1	Fire							Wind
17.737	Pl/1	Fire	Homes	City	Destroy/roars				
18.1	Pl/1	Smoke							
18.110	1/1	Smoke							
18.154	1/1	Fire							
18.207	1/1	Smoke/beacon		City	Gleam	Neighbors	Sunset		
19.17	2/1	Fire							
19.366	2/1	Fire							
19.374	1/1	Moon							
19.375	1/1	Fire		Mountain/farm		Sailors			(Wind)
19.381	1/1	Star							
19.398	1/1	Sun							
20.371	Pl/1	Fire							
20.423	1/1	Fire	Glens	Mountain	Destroy				Wind
20.490	1/1	Fire		River	Destroy locusts				
21.12	1/1	(Fire)/smoke		City	Destroy				
21.522	1/1	Star		Amid stars	Gleam/omen		Harvest/night	Gods	
22.26	1/1	Fire/sun			Gleam				
22.134	1/1	Fire							
22.150	1/1	Star		Amid stars	Beauty		Night		
22.317	1/1	Moon							
23.455	1/1								

1. FIRE SIMILES *(continued)*

Reference	Number	Source	Material	Locale	Effect	Witnesses	Time	Associated Divinity	Outside Force
Odyssey									
4.45[a]	1/1	Sun/moon			Gleam				
4.662	2/1	Fire			Gleam				
5.488	1/1	Fire	(Embers)	Far field		No one			
7.84[a]	1/1	Sun/moon			Gleam				
15.108	1/1	Star							
18.296	1/1	Sun							
19.39	Pl/1	Fire							
19.234	1/1	Sun							
24.148	1/1	Sun/moon							

[a] Repeated simile: *Ody.* 4.45 = *Ody.* 7.84.

2. LION AND BOAR SIMILES

Reference	Number	Animal	Victim	Hunter/Opposers	Attack	Response	Strength/Confidence/Fear	Locale/Time	Hunger/Thirst
Iliad									
3.23	1/1	Lion	Dead stag/goat	Dogs/Hunters	Devour				Hunger
4.253	1/1	Boar					Might		
5.136	1/1	Lion	Sheep	Shepherd	Attack	Wounded	Weakened/retreat	Sheepfold	
5.161	1/1	Lion	Cattle		Break necks			Thicket	
5.299	1/1	Lion					Might		
5.476	1/1	Lion		Dogs		Cower			
5.554a	2/2	Lion						Mountain peaks/thickets	
5.554b	Pl/Pl	Lion/boar	Cattle/sheep	Men	Snatch/raid	Killed		Farm	
5.782[a]	Pl/Pl	Lion/boar					Strength		
7.256[a]	Pl/2	Lion					Strength		
10.297		Lion						Night	
10.485	1/1	Lion	Sheep/goats/flocks	Shepherd absent		Attack			
11.113a	1/1	Lion	Young deer		Crushes/snatches			Lair	
11.113b			Mother		Scare	Trembles/runs		Forest	
11.129	1/1	Lion	Cattle						
11.172a	1/1	Lion	Single cow		Destroy/break with teeth/devour			Night	
11.172b									

193

2. LION AND BOAR SIMILES (continued)

Reference	Number	Animal	Victim	Hunter/Opposers	Attack	Response	Strength/Confidence/Fear	Locale/Time	Hunger/Thirst
11.239	1/1	Lion			Attack		High hearts		
11.324	2/2	Boars		Dogs	Attack				
11.383	1/1	Lion	Goats						
11.414	1/1	Boar		Dogs	Gnash teeth	Rush around/charge		Forest	
11.474a	1/1			Jackals over wounded stag	Devour			Mountains/grove	
11.474b		Lion		Jackals	Scatter/devour stag				
11.548a[b]	1/1	Lion	Cattle	Dogs/men	Vexes	Frustrated/departs	Fear	Farm/night	Hunger
11.548b					Depart		Sullen	Dawn	
12.41	1/1	Lion/boar		Dogs/men	Stand firm/attacks/killed	Like wall/javelins	Confident/No fear		
12.146	2/2	Boar		Dogs/men	Receives attack/noise of tusks/die			Mountains	
12.293	1/1	Lion	Cattle	Dogs/men	Attack	Killed		Fold	
12.299	1/1	Lion	Flock	Dogs	Snatch in jaws		No fear	Brush	
13.198	2/2	Lions	Goats	Dogs/men	Waits/Back bristles/eyes shine/whets tusks			Mountains/Lonely place	Hunger
13.471	1/1	Boar							

Reference	Number	Animal	Victim	Hunter/Opposers	Attack	Response	Strength/Confidence/Fear	Locale/Time	Hunger/Thirst
15.271	1/1	Lion	Stag/goat	Dogs/men	Scatters			Rock/thicket	
15.323	2/Pl	Lions	Cattle/sheep	No shepherd	Drives in panic			Night	
15.586	1/1	Lion	Dogs/men/cattle	Crowd	Kills/flees				
15.592	Pl/Pl	Lions							
15.630	1/1	Lion	Cattle	Herdsman	Tracks, attacks, scatters			Marsh	
16.487	1/1	Lion	Bull/cattle		Kills with jaws		Herd		
16.752	1/1	Lion			Ravages	Wounded	Confidence kills	Farm	
16.756	2/2	Lions	Hind		Fight each other		Confident	Mountain	Hunger
16.833	1/1	Lion	Boar		Kills		Confident	Mountain	Thirsty
17.20	Pl/1	Lion/boar			Exults		Courage		
17.61	1/1	Lion	Heifer	Dogs/herdsmen	Breaks neck/licks blood		Trust in strength	Herd	
17.109	1/1	Lion		Dogs/youth	Retreats		Heart chills	Farm	
17.133	1/1	Lion		Hunters	Stands firm		Glories in strength	With young	
17.281	1/1	Boar		Dogs/men	Scatters		Might	Mountain/glade	
17.542	1/1	Lion	Bull		Eats				
17.657[b]	1/1	Lion	Cattle	Dogs/men	Vexes	Frustrated/departs	Fear	Farm/night	Hunger
17.725	1/1	Boar		Dogs/hunters	Turns/scatters	Attacked/wounded	Confident		
18.161	1/1	Lion		Shepherds	Stays				Hunger

2. LION AND BOAR SIMILES (continued)

Reference	Number	Animal	Victim	Hunter/Opposers	Attack	Response	Strength/Confidence/Fear	Locale/Time	Hunger/Thirst
18.318	1/1	Lion	Cubs	Hunter	Tracks		Grieves/anger		Forest
20.164a	1/1	Lion		Men	Attacks				
20.164b				Youths	Gapes/froths/lashes tail/eyes glare/attacks				
22.262	Pl/Pl	Lions		Men	Show hostility				
24.41	1/1	Lion	Flocks		Attack		Strength/spirit		Hunger
24.572	1/1	Lion							
Odyssey									
4.335[c]	1/1	Lion	Fawns		Kills			Lion's den/thicket	
4.791	1/1	Lion		Men		Trapped	Fear		
6.130	1/1	Lion	Cattle/sheep/deer		Eyes glare/attacks		Might	Fold	Hunger
9.292	1/1	Lion							
17.126[c]	1/1	Lion	Fawns		Kills			Lion's den/thicket	
22.402	1/1	Lion	Ox		Devours		Bloody		
[23.48][d]	1/1	Lion					Bloody		

[a]Repeated simile: 5.782 = 7.256.
[b]Repeated simile: 11.548 = 17.657.
[c]Repeated simile: *Ody.* 4.335 = *Ody.* 17.126.
[d]= 22.402 and possibly spurious.

3. GOD SIMILES

Reference	God	Action	Other Men	Other God	Scene	Description
Iliad						
1.265	General	Appearance				
2.478	Zeus, Ares, Poseidon					
3.230	General					
4.394	General					
5.438	General					
5.459	General					
5.884	General					
7.208	Ares	Enter battle	Warriors	Zeus	Battle	
8.305	General					
11.60	General					
11.295	Ares					Plague to men
11.604	Ares					
11.638	General					
12.130	Ares					Plague to men
13.298	Ares	Enter, arm, give glory	Ephyri, Phlegyes	Phobos	From Thrace	Make men flee
13.802	Ares					Plague to men
15.605	Ares					Spearman
16.705	General					
16.786	General					
19.250	General					Voice
19.282	Aphrodite					Golden
19.286	General					
19.398	Hyperion					Shining
20.46	Ares					Plague to men

197

3. GOD SIMILES (continued)

Reference	God	Action	Other Men	Other God	Scene	Description
20.447	General					
20.493	General					
21.18	General					
21.227	General					
22.132	Enyalius					Warrior, waving plume
24.699	Aphrodite					Golden
Odyssey						
1.371	General					Voice
2.5		General				
3.468	General					
4.122	Artemis					With golden distaff
4.310	General					
6.16	General					Form, looks
6.102	Artemis	Roams, chases boars and deer, stands high		Wood nymph, Leto	Mountains (Taygetus, Erymanthus)	Archer
6.309	General					
7.5	General					
7.291	General					
8.14	General					
8.115	Ares					
8.174	General					
8.518	Ares					
9.4	General					Plague to men
15.414	General					Voice

Reference	God	Action	Other Men	Other God	Scene	Description
17.37	Artemis					Golden
	Aphrodite					
19.54	Artemis					Golden
	Aphrodite					
21.14	General					
21.37	General					
23.163	General					
24.371	General					

4. WIND AND WAVE SIMILES

Reference	Wind	Wave	Men Involved	Associated Divinity	Action	Object	Locale	Source	Time
Iliad									
2.144	Winds	Waves		Zeus	Raised to movement		Icarian Sea	Clouds	
2.147	Wind				Moved/bow	Corn	Cornfield		
2.209		Waves			Roars		Beach		
2.394a		Wave			Roar	Crag	Headland		
2.394b	Wind				Moves				
4.422	Wind	Wave		Zephyros	Moves		Beach		
5.499	Wind		Winnowers	Demeter	Blows	Chaff	Threshing floor		
5.522	Windless			Zeus		Clouds	Mountains		
7.4	Wind		Sailors	God	(Blows)	Sea			
7.63	Wind			Zephyros	(Blows)	Sea			
9.4a	Wind			Boreas/Zephyros	Move	Sea	Thrace		
9.4b		Wave			Rises				
10.437	Wind								
11.297	Wind				Rouses	Sea			
11.305a	Wind			Zephyros/Notos		Clouds			
11.305b	Wind	Waves			Rise				
11.747	Wind								
12.40	Wind								
12.375	Wind								
13.39	Wind								
13.334	Wind				Raise	Dust	Dusty road		
13.795a	Wind			Zeus	Roar	Sea	Earth	Lightning	
11.795b	Wind	Waves			Move				

Reference	Wind	Wave	Men Involved	Associated Divinity	Action	Object	Locale	Source	Time
14.16	Windless	Wave		Zeus	Heaves but no motion	Sea			
14.394	Wind	Wave		Boreas	Driven/roars	Shore			
14.398	Wind				Roar	Oaks			
15.381	Wind	Wave				Ship			
15.618	Wind	Wave			No motion	Crag	Near sea		
15.624	Wind	Wave	Sailors		Falls, hides, breaks mast	Ship		Clouds	
16.765	Wind			Euros/Notos	Shake, roar, break	Forest	Mountain		
17.263		Wave			Roar		Stream/Headlands	River mouth/Shore	
20.51	Wind								
21.346	Wind		Tiller	Boreas	Dries		Orchard	Autumn	
23.266	Wind								
Odyssey									
5.328	Wind				Blows	Thistles	Plain		
5.368	Wind				Shakes/Scatters	Heap of straw		Autumn	
6.20	Wind								

5. BIRD SIMILES

Reference	Number	Name/General	Place	Sound	Action	Attack	Victim
Iliad							
2.459	Pl/Pl	Geese/cranes/swans	Meadow by river	Cries	Fly		
2.764	Pl/Pl	Birds					
3.2	Pl/Pl	Cranes	Ocean	Cries	Flee storm	Bring death	Pygmies
5.778	2/Pl	Doves			Step forward		
7.59	2/Pl	Vultures	Tree				
9.323	1/1	Bird			Brings food		
13.62	1/1	Hawk	From rock to plain		Dives	Attack	Bird
13.531	1/1	Vulture					
13.819	Pl/Pl	Hawks					
14.290	1/1	Chalcis/Cymindis	Mountains				
15.237	1/1	Hawk					
15.690	1/1	Eagle	Riverbank			Attack	Geese/cranes/swans
16.428	Pl/Pl	Vulture	Rock	Cried			
16.582	1/1	Hawk				Attack	Geese
17.460	1/1	Vulture					
17.674	1/1	Eagle			Glances		
17.755	1/1	Hawk		Cries	Kills	Attack	Rabbit
18.616	1/1	Hawk	From sky		Dives	Attack	Starlings/daws
19.350	1/1	Hawk (?)	From sky		Dives		
21.252	1/1	Eagle			Swoops		
21.493	1/1	Dove	Hollow rock		Flies	Escapes attack	
22.139	1/1	Hawk	Mountains		Swoops	Attack	Dove
22.308	1/1	Eagle	From clouds to plain		Swoops	Attack	Lamb/rabbit

Reference	Number	Name/General	Place	Sound	Action	Attack	Victim
Odyssey							
1.320	1/1	Bird			Flies		
3.372	1/1	Sea eagle					
5.51	1/1	Cormorant	Sea gulfs		Hunts		Fish
5.337	1/1	Sea mew	Sea		Rises		
5.353	1/1	Sea mew					
7.36	1/1	Bird					
11.605	Pl/Pl	Birds			Terrified		
12.418	Pl/Pl	Sea crows			Float on waves		
14.308	Pl/Pl	Sea crows			Float on waves		
15.479	1/1	Sea bird			Falls		
16.216	1/1	Sea eagle/vulture			Laments		
21.411	1/1	Bird					
22.240	1/1	Swallow					
22.302	Pl/Pl	Vultures					
22.468	Pl/Pl	Thrushes	Thicket		Sing Snared	Attack	Birds
24.538	1/1	Eagle					

6. TREE SIMILES

Reference	Species	Locale	Action	Agents/Force	Tool	Purpose
Iliad						
4.482a	Poplar	Marsh	Fells	Chariot maker	"Shining iron"	Chariot wheel
4.482b		Riverbank	Lies drying (Fall)			
5.560	Fir		Resist	Wind/rain		
12.132	Oak	Mountain	Cut/brings leaves to ground		Bronze	
13.178	Ash	Mountain	Cut	Carpenters	Axes	Ship timber
13.389[a]	Oak/poplar/pine	Mountain	Stand unmoving			
13.437	Tree		Fears	Lightning of Zeus Viewer		
14.414a	Oak		Falls uprooted			
14.414b						
16.482[a]	Oak/poplar/pine	Mountain	Cut	Carpenters	Axes	Ship timber
17.53a	Olive	Lonely area	Raises	Man		
17.53b			Shakes/blooms	Wind		
17.53c			Uproots/lays on ground	Whirlwind		
18.56[b]	Sapling	Vineyard slope				
18.57[b]	Shoot					
18.437[b]	Sapling	Vineyard slope				
18.438[b]	Shoot					
Odyssey						
14.175[b]	Sapling					

[a] Repeated simile: 13.389 = 16.482.
[b] Repeated similes: 18.56–57, 18.437–38, and *Ody.* 14.175.

7. INSECT SIMILES

Reference	Group	Species	Sources	Action	Locale	Time	Enemies
Iliad							
2.87	Tribes	Bees	Rock	Come forth (2x)	Flowers	Spring	
2.469	Tribes	Flies		Roam	Farm	Spring/milking time	
12.167		Wasps/bees		Build home/defend	Path		Hunters
16.259a		Wasps	Nest	Attack	Roadside (2x)		Boys
16.259b				Defend			
16.641		Flies		Flit about/buzz	Farm	Spring/milking time	
Odyssey							
22.299		Gadfly		Attack		Spring	Cattle[a]

[a] This simile could well be a farm animal simile, but I am classifying it as an insect simile because the phrase "in the springtime" points to a common category in the insect simileme.

NOTES

CHAPTER ONE
Similes, the Shield of Achilles, and Other Digressions

1. La Motte 1716:263.
2. For recent studies of the Shield see Austin 1975:115–28; Andersen 1976; Atchity 1977:160–72; Taplin 1980:1–21; Lynn-George 1988:174–200; Hubbard 1992; Stanley 1993; Dubel 1995; Becker 1990; Redfield 1995:186–203; Stambury-O'Donnell 1995; Nagy 1997; Moog-Grünewald 2001; Snodgrass 1998:40–44; Edwards 1991:200–209; Alden 2000: 48–73; Scully 2003.
3. For a detailed study of the importance of the Shield in antiquity see Hardie 1985; Heffernan 1993:10–22.
4. For current studies of ekphrases see Heffernan 1993; Bartsch and Elsner 2007.
5. Catling 1977:78–79 describes Agamemnon's breastplate as an exceptional piece, meant not for the battlefield but rather for ceremony. He does find a statue that has cyanus as a decoration on the armor. Borchhardt 1977:50 gives known remains that parallel the description of Agamemnon's shield. But neither breastplate nor shield exists in a complete exemplar.

The cup that is similar to Nestor's cup is pictured quite widely—perhaps most easily available in Marinatos 1960, plate 188. Discussing 11.632–35, Hainsworth 1993 notes: "Commentators' conceptions of the vessel change as archaeological material accumulates."

6. For the technique of expanding arming type scenes see Armstrong 1958. The ornate breastplate is described as a guest-gift presented to Agamemnon when the Cyprian king heard of the Trojan expedition (11.19–23). For another special hero's cup see 16.225–26.
7. Homer calls attention to the continuing strength of Nestor in lines 636–37.
8. For recent examples see the illustrations in Hardie 1985 and Heffernan 1993:13–14 (Flaxman's sculpture); Heffernan concludes; "Exactly what Hephaestus wrought on the shield is ultimately impossible to visualize."
9. Becker 1990; Minchin 1999:49–64.
10. Dimock 1989:256–60 and Stanford 1958:8–24.
11. The audience is well prepared to interpret this sign at *Ody.* 16.281–98.
12. Though to some observers Penelope's approval of the contest lacks logic, see the discussions by Amory 1963; Russo 1982 and his introduction to his commentary on books 17–20, pp. 7–12; Marquardt 1985; and Felson-Rubin 1987.
13. See Austin 1975:205–38.
14. Scodel 1982:133 shows that the parable does have force: by suggesting that departure

is an appropriate event in a story touched by the ridiculous, Phoenix effectively dismisses departure as a choice. This dismissal is surely not accidental, and the shift of direction within the speech is evidently deliberate.

15. Athenaeus 192 d. For contemporary attempts to find relevance in the story see Burkert 1960; Bliss 1968; Braswell 1982; and C. G. F. Brown 1989.

16. Austin 1966 and Gaisser 1969 discuss the structure and function of Homer's digressions. Add the definition of "paranarratives" in Alden 2000:13–16: "In themselves they will not advance the progress of the main narrative, but will be related to it in some way, through similarities of pattern and detail, sometimes displaying significant differences from the main narrative."

17. Redfield 1994:187: "Against the similes we can set the Shield of Achilles. The Shield is intended as a systematic image of the wider world outside the *Iliad*. The patterns which emerge unreflectively in the similes have here been reflected upon and set into coherence. Yet this very difference makes of the Shield a kind of master simile; the pattern of the Shield can instruct us in our reading of the similes." Atchity 1977:160: "The shield plays a role like that of a simile." For a different point of view see Primavesi 2004.

18. Lessing called it "an epitome of everything that happens in the world." For more recent discussions about the broad design of the Shield see Reinhardt 1961:401–9 and Schadewaldt 1965:352–74.

19. Schadewaldt 1965:357: "Der Schild des Achilleus ist nicht in einer wirklichen Werkstatt, sondern der Gedankenwerkstatt Homers entstanden."

20. See the fine treatment of the use of the poetic gifts of Hephaestos in Tatum 2003:136–57.

21. For further examples see 5.87, 11.113, 11.474, 12.41, 12.146, 12. 299, 15.271, 15.381, 16.752, 20.164, and 21.573. See also discussion by Moulton 1977:46–49, esp. nn. 53 and 54.

22. For the best examples see chapter 5 for a discussion of *Iliad* 13 and 17, narratives that seem to wander randomly from one scene to another.

23. Stanley 1993:264.

24. Scott 1974:38–41.

25. Taplin 1992:285–93 lists suggestions for alternate book endings for the *Iliad*; Olson 1995:228–39 does the same for the *Odyssey*. Edwards 2002:38–61 proposes eliminating all book divisions.

26. This point is supported by the number of inessential narrative summaries at book junctures listed by Stanley 1993:249–61.

27. Stanley 1993:248–96.

28. Heiden in Jensen 1999. Among other earlier studies I note the strong trust in book divisions by Goold 1960.

29. This assumption is supported by early references to several sections of the *Iliad* and the *Odyssey* by the titles of episodes, which do not correspond to current book divisions. See Nicolai 1973:139–40; Richardson 1993:20–21; Stanley 1993:282–84; and Edwards 2002:152.

30. See Taplin 1992:288.

31. These are the considerations raised early in the book by Adrastos that cause Menelaus to think of sparing him (6.45–60).

CHAPTER TWO
The Simileme: The Background of the Homeric Simile

1. A. B. Lord 1991:18.
2. Bakker 1997b:87. See also discussion in Bakker 1997a and 1999.
3. Kirk 1966; Young 1967; Finnegan 1977; Ong 1982; Thalmann 1984; A. B. Lord 1991; Foley 1991, 1995 (esp. chap. 3), 1997, and 2002; Bakker 1992 and 1995, esp. chap. 3; Nagy 1996 and 1999.
4. Well stated by Bakker 1999, esp. on 46–47: "What is important is that we have a text whose essence lies in being performed, and which gives us ample information on its oral composition." Foley has given us the useful term "oral derived."
5. This split between immediate context (specific usage) and larger semantic field (generic usage) is clearest in the well-known contradictory epithets, such as the Greeks' "swift-sailing ships," "blameless Aigisthos," Penelope's "fat hand," and Nausicaa's "shining linen."
6. It is the effect of the "inherited conglomerate" on both poet and audience that separates the dynamics of the Homeric simile from those similes and metaphors created by poets who seek originality. For the theoretical background of such imaginative similes that do not come freighted with the immense weight of an oral tradition in their subject matter, their placement, and their phrasing see these recent works: Ortony 1979; Paivio 1983; Lakoff and Turner 1989; Goatly 1997. Such writers produce interesting comments that do have application to those similes, metaphors, and images with strong background in oral verse-making, but they lose contact with Homeric similes when they give too little weight to (or even omit) the force of the oral tradition. For example: "Imagery provides a rich storehouse of concrete memories that constitute our knowledge of the world. It provides an integrated way of organizing such information and ready access to the various components. It is also highly transformable or manipulable with relative freedom from the linear constraints that characterize language. Imagery is therefore the system par excellence for creative work, for unconstrained leaps of imagination. The verbal system, on the other hand, is relatively more efficient in symbolizing highly abstract concepts such as time, number, and relations. In addition, it provides an orderly sequence or logical flow to our ideas and thereby keeps the creative effort on track" (Paivio 1983:17) or "a metaphor is not a linguistic expression. It is a mapping from one conceptual domain to another, and as such it has a three-part structure: two endpoints (the source and target schemas) and a bridge between them (the detailed mapping)" (Lakoff and Turner 1989:203). There are many statements like these among contemporary writers on metaphor and simile. The problem for a Homerist is that there are familiar and attractive words ("storehouse," "a mapping from one conceptual domain to another") that introduce statements that seem perceptive and enlightening on the nature and usage of similes; but inevitably these writ-

ers do not acknowledge the traditional and limited nature of the majority of Homeric similes. For the most recent work in this area see Minchin 2001a:132–60.

7. Griffin 1986; Lohmann 1997; Martin 1989; Armstrong 1958; Krischer 1971; J. M. Foley 1990, esp. chap. 7; Lardinois 2000; and H. P. Brown 2006. Thalmann 1984 has analyzed many of the traditional storytelling methods.

8. For a listing of parallels that invite the audience to concentrate on both similarities and differences in these juxtaposed books see note 7 in chap. 3.

9. Coffey 1957 and Scott 1974.

10. See Minchin 2001a:137–39 on the functions of similes.

11. Notopoulos 1949 and 1957:326–27: "Why single out the similes as the sole evidence of Homeric originality, when it is becoming increasingly apparent that the whole texture of Homeric poetry—aside from the architecture, length, and perhaps characterization—is traditional, subject of course to the originality that is possible in using traditional material? Our aesthetic perceptions of the freshness of Homeric similes have blinded us to the fact that the similes, no less than the formulae, the type scenes, and the themes, are part and parcel of the oral tradition."

12. See esp. Fraenkel 1921: chap. 1; Bakker 1993 and 1997a, esp. 55; Rubin 1995:39–64, and Minchin 2001a and 2001b.

13. See also 12.282.

14. Redfield 1994:187: "The recurrent themes of the similes can be taken to reflect and express a substratum of the poet's mind or—since probably few similes are his original invention—of the poetic tradition in which he is at home"; J. M. Foley 1991:23–24: "A poet steeped in the traditional idiom *and its necessary implications* has harnessed them brilliantly, achieving an individual realization of traditional potentials and through the single text or performance providing his audience entry into the world of mythos."

15. See especially Calhoun 1935; Combellack 1959; Page 1959:227; Hoekstra 1965; Hainsworth 1968; Austin 1975:11–80; and Shive 1987.

16. See the chart in M. Parry 1928:50–51 or A. Parry 1971:39, where the phrase "swift-footed" occurs in two different formulations fifty-two times in the Homeric poems.

17. J. M. Foley 1991:22–29.

18. J. M. Foley 1991:7 and 2005: "Traditional referentiality, the idiomatic meaning attached—always implicitly, of course—to larger 'words.' This kind of signification differs in nature from discursive, metaphorical, or symbolic meaning in that it inheres in the specialized language used by generations of poets and audience to negotiate what Homer calls the 'pathways' of epic song. It is part of their way of transacting epic. . . . the idioms that populate Homeric diction and narrative carry with them added implications that enrich whatever individual situation they help to describe." See also the further exploration in this area by Danek 2002.

19. See the detailed discussion by Bakker 1997a:184–206.

20. The deletion of certain motifs and the addition of others are illustrated with special clarity in the discussion of wind and bird similes in book 2 (see discussions of the following similes in the section in chap. 3 titled "The Role of Similes in Book 2": 2.144, 2.147, 2.209, 2.394, and 2.459). There a continuing effort is made to omit items from the

simileme that would emphasize organized and purposeful activity in connection with the Greek army.

21. The combination of differing elements in a more traditional simile family is seen in those similes where an outside observer is added; for examples see, 4.275, 8.555, *Ody.* 6.102.

22. See the discussion by Armstrong 1958.

23. Krischer 1971:43 correctly comments that repeated similes affect the full narrative passage differently.

24. The task has been undertaken by several scholars: Wilkins 1919; Fraenkel 1921:15–97; Krischer 1971:36–75, and Scott 1974:56–95.

25. See Scott 1974:56–96, esp. the chart on 87.

26. See Scott 1974:127–40; only 5.782 = 7.256 are not placed in the same context.

27. Clearly there are fundamental semantic differences that separate families from each other. Lions and boars are dangerous animals and natural alternatives in many situations; however, lions and trees cannot be so related.

28. I am counting the repeated pairs of 18.56/57 and 18.437/8 as four similes.

29. Scott 1974:70–71.

30. Pucci 1987:157–61.

31. Nagler 1967:281.

32. Fillmore 1982:119.

33. Nagler 1967:281: "The Gestalt itself, in our case, would seem to exist on a preverbal level of the poet's mind, since we have found it impossible to define other than as a comprehensive list of all the allomorphs which happen to exist in the recorded corpus. But to approach accuracy this would have to be made an infinitely open-ended list, leaving room for all the allomorphs that escaped recording (the vast majority!) and even all possible allomorphs; it would not really be a definition at all."

34. Nagler 1967:291.

35. Supported by Bakker 1993:20–22 and 1997a:chap. 5, esp. on 99: "The core clause functions not as a flawed sentence to be repaired by subsequent additions, but as a starting point, a direction from which the detail added to later units is approached. The notion of a starting point or preview will remain central in our discussion; not only does it bind the syntactic and the suprasyntactic movement of Homeric discourse together, it also has more aspects to it than the preceding discussion has revealed."

36. Nimis 1987:18–19, drawing on Riffaterre 1978.

37. For comparison there is a simile of woodcutters on a mountain at 16.633.

38. In addition at 11.548 = 17.657 only the two introductory lines are varied. See Scott 1974:132–34.

39. Hainsworth 1962, 1968; Russo 1963, 1966.

40. This statement is deceptively simplistic. There are examples of similes that may or may not belong to a recognizable simileme; e.g., the subjects of snow, towers, or leaves, sand, and flowers; see Scott 1974:80–81. It is possible that these similes are drawn from a spectrum of possible sources ranging from similemes that are in the process of being formed to the independent observation of the poet. In addition, one simile subject

appears in one or more similemes, although there are few examples of overlap between the families most frequently represented in the texts. My own conclusion is that such raggedness is normal in a developing yet flexible system and may indeed offer the best proof that the system is continually evolving. Only through repeated usage will new similemes become established.

41. See chap. 6 for a further analysis of Homer's compositional method.

42. The charts and lists of variables are intended to serve as aids and possible analytic categories for modern critics; Homer needed no checklists to make his decisions.

43. Fraenkel 1921 provided a model for expanding a critic's view beyond the single point of comparison and for considering varied and multiple connections between simile and narrative. Lonsdale 1990:103–28 expands upon Fraenkel's work in showing that there is a greater structure to a separate story of animals and men than the simple simileme. But repetition shows that the simileme is a handy subunit of a longer tale — so handy and reused that it is best analyzed as a largely independent unit.

See also Morrison 1992:119–24, where he shows how easily Homer revises the Meleager story and Zeus' prophecies about Hector; "there is no monolithic version of a myth."

44. Mülder 1910:328–35; Lonsdale 1990:38–47.

45. Thus the question "Were there lions in Greece?" becomes silly; we never hear lions roar or see them exist in a "family" setting with father, mother, and cubs. The simileme has only certain limited areas that control the scenes presented in similes.

46. This is well summarized by Minchin 1992:234, drawing on the work of Schank and Abelson (1977): "Scripts are fundamental to our understanding of the world and to our ability to communicate with others. According to cognitive research, we all have a store of scripts, which contain information stored in sequential form about routine experiences."

47. Coffey 1957 and Scott 1974:28–31.

48. Scott 1974:71–72 and 77–79.

49. Lion similes describing Odysseus are common in the *Odyssey*: 4.335, 6.130, 17.126, 22.402, and 23.48. This comparison of Penelope to a male lion seems to be purposeful. Although Fraenkel 1921:92–93 has noted that lions are consistently male in the Homeric poems even in passages that describe activities usually associated with the female, there is parallel phrasing used at 21.483, where Hera taunts Artemis as being a "lion against women."

50. Scott 1974:67.

51. See Scott 1974:114–20.

52. For discussion on the role of the shepherd see Webster 1960:231–32.

53. See Williams 1993, chap. 2, who argues convincingly against Snell's nonintegrative reading of descriptions of the body (Snell 1953:1–22).

54. Yet these building blocks have their own kind of complexity because of their variety of previous associations inherited from the tradition.

55. The basis for this approach to Homeric composition is not new. See Notopoulos 1949: "Neither the poet nor his audience can divert their attention for any period of time to the whole; they cannot pause to analyze, compare and relate parts to the whole; the whole only exists as an arrière pensée which both the poet and his audience share as a

context for the immediate tectonic plasticity of the episode.... The poet selects his material and the unity of the larger whole may be on the minds of the audience. The oral recitation thus becomes a selection of parts whose whole is the inexpressed context of the traditional material" (21). More recently J. M. Foley 1995:208 has developed this premise: "Word-power derives from the enabling event of performance and the enabling referent of tradition."

56. Minchin 2001a:141–42, including n. 30.

57. See my full discussion in chap. 4.

58. See Morrison 1992 for a general treatment of Homer's handling of his audience's anticipation.

59. For discussions of the various functions that similes can perform see Fraenkel 1921:98–99; Martin 1997; Goatly 1997, esp. chap. 5; and Minchin 2001a:137–39.

60. Muellner 1990:66: "It is not that the longer Homeric similes are 'extended'; instead, all similes, including the longer ones, are 'condensed.'" Minchen 2001a:145 supplies a good explanation for the difference between the simple simile and the extended simile: "In the extended simile the relationship between the two domains is generally elucidated through a brief narrative or narrative fragment which incorporates a number of pertinent details: thus the simile maps itself more completely over what is now an event-sequence and through it the poet encourages the listener to envisage the scene and to complete the comparison, as he, the poet, wishes it to be seen.... by reinforcing his simile with further detail, the poet retains considerable, although not complete, control of our reading of both the simile and, therefore, the action."

61. Jong 1985.

62. However, one must always leave room for the development of special meaning in a type scene by its context and other scenes around it.

63. The ability of Homer to create is well stated by Minchin 1992:237: "So we should set aside the image of Homer the conformist poet, as he has been depicted in recent years, or of Homer the transmitter of chunks of traditional material, who nevertheless strains against the restrictions of his tradition. Rather, we can begin to think again of Homer as a creative poet who can work as he chooses — within the guidelines, of course, of his inherited stories."

CHAPTER THREE
Homer's Use of Similes to Delineate Character and Plot

1. See the most recent study of this mutual dependency by Dickson 1995:123: "Situation and ethos are thus best understood not in isolation but rather as interlocking elements or, better, as the warp and woof of a single narrative fabric."

2. The most relevant discussions would be A. B. Lord 1960; Patzer 1971; Page 1973; Fenik 1974; Nagler 1974; Edwards 1975; and J. M. Foley 1991 and 1995.

3. See the basic study by Kullman 1960.

4. This section on book 2 of the *Iliad* appeared in an earlier form in Rabel 2005:21–58.

5. The following publications have been of special importance for this section:

Jachmann 1958; Nagler 1967, 1974; Scott 1974; Kirk 1985; Taplin 1990; Edwards 1991; Minchin 1992, 2001a; Schank and Abelson 1977; and Schank 1999.

6. For a summary of current research on the Catalogue and its function in the narrative see Danek 2004.

7. A series of parallels between books 1 and 2 suggests that Homer intended these two books to provide a continuing characterization of Agamemnon, just as books 23 and 24 provide a continuous presentation of Achilles (Scott 1997):

Book 1	Book 2
8–52: Agamemnon proposes to do the reverse of a priest's wishes	1–75: Agamemnon proposes to do the reverse of Zeus' instructions
53–307: a meeting in which Nestor supports Agamemnon	76–85: a meeting in which Nestor supports Agamemnon
308–57: Agamemnon asserts his will over Achilles	86–154: Agamemnon asserts his will over the army
	155–210: Odysseus and Athena restore order
357–427: Achilles complains to Thetis about Agamemnon's arrogance	211–42: Thersites complains to the army about Agamemnon's arrogance
427–56: Odysseus restores order by returning Chryseis	243–77: Odysseus restores order
	278–393: Odysseus and Nestor encourage men to a continued war effort
457–75: Sacrifice to Apollo	393–432: Sacrifice to Zeus
[1.458–69 = 2.421–32 (except 425–26)]	
493–530: Thetis and Zeus = unity	486–760: Catalogue of Greek Ships = unity

8. Even Agamemnon talks about the army in terms of numbers at 2.123–30.

9. Bluntly stated in line 2.38–40; see Owen 1946:20–22. For discussions of the status and performance of Agamemnon see Fenik 1986:22–27; McGlew 1989; Taplin 1990; Rabel 1991 (with bibliographies); and Hammer 1997, 2002, chap. 3.

10. Scott 1974:12–95.

11. See charts in appendix.

12. The simile at 12.167 places wasps and bees within the same simileme by offering them as alternatives.

13. See Scott 1974:58–68, 76–77.

14. This sense of the simile is confirmed in the description of the meeting place as confused (95) and filled with noise (96).

15. Leaf 1900 (on line 146) entertained the possibility that one of these two similes (probably 144–60) would have to be rejected. However, the juxtaposition of such different subjects within a tight narrative frame demonstrates the ability of each simileme to be adjusted in order to emphasize the varied tonal qualities of specific narrative situations; see Edwards 1991:40.

16. This structure is probably related to those similes that offer alternative topics, such as "Not so great is the might of a leopard or of a lion or of a wild boar" (17.20–21); see Edwards 1991:37. Each of these alternatives has appeared alone, but the series of nouns suggests that the poet is striving to emphasize the narrative direction by repeating elements of like tone.

17. Nimis 1987:50–55 finds a different potential in the similes at 11.548 and 558 that describe the same subject (Ajax) in close proximity: "A simile is generated to handle the development (548–55), but the lion simile gets the appetite seme wrong. . . . Homer . . . leaves it and takes another shot, this time focusing on the woodman simile more sharply and adjusting the transformation of the appetite seme in the lion simile (558–63)" (55). This seems his general approach to double similes (p. 111): "Homer's similes are often attempts to exercise control over the course of the narrative; for this reason, they are at one level symptomatic of a certain *lack of mastery*. In fact, a dense accumulation of similes in Homer often signifies textual complexities." I can find no good parallels to this type of juxtaposition; most joined similes reinforce the surrounding passage.

18. The best examples are those already discussed above (from 15.624, 13.795, and 16.765), but 9.4, 11.297, and 11.305 can also be added.

19. The similarities of items in 2.209 and 13.795 show that they arise from a common simileme. The items added to 13.795 are the thunder of Zeus (source); the scale of the wind, which is not only at the beach but also blows over the plain (location); the mixing of wind and water (alternatives within the simile family); the succession of waves (repetition); and the addition of adjectives (*argaleon, thespesios, polla . . . paphlazon*). Through these choices the simile at 13.795 illustrates the controlling force of Zeus and the appropriately enhanced scope of the action.

20. Minchin 2001a:29–30 quite rightly notes the variety of sources from which similes are drawn: "Professional storytellers work not so much *from* memory, but *with* memory. That is, when singers are confronted with the task of drawing from memory a sequence of events which will be the foundation of a good story—and the words to express it—they employ a number of memory-based functions: memory for typical scenes . . . visual memory, spatial memory, and auditory memory."

21. *Iliad* 15.618 is, in fact, a double simile opening with "they held fixed like a wall" (*pyrgedon*), thus focusing on the army's resistance. See comment by Janko 1992 on 618–36 for the structure of the larger passage.

22. *Elibatos* is a word that also suggests great size and strength: e.g., the massiveness of the rock with which Polyphemus seals his cave, and the size of the cliffs protecting a harbor (*Ody.* 9.243, *Ody.* 10.88, and *Ody.* 13.196).

23. This is a suggestively complex simile allowing the audience to structure a unified "plot" from the juxtaposed elements: the sailors have put to sea and are being driven farther away from the shore by a storm; they can only see the distant fire in the hills marking their friends' farm. The sentimental tone in the unwilling journey away from friends has roots in the surrounding narrative: 365–67 ("into his heart entered unendurable grief"), 387–91 = 16.140–44, and 407–17 (all reminders of Achilles' role in Patroclus' death). See Jong 1985:276 and Edwards 1991 on 372.

24. Scott 1974:77–79. 2.459–63 seems to stress both the size of the Greek army and the noise of its advance; see Kirk 1985 on 465–66.

25. Line 304 is difficult to understand; see Russo, Fernández-Galiano, and Heubeck 1992 on *Ody.* 22.304–6 for alternate interpretations.

26. Leaves within similes have other connotations, but in 2.468, 2.800, and *Ody.* 9.51 they are marked in the passage as referring to numbers. Both 6.146–47 and 21.464 are likewise marked within their passages as referring to natural qualities of the leaves; *Ody.* 7.106 is ambiguous.

27. See Scott 1974:74–75 and 81.

28. See discussion above about 2.87. Kirk 1985 on 473 notes that Homer returns to the narrative with a sentence that ends with *diarraisai memaotes*, "a deliberately harsh formula in contrast with the pastoral scene."

29. Also 13.298 (although the extension of this simile adds Phobos as a mark of warrior spirit) and *Ody.* 6.102.

30. There is one other triple comparison at 14.394–400.

31. For discussion of passages where the poet chooses to use more direct descriptions, see the discussion of locations where a simile is not used at the end of this section on book 2.

32. In addition to the similes cited here see 5.161, 12.293, and 17.542. However, similes of farm animals are not used with high consistency in the Homeric poems; see Scott 1974:79–80. In 21.237 and *Ody.* 21.48 the bull is not a victim but is used to describe sound, and in the later example the bull is grazing peacefully in the meadow.

33. See fuller discussion in chap. 5 on the simile at 17.4.

34. See 13.242 and 22.26.

35. "The lack of a qualified herdsman" may be a motif in book 15 representing the Greek army without Achilles; see 15.325. Achilles' absence is emphasized at 59–65 and 395–404.

36. Moulton 1977:27–33 provides an extended discussion of the signs of internal organization in the full series of seven similes in book 2: "The entire movement . . . clearly exhibits a contraction of the frame, until the audience is finally brought to concentrate on the supreme leader of the expedition" (33). He bases this conclusion on a series of words that seem repeated from earlier similes. On the verbal level it is highly likely that such repetitions may take place. But the choice of topics and the development of those topics seem less ordered and are more likely the results of the poet seeking a common effect through a series of different simile families, all of which can be organized into a unity under the general concept "images of peace undercutting the army's potential in war." Moulton insists that the series develops until "Agamemnon is at last singled out in glory," although he further states: "Whatever equivocal impressions we may have of him after his foolish conduct earlier in this book seem to give way to the description of his powerful external image" (33). I would argue that the sequence shows no such development when each simile is considered against the audience's familiarity with the more customary directions in which each simileme has been developed elsewhere in support of battle scenes; I have the same problem with his discussion of the repeated simile subjects from 87–394 on pp. 38–42.

For a more adequate discussion of the repetition of words and phrases within the simile cluster see Kirk 1985 on 2.467–68.

37. There are similes that suggest a sound even though no words directly express it; see the earlier discussion of the simile at 2.394. 15.381 also implies the noise of attacking troops.

38. Scott 1974:66–68.

39. Van der Valk 1964:II:475–77 interprets this simile as an element in a strategy to show Homer's judgment against the Trojans as parallels to Typhoeus defeated by Zeus. Such a reading does not sit well with the role of Zeus at the end of the *Iliad*, where he considers saving Hector, presses Achilles to return the body, and sends Iris to urge Priam to go to Achilles' tent (22.168–76; 24.104–19 and 144–58). It seems to me that the evidence of judgment against the Trojans is not developed consistently enough to define it as a pervasive theme in the poem. See also Erp 2000.

40. In book 2 the phrase "here and/or there" seems a sign of weak leadership: see 90, 397, 462, and 476 (all in similes). In confirmation see 779 where the Myrmidons are singled out as roaming "here and there yearning for their leader." 812 uses the phrase in a different sense. See Muellner 1990:65–68.

41. For the consistent attitude toward children in simile and narrative see Ingalls 1998.

42. Wyatt 2002 has a much tighter reading of Zeus' intention in book 2, but we agree that Agamemnon is deceived into misunderstanding Zeus' words and weakening the Greek troops. See further McGlew 1989 and Cook 2003.

43. All of the similes in the rest of the book are short. 764 and 800 recall topics from earlier in the book—birds, leaves, and sand. When Iris describes the Greek army, she says that they are as numerous as leaves and sand (800 vs. 468). Because most subjects after the catalogue echo similes earlier in the book, the audience that has earlier heard the description of flowers, leaves, and birds can realize how terse and direct this simple unmodified description is. 754 and 872 are within catalogues, thus providing too little content or context to contribute meaningfully to the book's ongoing theme.

44. See Scott 1974:15–20.

45. As contrasts there are scenes where the passing from one area to another is a sufficiently important event in the narrative to receive an extended simile, e.g., *Ody.* 5.51 or 5.864.

46. See Scott 1974:38–41.

47. As examples, see 11.548 and 558 (Ajax) and 17.4 (Menelaus).

48. As examples see 8.18 (the Golden Chain speech to emphasize the power of Zeus) or the first three similes in book 15 at lines 80, 170, and 237 (reinstatement of Zeus' plan).

49. See 8.555, 22.317, and *Ody.* 21.406 + 411.

50. Scott 1974:38–41.

51. Scott 1974:28–31.

52. The potential complexities that could be opened by enhancing the scene with Thersites are discussed by Thalmann 1988 and Kouklanakis 1999.

53. For an analysis of Nestor's role, see Dickson 1995.

54. The most useful studies of these two books are Segal 1972; Moulton 1974b, 1977; Bremer 1985; Richardson 1993; and Redfield 1994, chaps. 3 and 4.

55. This "reversal of fortune" theme is signaled at the beginning of the book: the locale of the opening charge of Achilles is described as the field where Hector dominated the battle only the day before (4–5).

56. See Fenik 1968:214, Edwards in Bremer 1987:50–52 and Edwards 1991:19, and Richardson 1993 on 21.514–611 for the themes of book 22 that are anticipated in 21. Whitman 1958:272–73 discusses the unity of the two books.

57. A. B. Lord 1962:200–201 argues that Homer's language focuses on the river as the setting for the battle: "The river Xanthus is placed explicitly at the beginning, middle, and end of this passage and is reflected acoustically throughout" (201). Cf. Elliger 1975:54 and 72–73.

58. Such language is consistently used in this book to describe the river:
My lovely streams are filled with corpses
and I cannot carry my waters to the shining sea
since I am choked with dead bodies . . .

(21.218–20)

In addition, see Richardson 1993 on 21.1–2 for a listing of phrases referring to the river Scamander, most of which emphasize its lyrical, peaceful qualities. Together these phrases are close to being a formular system. Rivers and the ocean generally attract lyrical epithets, but they are extraordinarily frequent at the beginning of book 21 (e.g., *argurodines, bathydines, bathyroos, dineentos, eurreios*). Mackie 1999 shows how Homer develops the beautiful river into a virtual underworld place of suffering—a "Hell on earth"—through the actions of Achilles and his Olympian allies.

59. Compare the parallel act of Achilles, taking Isos and Antiphos as they were herding sheep and returning them for ransom at 11.104–6.

60. Book 21 is pervasively conscious of the coming battle in book 22 between Hector and Achilles. Hector is introduced frequently as background in book 21; see 21.5, 95–96, 225–26, 279–80, and 296–97.

61. See Leaf 1902:382: "The best excuse which can be made for it is to regard it as an early parody, a precursor of the Battle of the Frogs and Mice."

62. This second drama is introduced early, at line 6, as Hera pours a mist around the Trojans to hinder their flight.

63. This is specifically said at line 264, an important statement in a book where comparisons of strength and significance are a major topic: Achilles measures the worth of Lycaon and Asteropaeus, the gods are aware of dominating men, and they boast of their own warlike abilities (107, 184–99; 462–67; 357–60, 369–76, 410–15, and 487–88). Cf. 1.573–76 and 8.427–31.

64. The futility of human acts is made clear even in the small action where Hera picks up a boundary stone to strike Ares: a stone "lying on the ground, black, jagged, and huge, which earlier men placed there to be a boundary for their field" (403–5).

65. See Griffin 1980:179–204; Richardson 1993 on 21.383–513.

66. Achilles' invincibility is stressed when Homer opens this book with the compari-

son of the panicky state of the Greeks on the previous day before Achilles entered the battle (21.4f.).

67. *Iliad* 21.12 and 22 join to present a complex initial image of the vindictive Achilles. The focus in scene and simile stays on the river/harbor (8, 13, and 25); cowering and fear unite narrative and simile (14, 24, and 29). The surrounding narrative provides the noise and confusion (9–10 and 16), while the similes concentrate on the fear caused by destructive forces.

68. Scott 1974:68–70. In fact, this theme may begin earlier, with the similes at 20.447 and 493, where Achilles attacks Apollo and then presses his battle toward the city. It is continued at 21.522, when Achilles destroys the Trojans as the gods destroy a city.

69. This story is brought into the narrative three times in the first hundred lines: 35–46, 54–59, and 74–82.

70. Lycaon's defenselessness is stressed in line 50.

71. *Iliad* 22.138 repeats the bird of prey simile to describe Achilles; similarly aggressive eagles appear at 15.690, 17.674, 22.308, and *Ody.* 24.538.

72. "The simile as a whole makes a delightful contrast with the scene in the narrative. . . . in the narrative all is noise and confusion, whereas in the simile we have a typically peaceful scene from daily life" (Richardson 1987:173).

73. *Iliad* 21.493 is unique among these similes in exempting the dove from danger. In fact, there is a wide variety of tones in bird similes accompanying narrative scenes of attack. *Ody.* 22.302 is the strongest version within the simileme:

As vultures with crooked talons and hooked beaks
coming from the mountains rush on small birds
who dart over the plain fleeing away from the clouds,
but the vultures pouncing upon them slay them and there is no defense
or flight. And men rejoice in the hunt . . .

74. This simile is probably derived from the fire simileme; see Scott 1974:66–68. There are parallel similes at 17.737, 18.207, and 22.410. For the mention of the gods' wrath at 523, see Moulton 1977:35–37 and 110–11.

75. There are only two other similes containing leopards (13.103 and 17.20), but in both they are grouped with major animals of prey (jackals, wolves, lions, and boars).

76. Leaf 1902:427; Nikolai 1973:112f. and 114; Stanley 1993:212–14f. and 383n1.

77. See Moulton 1977:76–87; Richardson 1993:introduction to book 22.

78. See especially Schadewaldt 1943, chap. 4.

79. See especially Bassett 1938:187–93; Redfield 1994, chaps. 3 and 4.

80. Richardson 1993 on 22.248–366 comments on the different quality of the narrative in book 22: "We are constantly aware of the reactions and emotions of the two contestants, of the issues behind the action, in terms of the future fate of Hektor's body and the fate of Troy itself, and also of the divine hand at work directing the course of events to their inevitable outcome." See Bassett 1938:109–10; Schadewaldt 1965: 311–23.

81. Such as the formal arrangements between Menelaus and Paris in book 3 and Ajax and Hector in book 7; the agreement between Diomedes and Glaucus in book 6 is similar.

82. Segal 1972:33–47.

83. See Moulton 1977:76–87 for a clear presentation of the linkages and echoes among the similes of book 22 on the basis of a ring-compositional structure.

84. Neither 22.410–11 nor 460 show enough difference between the content of narrative and the suggested comparison to be full similes, even though the phrasing is suggestive.

85. *Iliad* 3.33 is the only other simile to include a snake, but this simile is predominantly about the frightened man and — in any case — provides minimal description of the snake; 12.200–207 shows the snake's feisty behavior (Fraenkel 1921:69). Fenik 1978:83–84 reads this simile very sensitively in terms of both its language and its position. Jong 1987:129–30 comments that the snake in book 22 feels small compared to the *pelorion* figure bearing down on it, and she is followed by Bremer 1985:370: "The impact of the simile is thus twofold or ambivalent: it conveys that Hector, seeing Achilles approaching, feels himself overpowered and threatened; but at the same time it shows Hector determined to fight and kill Achilles if he can."

86. For parallel similes expressing the victim's weakness see 4.243, 10.360, 13.101, and 21.29. This simile at the beginning of book 22 anticipates the coming simile at 188. See Moulton 1977:78–80.

87. The tone of this simile in the larger context has been puzzling. Moulton 1977 argues for a double vision of the same event: "The poet has no other way to emphasize two separate aspects of the race: seriousness and speed. He must accord each aspect its proper emphasis successively in a linear progression." Griffin 1980:139 melds narrative and simile: "It almost was an athletic spectacle of the conventional sort — except that the gods were the audience and the stake was the life of Hector"; also Bremer 1985:371. Jong 1987:130–31 separates narrative from simile on the basis of different focalizers: "The mortality of man is placed against the background of the immortality of the gods, for whom human misery is like a tragic play."

88. For parallel attacking eagles see 17.674 and 21.252; Lonsdale 1990:114 discusses the broader uses of such language. Moulton 1977:81–82 develops the implications of using such similes.

89. And, in fact, this simile reverses the equation in 22.139 and 189: threatening animal = Achilles / timid animal = Hector. Stanley 1993:217–18 sketches the tightening linkage of Achilles and Hector through motifs and similes in book 22. See further Richardson 1993 on 308–11: "The dark clouds are effective: the eagle suddenly appears through them, swift and menacing. There may be a contrast between the eagle in the dark clouds and the radiance of the evening star against the darkening sky in the simile which follows at 317–21, symbolizing Akhilleus' victory and Hektor's doom."

90. E.g., Hector's choice to run from Achilles, his desire to seek a self-protective compromise for the loser's body, and his reliance on the image of Deiphobos.

91. For earlier imagery of fire describing Achilles see 18.135–36, 18.609–10, and 22.26 and the full discussion by Whitman 1958:128–53. For other fire similes see Scott 1974:66–68.

92. Lonsdale 1989:408–9 compares the addition of protection for the dove in 21.493 ("it was not fated for her to be taken") in a context where death is impossible.

93. Schadewaldt 1965:308; Elliger 1975:58–95; Griffin 1980:21–22 and 112.

94. The horses in the similes at 22 and 162 receive the same epithets (*aethlophoros/oi* = "prize-winning") and also provide a prelude to book 23 (Dunkle 1981:11–18). While there are not enough parallel horse similes to derive a simileme, the light and unthreatening tone conveyed by these horses is also found at 6.506 = 15.263 (a repeated simile).

95. Parallel star similes describing shining weapons are found at 5.4, 11.62, and 22.317. Moulton 1977:26–27, 80–81, and 85–86 links this simile in a pattern with 317. Tsagarakis 1982:140 sees line 30 as evoking the reactions of Priam as he watches Achilles approach Hector. Bremer 1985:369–70 develops this idea, as does Jong 1987:126, who identifies two functions for the simile, the second of which is the expression of Priam's feelings.

96. It is significant that the gleam to which the fairest star is compared comes from the immortal weapon that guarantees his victory in war and that this simile follows a section which focuses on this armor (311–16).

97. Good discussions are presented by Scott 1921, chap. 7 and Redfield 1994, chap. 4: "At the end he can do nothing with his fate except know it. Hector dies because there is nothing left for him to do, because for him there no longer exists a world in which he can act" (159).

98. Lonsdale 1990:110, on the animal imagery in book 22 that was earlier applied to Hector at 16.756 and 823: "Achilles . . . borrows Hektor's imagery, much as Hektor wears Achilles' fatal armor"; see also 90.

99. Book 21.12 and 522; 118 and 227; 252 and 493. Book 22.1 and 189; 26 and 162; 26, 134, and 317; 139 and 308. See a similar technique in book 2.144, 147, 209, and 394.

100. This section appeared in an earlier version in *Classical Philology* 101 (2006): 103–14.

101. Useful discussions are Schadewalt 1943; Scott 1974; Moulton 1977: 96–99; Fenik 1968:78–114 and 1986:5–21; and Hainsworth 1993.

102. In his *Iliasstudien* Schadewaldt 1943 made clear the pivotal nature of book 11 in the *Iliad*, as well as its tight structure, yet since the appearance of this study there have been few attempts to extend his conclusions by probing the inner structure and fine detailing in the book. Owen 1946:110–18 has ordered the events as they move from scene to scene. Fenik 1968:78–114 has identified the typical elements from which Homer has shaped the narrative, and in a later study he summarized his analysis of the careful structuring of the book by comparing it to book 6: "The style remains the same, only exercised this time at a longer stretch. It is less intense but more varied, less self-contained but more firmly grounded in the plot. In neither case are episodes strung together like beads. Interdependencies bind them. They are absorbed into overriding structures and play on our imagination as a set. We are invited to compare and infer, to ponder each event in relation to the rest" (Fenik 1986:21). Indeed, the organization and interplay of the various scenes and characters have generally been admired. Even Leaf 1900:466, in the introduction to book 11, praised its style: "The book, however it was developed, has attained a splendid force and vigour, equal to that of E at its best, and superior in variety of scene and mood, with its alternation of battlefield and camp, of rest and action."

103. Schadewaldt 1943; Austin 1966: 306. Hainsworth 1993:211 defines the role of book 11 in the larger structure of the *Iliad*: "The Great Battle of the central books of the *Iliad* is

related in two roughly parallel episodes, 11–12 and 13–15, each beginning with Achaean success and ending in Achaean disaster."

104. See the summary of positions on the *Doloneia* in Hainsworth 1993:151–55 and Stanley 1993:118–28.

105. For an evaluation of Agamemnon's arming scene expressing both the impressiveness of the king and an air of anxious discouragement see Armstrong 1958. In addition, in lines 45–46 (cited by Fenik 1968:79 as unusual) Athena and Hera thunder to honor Agamemnon; Hainsworth 1993 on 44–45 notes that Zeus, the usual thunderer, is at the moment supporting the Trojans.

106. Nicolai 1973:100–101; Fenik 1986:5–21; Hainsworth 1970 and 1993:212; and Stanley 1993:128–36.

107. Schadewaldt 1943:14–17 and passim presents the fullest argument for this structure.

108. Although at 11.504–15 Homer specifically mentions the Greeks' concern at the thought of losing their healer.

109. This structure is close to that proposed by Hainsworth 1993 and Stanley 1993:28–36 and 359n3.

110. It is clear in Zeus' imperatives to Iris that Hector is the agent of his plan. At line 189 Zeus uses third-person imperatives, which are correctly communicated by Iris in line 204 as direct imperatives; cf. 5.174 and 20.375. If Zeus were merely warning Hector of danger, he would offer Hector choices; cf. Athena's words of persuasion to Achilles at 1.207–14, especially *ai ke pitheai* (207).

111. Not only does Homer give Hector two similes (62 and 66); he also provides him with a listing of accompanying warriors. Such a catalogue introduces the individual actions of other warriors: see 5.25–83 (catalogue of killings by individual Greek heroes before Diomedes' aristeia); 7.161–69 (list of volunteers for individual combat with Ajax); 10.227–32 (list of those eager to accompany Diomedes on the night expedition); and 16.168–97 (list of Myrmidon commanders who will accompany Patroclus).

112. Fenik 1968:55–56 and 86 discusses the emphasis provided by the extended second telling of an event. In these lines the agency of Zeus is stressed.

113. For a similar list of slain enemies marking the entrance of a hero see 5.144–65.

114. Hainsworth 1993 on 27–28 suggests that such a *teras* can cause encouragement or dismay; this simile reinforces the actual *teras* reported at 11.4. There is a dark undercurrent to Agamemnon's aristeia; Armstrong 1958:345: "Homer creates here through suggestive association an atmosphere of foreboding uncertainty."

115. Stanley 1993:360n10 calls these elements "mixed signals." The importance of the similes in the compressed passage describing Hector and the first encounters (56–73) is clear in the appearance of six similes within eighteen lines (two are short) — unique for book 11 and even more concentrated than the "three similes in thirty lines" formula that I used earlier for defining simile clusters (see the subsection titled "The Clustering of Similes 2.455–83" in chap. 3). There is a similar clustering of four similes at 11.291–309 (one is short); both clusters mark important structural transitions in the narrative.

116. See W.-H. Friedrich 1956:61; Fenik 1986:87–88. Hainsworth 1993 on 137 points out

that Agamemnon's implacability seems characteristic throughout the *Iliad*: "No less than seven of Agamemnon's 46 speeches . . . are introduced as 'stern' or 'pitiless.'"

117. Except for one wolf simile and the comparison to Ajax to an ass, animal imagery in book 11 is restricted to lions.

118. Regarding line 113, Rabel 1990 and Lonsdale 1990:58–60 show how the brief story about the warriors' earlier capture by Achilles is echoed in the simile, and Rabel traces the growing ferocity in the fighting from this simile to its culmination in book 22. Both note that this simile is one of the few that attaches to the narrative by focusing originally on the lion (Agamemnon) but rejoins it by turning to the doe (the Trojans).

119. The extended lion similes in book 11 are drawn from the more physical and bloodthirsty descriptions of the "attack" motif that are best exemplified in 5.161, 17.61, and 18.583. See especially 5.136, 5.554, 11.414, 11.548 = 17.657, 12.229, 16.487, 17.61, 17.133, 17.725, 17.737, 20.164, and 20.490.

120. For discussion of the effect of this simile see Moulton 1977:97–99 and Stanley 1993:133. In contrast see Holmes 2007, who finds Homer using this simile to challenge the usual heroic exchange of time for blood.

121. This is the second clustering of similes in this book, each of which marks a transitional scene in this carefully structured book. Stanley 1993:134 contrasts the simile-less entrance of Agamemnon at 215ff.

122. See the discussion of a traditional form underlying this scene by Fenik 1968:90–91; he presents an outline of the similar passage at 8.332 that contains a hunting simile.

123. Compare also 11.414, 11.548 = 17.657, 17.61, 17.133, and 17.725.

124. For discussion of the typological qualities of hunts, winds/waves, and gods in similes see Scott 1974:72–73, 62–66, and 68–70.

125. Hainsworth 1993 on 292–93 feels that this simile "sounds the keynote of the narrative from this point: the Achaeans . . . are hunted beasts," and Stanley 1993:134 interprets the hunter simile as reversing the series of lion similes in Hector's favor. However, Lonsdale 1990:77n16 notes the strong association between Hector and hounds/hunters. In view of this continuing theme it seems more faithful to the developing text to acknowledge that the situation of the attackers in this simile is precarious. The lion is still the strongest animal, and any hunter who easily sends his dogs out to kill such a "wild beast" has not been reading such similes as 3.23, 5.476, 11.548 = 17.281, 12.41, 12.146, 12.299, 13.198, 13.471, 15.271, 17.61, and 17.725. Yet some of these scenes end in a draw, and some versions of the simileme place the dogs in the dominant position: 8.338, 11.414, and 17.109.

126. It is significant that the narrative specifies no single opponent to be compared with the simile's lion.

127. The closest parallels to the boar in line 414's simile are 5.782, 12.146, 13.471, and 17.281 and 725; see also *Aspis* 386–91.

For parallels to the spoliative lion of line 474 see 3.23 and 13.198. Moulton 1977:45–49 and Lonsdale 1990:72–74 describe the connections between this simile and the surrounding narrative, and Hainsworth 1993 on 459–88 shows the parallel structure in the two similes 414 and 474.

128. For parallels to the raging river see Scott 1974:76–77. For placement in a typical scene see Fenik 1968:84–85. In addition, Ajax's shield is "like a tower" (485).

129. Zenodotos omitted the simile beginning at line 548; see Fenik 1968:110–11 and Hainsworth 1993 on 548–57.

These three similes are not as tightly juxtaposed as at 2.144/147, 468/469, and 14.394. There are intervening narrative lines, and the similes do not reinforce the same message. This is a series of similes focused on the same object in the narrative from two different perspectives — Ajax's reluctance and the frustration of the Trojans' effort. There is no good parallel to this loose structure, which for a long time has produced disagreement: e.g., Hermann 1877:11–23 felt that these juxtaposed similes weaken each other and confuse the audience to the extent that they are probably the product of two poets; see also Mancuso 1915.

130. This element has no parallel in the surrounding narrative, where Hector is extremely active. The half-line may be added because of its association with Hector's fate.

131. See the careful analysis of the scene by Minchin 1991 and 2001a:192–94.

132. See the chart in Scott 1974:87.

CHAPTER FOUR
Similes to Delineate a Narrative Theme

1. Homer seems conscious of the need for such motivation at 12.465–66 and 13.1–9. For the clearest discussion of the close relationships between books 12 and 13 see Stanley 1993:136–52.

2. The most useful studies for the similes in book 12 are Moulton 1977:64–67; Fenik 1986:28–33; and Hainsworth 1993:13–66.

3. My general interpretation will follow Fenik in focusing on the organization of the narrative around the wall rather than the consistent description of battle arrangements, the clear division of the troops, their subsequent deployment, and the adequate usage of all characters who are introduced early in the book.

There is a long-standing debate about the interpolation of the wall that does not particularly belong in my argument because I will be focusing on the similes' function within the full text of book 11. See Page 1959:315; Tsagarakis 1969; West 1969; Thiel 1982:33–50.

4. Homer's focus on the wall is made clear in the three successive attacks that structure the book. The organizing force of the wall is clear from its position as a frame to the narrative, its role as the goal to be achieved, and constant references to it as the locale of battles throughout the book. Owen 1946:119: "What happens in Book XII could be stated in one sentence — Hector crosses the wall." Although Hainsworth feels that the book is weakly organized, he does out point out Homer's strategy of emphasizing the wall from the very beginning of the book: after a two-and-a-half-line connection to book 11 "a simile to illustrate the ferocity of the fight could be expected to follow, but the description of battle is overtaken by the digression about the Achaean wall" (line 3). For a different perspective see Jong 1987:88–89.

5. It should be remembered that the first lines in book 12 report that the plan of Zeus

continues to operate: Patroclus remains behind, helping Eurypylus from book 11 through 15. The Greeks will be driven back as Zeus promised in book 1 (thus the success of Hector in books 12 and 15), but at the same time sympathy for the dying Greek warriors develops within the Greek camp and is aroused in Achilles by the weeping Patroclus in book 16.

6. For discussion of the parallelism between the attacks of Asius and Sarpedon, see the recent discussions by Fenik 1986:30–33 and Hainsworth 1993:348–49.

7. Hainsworth in his introduction to book 12 presents the evidence for disorganization in the narrative both in the physical features of the battlefield and in the movements of the five (?) divisions. These comments are correct, but I have focused on the elements which Homer has expressed clearly in his general battlefield scene: the wall, the series of individual heroes, and the guiding power of Zeus. I would leave in the background such questions as what happened to the divisions of Paris and Aeneas, which were introduced pointedly at 88–107. They do not seem to occupy Homer's mind.

8. Hector is the first hero singled out at line 38, and he is immediately described by two similes; he is then offered advice by Polydamas, and there follows a catalogue of Trojans (38–107).

9. See earlier discussions of juxtaposed similes in chap. 3.

10. The scholiast suggests that 12.40 may even point toward this passage in the phrase "as before."

11. Cf. 11.414 and 11.293. This is one of the similes that seems to go further in its development than the narrative scene. The lion fights unceasingly until he is slain, even though Hector is very much at his liveliest in the surrounding narrative; there are similar inconcinnities at 5.87, 11.113, 11.474, 12.41, 12.146, 12. 299, 15.271, 15.381, 16.752, 20.164, and 21.573. This instinctive willingness to risk all makes a more important contribution to the passage than the close matching of details (Fenik 1968:58).

12. Lonsdale 1990:62 remarks on the simile's mixture of tactical and animal vocabulary.

13. The relationship of this simile to the surrounding narrative has long been a concern; see Murray 1907:245–49. The heavily enjambed quality of these lines may testify to the careful composition of both simile and narrative. While there are admitted discrepancies in the object-for-object points of comparison, still the hunting scene pitting man against animal is appropriate as a psychological parallel to Hector's entrance into this book; there is no victim included, no locale, no time, and no driving hunger or thirst. All is focused on the valor of the contestants. See discussions by Fraenkel 1921:66–67; Scott 1974:61; Moulton 1977:47–48; Thiel 1982:36–37; Hainsworth 1993 on 41–48; and Erbse 2000:260–63.

14. This catalogue appears to be designed and placed to enhance the image of Hector as the leader of the Trojans. The Trojan army is not organized in this way anywhere else (see parallel listings of Trojan captains at 13.790–94, 14.425–26, and 17.215–18, none of which seem built on the same tight structure); the order of commanders is not apparent in the form of the following narrative. There are not five gates in the Trojan wall. Probably the main contribution of this rigidly constructed catalogue (5 commander + two subordinates) is the image of an organized army serving its general (Hector) and moving as a unit

to battle; this sets the background for the independent action of Asius. See Hainsworth 1993 on 87–107.

15. Cf. 4.295–96; 5.43–83; 16.168–97.

16. Part of the complexity of this simile is the two-part development in the simile that moves the narrative ahead in time. The heroes take a stand before the gates as the two boars do; then the boars, in charging sideways, noisily break through surrounding trees. Similarly, the armor of the heroes resounds when struck. Cf. 13.492 and 15.623 as examples of such double-sided similes.

17. Scott 1974:58–62 and 68–71.

18. There are several traditional elements in this simile; see Hainsworth 1993 on 167–70. The closest parallels in subject are 16.259 and 2.87; the tone seems appropriately warlike, but in the general category of insects the breadth of elements is remarkable: see 3.151, 16.641, 17.570, and 21.12. For the theme of parents defending their young in similes see 16.259, 17.133, and *Ody.* 20.14.

19. In addition, Damon 1961:262–63 sees a warlike tone in 278–80.

20. Polydamas' sequential warnings play a role in the long-range undercutting of Hector's strength. The clear contrast between his first and second attempts to advise Hector is marked by the same introductory line 60 = 210. The first time Polydamas speaks in reasonable terms, Hector accepts his idea and is gracious in response; all is different the second time and begins to reveal the weakness of Hector's position: "Hektor's scorn for omens is hardly sensible and borders on blindness and delusion" (Willcock 1976 on 237–38).

21. Hainsworth 1993 on 156–58: "The parallelism between the assault of Asios and Hektor's first attack is emphasized by the relative rarity and brevity of other snow similes."

22. Along with 3.222 and 19.357, there are only four similes in which the prime subject matter is snow; together these similes suggest a model for the simileme. The two in book 12 develop the same elements in different ways to make the similes responsive to the narrative's needs: the elements from the simileme would be wind/no wind, emphasis on breadth of geographical coverage, and clouds vs. Zeus as the source of snow. The effect of these choices among customary elements in storm scenes is a contrast between the thick and fast storm driven by the wind and the continual snowfall that is caused by Zeus. See Moulton 1977:64–67.

23. The identification of the heroes around whose accomplishments book 12 is built is emphasized by the close matching of motifs in the lion similes at 41 and 299; see Lonsdale 1990:60–65.

24. The continuation of the same subject in juxtaposed similes appears also at 11.297 + 305–8 and 13.298–303; see the discussion by Moulton 1977:19–22.

Hainsworth on 299–306 cites *Ody.* 6.130 as a parallel simile. This pairing shows how the poet can vary the same elements of the simileme (the lion's motivation for attacking) to suit the surrounding narrative; see also the discussion by Pucci 1987:157–61.

25. The momentum of the ravenous lion is checked by the famed statement of Sarpedon to Glaucus, thus both postponing the entrance of the hero and explaining his motivation by restating the forces in the simile in human terms; see Lonsdale 1990:64–65.

26. For formulaic repetitions with connotations of power see 20.51 and 11.747. Hains-

worth 1993 on 375: "A storm is a favourite image for Trojan attacks in this part of the *Iliad*"; see 11.297 and 306, 12.40, 13.334 and 795.

27. Even at this point of major achievement only the protection of Zeus permits Sarpedon's feat (12.402–3).

28. See chart in Scott 1974:87.

29. For parallels featuring craftswomen, see 4.141 and 23.760.

30. Zenodotus omits line 450, and later editors athetized it on the grounds that it would lessen Hector's strength. This reading is correct—in fact, the weakening of Hector's strength is a continuing theme of the book and appropriately appears in this last scene. For the forceful presentation of a similar scene without the simile see 16.733–36.

31. At least this is the possible interpretation of comparisons to the night for entering enemies at 1.47 and *Ody*. 11.606.

32. The book's ending contains a revealing phrase at 465–66: "No one confronting him would have held him back except the gods."

33. It is important to the design of book 12 that the battle be presented as even so that Hector can achieve a victory over stout resistance. Yet in each case where a simile is used to stress the balance between the two sides, the topic is drawn from an unlikely peaceful context (155, 278, 421, and 433).

34. In addition, Zeus' eagle flies off on a gust of wind at 12.207.

35. See 2.455–83 and 872, 3.222 and 230, 4.253 and 275, and 10.154.

36. The following studies have been useful throughout this section: Erbse 1961; Fenik 1968, esp. 9–77; Moulton 1977: 58–64; Andersen 1978, esp. chap. 4; Kirk 1990:51–154; Stanley 1993:75–86.

37. The scenes at 4.364–421 and 6.119–236 seem self-contained incidents in larger scenes; only 6.96–101 seems to depend on an awareness of Diomedes' actions in book 5. The specific linkage from books 4–5 is focused on Athena (4.541–42 + 5.1–2); that between books 5 and 6 centers on *oiothe*, summarizing the departure of the gods at 5.907–9 (identified by Stanley 1993:259 as a "retrospective closure"). For a discussion of larger patterns bridging these book divisions see, e.g., Latacz 1977:81–95.

38. The importance of this involvement is signaled in the first line of the book, and the direct effect on the battle is reported as early as 29–36.

39. Stanley 1993:75–86 ends a major section at 471, marking off 431–70 as central to the structure of book 5 since it is the point at which Diomedes' "tendency to overreach ... overwhelms him"; such a structure is, however, centered on Diomedes as the key to understanding book 5. If the perspective is broadened to the interaction between gods and men, the moment when Ares replaces Aphrodite/Apollo becomes a recognizable structural division; see Erbse 1961 and Moulton 1977:58–64. Such intertwining of main character and theme is well paralleled in book 6, where Hector carries the plot from scene to scene while the theme of warrior vs. human is developed throughout the separate scenes; see discussion by Schadewaldt 1965:207–33.

40. Cf. 5.99–101. For Diomedes as surrogate to Achilles see Schadewaldt 1965:60–61 and 155; Scheliha 1943:184–87; Erbse 1961; Lohmann 1970:221; and Kullmann 1984:313–15.

41. This ineffectuality is signaled immediately in the first incident, when Hephaestus

saves one of the two brothers from certain death at 5.22; in the other scenes where Diomedes slays two brothers, both are killed.

42. Appropriately, the book ends with the return of Athena and Hera to Olympus after they have frustrated the action of Ares; but even his wound is soon healed and he sits in glory next to Zeus.

43. When the action in one book has had a large effect on the ongoing narrative, this is often marked by a response at the beginning of the next book, e.g., book 9: the Trojan advance causes Agamemnon to hold a meeting; book 13: Poseidon enters the battle in support of the Greeks after Hector breaks through the wall; book 17: Menelaus moves to protect Patroclus' body after Apollo has killed him.

44. This is typical. The only mortals that suffer direct vengeance from the gods are Patroclus in 16.705–11 + 783–804 and Niobe in 24.602–17. More normally gods do not seek vengeance for such wounds; see 5.382–402.

45. The specificity of these instructions is enhanced by the repeated *ge* in 130 and 132.

46. The only direct reference to the judgment of Paris is 24.28–30, but there are allusions to Aphrodite's special regard for the Trojans at 3.374–420 and 5.423.

47. For the full discussion of the meaning and tone of this passage see Andersen 1978: 61–73.

48. There is plenty of room for confusion: Athena appears without disguise to Diomedes at 121–32 and gives him specially clarified sight; at 432–44 Diomedes is able to recognize Apollo, yet despite the explicit command of Athena at 129–32 he shows no hesitancy in attacking the god until he is strongly rebuked; Diomedes' vision is still clarified when he identifies Ares supporting Hector at 601–6, yet in spite of Apollo's rebuke he unquestioningly accepts Athena's command to attack Ares. A normal mortal, caught up in such a nexus of desires and commands, ought to raise some questions.

49. The rareness of such attacks is brought pointedly into the narrative by the limited catalogue of such events given by Dione at 382–402. On the function of the scene with Dione and the theme of book 5 see Andersen 1978, esp. chap. 4.

50. = 4.223–421.

51. For a parallel entrance scene and simile see 22.26. This first simile of book 5 describing the entrance of the Greek champion is balanced by the darkness describing Ares, the supporter of the Trojans, at 864. Stanley 1993:75 also comments on the structural importance of 506–11, which contains the darkness spread by Ares.

52. In this book Diomedes has an inordinate interest in horses: 199–203, 221–38 (although earlier Aeneas was foot; see 166–70), 263–72, and 310–30.

53. This scene, built on an exchange between gods who support opposed sides, is appropriate for a moment when Diomedes is on the verge of a series of strong acts that will turn the battle in favor of the Greeks; in addition, it emphasizes the constant interplay between gods and mortals that is the major theme of the book.

54. Kirk 1990 on 87–88 shows how this simile quite precisely focuses on the destruction of both the artificial embankments and the phalanxes on the battlefield.

55. Kirk 1990 on 144–65 notes victims sharing a chariot as a typical motif of the *Iliad*, as well as the emphasis on pairs of brothers (cf. Fenik 1968:11).

56. This third entrance into battle is carefully constructed to emphasize the power of Diomedes: entrance with simile (136) + list of brothers slain in chariots + final slaying of brothers with simile (161). Lonsdale 1990:53 notes that 161 is the resolution of the lion's uncompleted killings in 136.

57. Fenik 1968:22–23 makes clear the typical nature of the heroic entrance scene, and Kirk 1990 on line 134 notes on the frequency of similes.

58. Kirk 1990 on 135–36 comments on the wide divergence between this simile and the surrounding narrative: "For it is the wound itself that increases the lion's *sthenos* (139), whereas the increase of *menos* in Diomedes is caused by the goddess, and the wound is ignored." But the comparison, while joining other similes that seem to develop in relative independence from their context, may extend beyond the immediate context. Kirk notes that it is probably impossible to determine the subject in lines 139–40. I am assuming that the following is the correct reading: "The wound increases the lion's wrath, and the shepherd no longer defends the sheep, but he (the shepherd) lurks around the sheep pens and fears the open areas. The sheep are heaped upon one another in piles, but the lion in his fury leaps out of the high enclosure." This version has the advantage of emphasizing the broader passage, both the lion and the shepherd; this double focus reflects the return of Diomedes as well as Pandaros, who is conscious of his failure (180–91). For a full presentation of the problems in understanding this simile see Kirk 1990:70–72.

59. See Moulton 1977:61 on reinforcement of the two similes.

60. For parallel scenes see 8.330–34 = 13.419–23, 17.4, and 17.132. The last two are especially good comparisons because they show the subtlety possible in varying the simile subject. The use of a simile is typical, but each scene is individually suited to its context (Fenik 1968:33–34).

61. See Scott 1974:68–70.

62. This is emphasized in line 457: "who now would fight even father Zeus."

63. The care with which the book is constructed is shown in Apollo's invitation at 455–59 (455 = 31), which balances Athena's encouragement of Ares' withdrawal at 31–34.

64. For discussions of the setting of this simile in the fuller passage see Jachmann 1958:243–49 vs. Fraenkel 1921:21–22 and Fenik 1968:55–56. Moulton 1977:63 associates the two similes at 522 and 864 as illustrating the dramatic development of the narrative. Kirk 1990 on 522–27 and 864 calls attention to the change from the simplicity of 522 to the obscurity of 864. See the inverse simile drawn from the same simileme at 16.297.

65. Scott 1974:62–66.

66. Fenik 1968:58 notes that this is the only lion simile where both the heroes in the narrative and lions die. Moulton 1977:60–61 sees this simile as a reversal of 5.136, which echoes the direction of the narrative.

67. Lonsdale 1990:55 points out the unity of similes and narrative from 5.541–60. In addition, there seems to be a scaling in the relative strength/weakness of trees within the tree simileme: oak trees are consistently strong (12.132, 13.389 = 16.482, and 14.414) vs. saplings that are vulnerable (17.53, 18.56 + 57 = 18.437 + 438, and *Ody.* 14.175). Thus the fir trees in the short simile at 560 would echo the position of the lions in 556, who are stronger than

the cattle and sheep but are slain by men. For parallel tree similes describing fallen warriors see 4.482, 13.178, 13.389 = 16.482, 14.414, and 17.53; also Scott 1974:70–71.

68. Moulton 1977:61–62. For a parallel context with another simile subject see 3.33.

69. See Moulton 1977:60. The repeated line 31 = 455 emphasizes the stages in the narrative that are marked by the entrance of Ares.

70. For parallel comparisons for distance see 3.12, 16.589, 23.431, and 24.317.

71. The effect of doves in a war setting is difficult to determine, but in other passages they are consistently presented as weaker birds victimized by falcons, hawks, or eagles (see 21.493, 22.140, *Ody.* 15.527, and *Ody.* 20.243); Stanley 1993:84f. thus finds meaning in the juxtaposition of 778 and 782: "Like the heroes they imitate, the goddesses betray the very values they mean to defend: Athena's descent into battle, equipped with her threatening armor and horrific aegis, dissolves in the absurd collocation of similes in 782ff., where both goddesses, strutting like timid doves, approach the men fighting like lions rending raw flesh, or wild boars, as Hera bellows like fifty." Cf. *Hymn. Hom. Ap.* 114.

72. This simile is repeated to describe the effect of Poseidon at 14.148.

73. For discussion of the proper translation see Kirk 1990 on 864–67.

74. For a comparison of the elements of divine participation in books 5 and 8, see Reinhardt 1961:138–49; he finds book 8 parallel to book 5, but similar motifs have a focus and intensity that they lack in the earlier book. He attributes this difference to the relative lateness of book 8, but it is more likely that the shift in theme from the confusion and motiveless interaction of men and gods in 5 to a more rigid handling and direction of the battle under the command of Zeus in book 8 is responsible for the latter's tighter organization.

75. Andersen 1978 treats Diomedes as a character who is consciously developed in the course of the *Iliad*; e.g., 9.33–56 presupposes the quarrel with Agamemnon in the *Epipolesis*, and book 8 explains the easy relationship between Nestor and Diomedes. Yet it seems to me that the *Iliad* throughout depends on preexisting archetypes as major elements in Homeric composition. On this assumption it is more probable that these relationships were drawn from traditional story material, often unknown to us. Thus each major character can be called forth with little concern for previous contact with them in the scene or motivation to support the narrative. Each time Diomedes appears he is the attractive, spirited, and somewhat naive young warrior; he is thus perpetually ideal for book 5, with his respect for his father and his gods and his characteristic silence before confusing situations.

76. The second occurrence of this scene is a parallel event at 159–65, but the third at 230–38 is extended to include Pandarus' frustration. There is sufficient variation in the action that a simile is not needed.

77. For contrast see Agamemnon's entrance into battle at book 11.84–162. Here the slaying of three sets of two warriors is the sum total of Agamemnon's successes before he is wounded and must withdraw. The poet's task is to make these three quite similar incidents seem big. He does this by including descriptions of woundings, some genealogy and history of participants, speeches of participants, and four similes (two long, two short) at 113, 129, 147, and 155. The passage of parallel repeated actions needs these additions to seem varied, since there is little development in plot, character, or theme.

78. The following studies have been useful throughout this section: Stanford 1958; Fernández-Galliano in Russo, Fernández-Galliano, and Heubeck 1992; and Nannini 2003.

79. At *Ody.* 21.38–41 the bow is marked as a sign of rulership rather than a weapon of war.

80. At *Ody.* 24.463–64 more than one-half of the relatives of the suitors will feel that they deserved death at Odysseus' hands.

81. For a full discussion of the complex relationship between Athena and Odysseus see Clay 1976:313–26 and 1983.

82. At this point, when both sides arm themselves and use spears, the conflict becomes more Iliadic, opening the possibility of a fuller battle narrative; see the comment of Fernández-Galliano in Russo et al. 1992 on 126–202.

83. There is little agreement on the division of this book. Stanford 1958 splits the initial three sections differently but does agree on the last three. Fernández-Galliano in Russo et al. 1992 feels that the structure of the book is unsatisfactory, and he becomes involved in identifying passages that have been inserted in the process of reworking. I am arguing for an understandable building of a theme through the six sections by one poet.

84. There is a short bird simile describing Athena at 240, but her role in the battle among men seems abstract in this book. The text specifically states that Athena did not give Odysseus strength sufficient to turn the battle (236).

85. For a current attempt to sort out the precise meaning of this simile see Fernández-Galliano in Russo et al. 1992 on 304–6 and Jong 2001 on 299–308.

86. *Iliad* 12.167, 16.259, and 17.570.

87. *Iliad* 16.428, *Ody.* 16.217, and *Shield* 405.

88. Schnapp-Gourbeillon 1981:33–34. The peaceful quality of life in this simile is stressed at *Ody.* 22.301, which is repeated in Odysseus' challenge to Eurymachus for an even, nondestructive contest in the countryside (*Ody.* 18.367). A similar tone is attached to the formulaic *horei en eiarinei* at *Iliad* 2.471 and 16.643.

89. Even the short simile describing Athena as she flies up to the roof in the disguise of a swallow matches this tone (240). Though a bird is a normal simile topic for a god or goddess (Scott 1974:77–78), the swallow is one of the mildest birds in the simileme. This quality is continued from *Ody.* 21.411, where the bow of Odysseus sang sweetly like a swallow.

90. The moment of being hunted and caught is omitted when the fish are not speared (*Ody.* 10.124), caught on a hook (*Iliad* 16.406), or cowering in terror before a larger predatory fish (*Iliad* 21.22). See Jong 2001 on 381–89.

91. R. Friedrich 1981:128–31.

92. Although Stanford 1958 on 465ff. makes a noble effort to describe the parallels in physical arrangements, the details of the trap within the simile are unclear, as are the details of the mechanism for hanging the maids; see Fernández-Galliano in Russo et al. 1992 on 468–73 for a more realistic assessment of the problems in this passage.

93. There are a number of specific items which suggest that Homer presents a complex victory—bloody but just: Philoitius characterizes his slaying of Ctesippus as a compensatory "guest-gift" (290–91); the herald Medon is spared so that he may encourage good

deeds (372–74); Phemius ponders seeking safety at the altar of Zeus Herkeios, "where Laertes and Odysseus had burned many thighs of cattle"; and later he and Medon do sit by this altar while Odysseus sees to the cleansing of the megaron (334–36 and 379), asks Eurycleia to identify those maids who are guilty of dishonoring the house and those who are innocent, claims that the *moira theon* and the suitors' cruel deeds have earned them a shameful death (413–16), and pledges to cleanse and purify his hall at the moment he summons Penelope and assigns punishments to those who have wronged him (481–82). See the recent discussion of this theme in book 22 by Dimock 1989: 295–315, esp. 296: "What might appear at first cruel and cold-blooded calculation is revealed to be in fact the emotional essence of Homeric justice."

94. See Scott 1974:38–41.

95. See Scott 1974:31–33.

96. The text specifically states that Athena did not give Odysseus strength sufficient to turn the battle (236). This passage introduces an issue that is problematic throughout both the *Iliad* and the *Odyssey*: in clearest terms: does a god or goddess ever so dominate mortal action that humans lose their role as motivators of the story? Lesky 1961 argues that rhetorically they do on some occasions, but on others men are said to cause actions, and often both are combined. But he also makes it clear that these are merely different ways of looking at the same act. In other words, Homer can introduce gods as complementary motivators or even narrative aids that allow the story to develop easily once he has outlined the values basic to the plot. This seems to describe well the limited role Athena plays in the battle of *Odyssey* 22.

97. The repeated line (256 = 273) emphasizes the same results to the sequential stages in this unit.

98. Dimock 1989:304: "To us it may well seem 'natural,' in accord with the nature of things, that the guilt-ridden suitors should undergo panic at this point. If we can accept that in Homer the gods embody the nature of things, we can happily see the victory as primarily Athena's — good luck, bad consciences, panic, and all."

99. See Scott 1974:28–31; close examples of this use of the simile are *Ody*. 5.394 and *Ody*. 23.233.

100. Throughout this discussion the following studies have been the most useful: Hainsworth 1988; Dougherty 2001; and Nannini 2003.

101. The time required for this book's action is at least nine days; see 225 + 262 + 388–90.

102. See discussion by Vernant 1991:104–10.

103. Thus the *Odyssey* story opens with a strong parallel to the *Iliad*. There Zeus, at the behest of a goddess, opposes another powerful Olympian in fulfilling a mortal's desires — and this human desire lies at the core of the epic.

104. Probably the strongest argument for the appropriateness of the divine council that opens book 5 is the powerful introduction of the theme of Zeus' protection as Odysseus breaks from Calypso. The first council merely indicated that the gods would think of ways for Odysseus to return home safely (1.75–79); the second council emphasizes more precisely the elements of Zeus' plan for Odysseus until he arrives on Ithaca. In addition,

the version in book 5 is significantly changed to emphasize the need for the gods to reward good kings, Odysseus' desire for vengeance, his lack of equipment to make the return trip, and the threat to Telemachus. For a summary of recent discussion on the second council of the gods with bibliography, see Hainsworth 1988:251–53. See also Rengakos 1995, 1998.

105. There are many signs of Odysseus' lack of awareness of the true situation, but probably the most dispiriting falls at 303–5, when he assumes that Zeus is seeking his destruction.

106. Yet this description has sinister overtones: see Parry 1957 and Hainsworth 1988 on 63–74. I would add: the remoteness of the island, indicated by the description of Hermes' journey (44–55); the fire in Calypso's cave, which dominates the island's atmosphere (59–61); the emphasis on the cave's large size (57–59); and the description of the cave as the source of all growth, shelter, and water. See Güntert 1919 for a full analysis of allusions to wider mythical sources and the function of Calypso's realm in Odysseus' travels.

107. The interlinkages between the four incidents in section 3 (283–493) are signs of careful structure. The first two scenes are linked especially by the appearance of the helpful female divinity and the parallel threatening speeches of Poseidon at 286–90 and 377–79, both of which end with the direct threat of evil. In addition, the introductory sections of each speech are marked with similar rhetoric: 282b = 375b and 285 = 376.

All four of these sequential scenes are unified by the repeated lines 298–99, 355–56, 407–8, and 464–65, each containing an *o moi ego* type of phrase, and three followed by a *deido me* fearing clause.

For discussion of the repetitions and doubling in the structure of this series of four scenes see Fenik 1974:143–45; Bannert 1988:151–56; and Hainsworth 1988 on 297–387 and 458–90.

108. The placement of this simile is typical on two grounds. Similes often describe the journeys of gods, and the bird simileme is customarily used to describe gods (Scott 1974: 15–20 and 77–90, and Moulton 1977:138).

109. Seldom are the comparanda between simile and narrative so transparent (wind = wind). The closest parallels are those occasions when a god rises like a bird that receives comment from characters in the narrative; these cases are as much a metamorphosis as they are a simile. *Ody.* 3.372 may not even be a proper simile, because *eidomenos* usually introduces the transformation of a god into a character; *Ody.* 1.320 has the form of a simile, though closely tied to the action in the narrative.

110. Moulton 1977:19–27 discusses Homer's use of paired similes; here they seem to underline the additive structure of the second part of the book. The closest parallels are 5.499 and 13.334.

111. Cf. 15.624 and perhaps 15.381.

112. This simile seems awkward in its connection to the narrative: "The point ... is ... that the skin of his hands is left clinging to the rocks as the pebbles cling to the suckers of the octopus. The imagery in fact is slightly confused, since the octopus suffers no injury" (Hainsworth 1988 on 432–35); see also Primavesi 2004:136–37. However it is possible that the poet is trying to mitigate the impression of serious lasting damage in the narrative, since Odysseus has been protected since the opening of the book.

113. When Demodocus tells the tale of Troy, Odysseus weeps like a woman who sees her husband cut down before the gates of the city (*Ody.* 8.523). Odysseus and Telemachus meet in the swineherd's hut and wail like birds bereft of their young (*Ody.* 16.216). Images of the father-son relationship come easily to Telemachus: he tells Athena-Mentes that he is as kind as a father is to a son, and he reports to Penelope that he was welcomed by Nestor as enthusiastically as a son is welcomed by his father (*Ody.* 1.308 and *Ody.* 17.111); Eumaeus greets Telemachus as a father greets his only son (*Ody.* 16.17). Penelope, as she tells of her vacillation before the suitors, is like Aedon lamenting the death of her son (*Ody.* 19.518).

114. There is probably an allusion to this simile (and its narrative situation) at *Ody.* 23.233-38, where Penelope welcoming Odysseus is like the sailors who welcome the land that provides them an escape from death. For discussion of the subtleties in this artful simile see Fraenkel 1921:94-95; Mattes 1958:135-37; Podlecki 1971:88-89; Moulton 1977:129-30; Foley 1978:7-8; R. Friedrich 1981:133-37; and Jong 2001 on 394-99.

115. For discussion of this theme see Segal 1962:17-64 and Podlecki 1971.

116. Primavesi 2004:138-39. Fire vs. water may be a standard epic contrast. The most famous and fully worked version of this contrast is in book 21 of the *Iliad*. The terms are not so directly opposed in *Odyssey* book 5, but there is so much water in the narrative that the role of the survivor/opponent would naturally be fire.

117. Primavesi 2004:131-51.

118. Ibid. In *Ody.* book 5 this simile topic is reinforced by 234-60, in which Calypso provides the tools, and Odysseus, as the craftsman, cuts trees, works them, measures, drills, fits, and outfits his raft. When he sets sail at 270, he directs his raft *techneentos*. This theme is followed at *Ody.* 21.307-400, when the suitors call him a connoisseur or maker of bows (*Ody.* 21.307-400) as he threatens to string the bow.

119. For the fullest discussion of the raft in the thematic development of the *Odyssey* see Dougherty 2001.

120. Through this study I hoped to show that the poetic techniques or the *Iliad* are largely those of the *Odyssey*. Nannini 2003 argues for a usage of several similes in the *Odyssey* that is different from that in the *Iliad*. The point is well summarized on 121-27. There are certainly reversed similes (Foley), oddly contorted similes that develop in unexpected directions (*Ody.* 5.394 and *Ody.* 23.333), and continuously interrelated series of similes over broad spans of the narrative. But I cannot accept her thesis that the composition of the similes is different because each epic was written by a separate author. She never adequately discusses the idiosyncratically structured plots, the varied atmospheres surrounding each tale, and the different approaches called for by themes of the two poems. In defense of her theory I must admit that the very similes she cites as primary evidence do not seem to be derived from similemes that are any more comprehensive than the ones presented in this study. Yet a question remains: do the similes provide evidence for a whole different set of similemes that are not represented in the *Iliad*, or is there a different singer? She does not provide enough evidence to determine this.

121. This organization is also found in the first third of the *Iliad*. In book 1 Achilles makes his choice between the materialistic definition of the heroic code used by Agamemnon

and his own more idealistic view of his life's worth. In books 2–8 the author presents several heroes responding in their own ways to the demands of the code; against this background there is a much profounder presentation of Achilles' choice in book 9 through his responses to the three ambassadors. In addition, it is in the first book that Achilles receives Zeus' promise that he will be able to carry out his choice as he wills it; similarly, in book 5 Odysseus is given divine protection so that he can reach Phaeacia.

122. The unwarlike qualities of the horse are shown in the repetition of this simile to accompany the reentrance of Paris to the battlefield after his brother has chastised him (6.506):

What's this? It is not good to place this anger in your heart.
Your people are dying in battle around the town
and the steep wall. It is for your sake that cries and warfare surround
this city. You yourself would rebuke any other man
you saw fleeing from the hateful war.
Rouse yourself before the town is consumed in blazing fire!

(6.336–41)

CHAPTER FIVE
Problem Books

1. The following studies have been useful throughout this section: Winter 1956; Fenik 1968:115–58, 1986:35–43; Michel 1971; and Janko 1992:39–148.

2. Leaf 1902:1. Cf. W.-H. Friedrich 1956:69–70 and Michel 1971 passim.

3. Perhaps this larger unit even begins in book 12; see Bethe 1914:I:293: "Die ganze Hemmung und Rückstauung der Handlung, die durch 13, 14 und 15 hindurch anhält, so dass sie erst 15.367 wieder auf demselben Punkte wie 12.471 anlangt, ist durchaus einheitlich und nach einem Plane mit Benutzung älterer, fertig übernommener Stücke . . ."; see also Stanley 1993:136–37 and 150–52. For more internal arguments for the unity of book 13–15 see Owen 1946:126–33; Winter 1956; Reinhardt 1961:278–92; Fenik 1968:115–58; Michel 1971; and Janko 1992, esp. 39–41.

4. For an earlier review of such analytic criticism see Ameis and Hentze 1897:II:119–24, and for a contemporary version see Thiel 1982:51–122.

5. Rengakos 1995:25–28 argues that the action at the end of 12 is simultaneous with the activities in books 13–15. His study of the implications of Zielinski's "law" is based on analyses of several scenes showing that simultaneous action is a characteristic of Homeric presentation.

6. The opening lines of book 13 (1–9) promise disorder: Zeus, who has organized the action since book 8, now averts his gaze to distant locations, trusting that no other god will enter the battle.

7. There is a fair amount of agreement in determining the larger units composing this book, even though critics organize the subsections differently. See especially Michel 1971:95–101; Fenik 1968:115–58, esp. 119; and Stanley 1993:142–52.

8. Fenik 1968:119 has presented a structure for book 13 based on finding two sections

of parallel actions; in establishing the break between the two sections so early in the book he does not focus on the major recapitulation at 345–60. Leaf 1902 on 345 comments that this passage "is clearly out of place; there appears to be no other case of such lengthy and superfluous recapitulation in H." Fenik himself lists parallel passages that show that the statement of divine purposes is not all that unusual (54–55, 130), as does Janko 1992 on 345–60. I would argue against both that this statement serves as the major dividing mark in book 13.

9. On lines 39–40, Janko 1992 suggests a kind of hendiadys in which "gales whip up fires" (see 17.737 and *Ody.* 12.68); but the commonly used simile phrasing "x or y" probably indicates that both similemes occur to the poet as alternatives (see, e.g., 14.396 and 17.20).

Phlogi eikelos appears six times in the *Iliad*: five times describing Hector and once Idomeneus (13.53 and 688, 17.88, 18.14, 20.423; 13.330). While fire is a common simileme for a fighting warrior, Hector perhaps attracts this formulaic phrase because of his driving intention to burn the ships; see Whitman 1958:128–53 and Janko 1992 on 53.

10. Scott 1974:66–68, 62–66, and 71; jackals occur only at 11.474.

11. Janko 1992 on 102–4: "The deer, a common victim, connotes cowardice: cf. 4.243, 21.29, 22.1, *Ody.* 4.334ff."

12. The strongest simile from this simileme is *Ody.* 22.302; the closest parallels to 13.62 are 16.582, 17.460, and 17.674. For a broader discussion of gods being compared to birds see Bannert 1988:57–68.

13. See the analysis of 136–42 by Janko 1992: "The simile thus presages the failure not of this attack only, but of Hektor's entire drive to the sea."

14. Fenik 1968:125–28 offers the most detailed analysis of the typical elements that underlie this scene.

15. See Shannon 1975:57; he provides sufficient evidence to establish this connotation throughout the *Iliad*.

16. See chart 6.

17. For an analysis of the components of this simile, see Minchin 2001a:146–47. W.-H. Friedrich 1956:67–70 shows the parallels between this passage and 4.473–87. Moulton 1977:23 notes the difference in tone from 13.389, which he attributes to the more significant role of Asios as a leader of the attack on the wall in book 12; more likely the tone of 13.178 is determined by the narrative needs of the passage (see further discussion in chap. 6).

18. The use of two lions or a single lion confronting dogs or goats seems standard language for dominance and intimidation. The elements are all present in the lion simileme, especially at 3.23, 5.554, 10.297, 11.383, 15.324, and 18.579. See Schnapp-Gourbeillon 1981:77–79.

19. The tone for this simile may be set in the ball game in the *Odyssey*'s Nausicaa episode (book 6). There are two other similes that seem to dehumanize or trivialize warriors by comparing them to inert objects or toys: 11.147 and 14.413 (another possible parallel is 14.499). In each case the warrior has been decisively overwhelmed.

20. The only precise parallel is at 11.66. The interesting feature of this simile is Homer's

identification of Idomeneus' entrance to the battlefield with the will of Zeus, whereas Zeus is absent from the battlefield and, in any case, is supposed to be strengthening the Trojans. This is one of the clearer pieces of evidence that individual similes can develop elements from the simileme that take on a life of their own independent of the surrounding narrative.

21. The comparison to Ares is introduced at 295 and reinforced at 328; see Moulton 1977:21 for a discussion of associative composition.

22. Scott 1974:68–70; for comparisons of humans to specific gods see 2.478, 7.208, *Ody.* 6.102.

23. The closest parallels in subject are 3.10 and 5.499, but in neither case is there a comparable extension. All three of these similes express the weakness of the wind; in each case the battle is beginning or balanced. In contrast, the strongest similes developed from the wind simileme are 15.624 and 16.765.

24. See the detailed discussion in Michel 1971:51–62.

25. Michel 1971:48–51; Fenik 1968:128–37; Reinhardt 1961:294–99; Janko 1992 on 206–45, 210, 242–45, and 298–303.

26. For a discussion of the typological qualities of this scene see Fenik 1986:34–37.

27. Note the careful parallel to the first Trojan slain in section 1, Imbrius, a son of Priam (178).

28. Of course, these elements were chosen again, since this simile is "repeated" at 16.482; for the parallels to the Sarpedon scene see Fenik 1968:61; Schoek 1961:61–64; and Janko 1992 on 13.383–401 and 389–93. Both passages stress the agent (Idomeneus/Patroclus), who is fulfilling the plan of a god (Poseidon/Zeus). A parallel to the repeated simile occurs at 4.482, where a human uses the tree to make some object. Minchin 2001a:146–47 reaches a different conclusion about the relationship between simile and narrative.

29. For the connotation of steles in similes see Scott 1974:72.

30. Fenik 1968:130–36.

31. This is a unique juxtaposition of two similes that intensify the comparison through their opposition; the first is the negative statement that is then reversed in the following positive statement.

32. Similes of farm animals can express a variety of tones depending on the surrounding narrative: see 3.196 and 4.433; for the shepherd see 8.559. When there is such a different quality to each of the similes, one must ask whether there is only a partial simileme behind the group, i.e., a collection of elements that would be familiar from a farming scene, none of which have an established range of behaviors and therefore range from strong to weak. Indeed, during this simile the narrative shifts from the leadership of the group to the joy of the commander; Aeneas seems to shift from the ram to the shepherd. Fraenkel 1921:6–7 calls such similes "double-sided"; see also 13.795 and 15.624.

33. The simile reveals the complexity in the full scene. The similes at 470, 471, and 492 together present a rejoined battle with a focus on the single heroes, Idomeneus and Aeneas; Fenik 1986:37: "The similes at the start and finish establish antithesis, with the violence of the boar hunt set against the closing pastorale."

34. There is no clear parallel for the subject and narrative setting of this simile, but the

closest in presenting the effective ferocity of the men and beasts are 11.414, 12.146, and *Shield* 386–91.

35. As Janko 1992 notes on 531–33, it appears that Homer has repeated the ingressive action of Meriones especially to introduce the simile and perhaps to emphasize the assignment of individual heroes in furthering the attack of Poseidon's intentions in the second half of the book (see simile at 13.62).

36. Such extreme extension of the simileme into future time is paralleled at *Ody.* 5.490, where the traditional fire simileme for the hero Odysseus at a low moment is reduced to a mere ember.

37. For parallels to a bull being mastered by men see 17.520 and 20.403 (cf. 16.487); however, as noted earlier in note 32, the whole family of farm animals seems to be a simileme without fixed tones of stronger vs. weaker. All three of these bull similes take their tone from the narrative.

38. Janko 1992 on 564–66 calls attention to the verbal echo in 654, even though the immediate context is different.

39. For the closest parallels to this scene see Janko 1992 on 703–7.

40. This is a difficult simile to interpret; see Michel 1971:128 or Janko 1992 on 754–55. Either size or impressiveness must be intended; it is important that there is no lessening of the threat posed by Hector.

41. For both similes see Janko 1992 on 795–99.

42. For the swiftness of hawks see 13.62–65, 15.237, and *Ody.* 13.86. Janko 1992 on 821–23 notes that the hawk metaphor produces a real bird of omen.

43. 13.389 = 16.482.

44. For this section the most useful studies are Fenik 1968:159–89; Thornton 1984; Edwards 1991; and Stanley 1993:175–85.

45. E.g., Leaf 1902:II:217–18: "The logical conclusion seems to be that we have a narrative which has developed by successive stages from a comparatively short combat over the body of Patroklos between Hector on the one side and Aias and Menelaos on the other. . . . We have reached a gap in the story of the *Menis* which can only be filled by useless guess-work."

46. The "rebuke" pattern in book 17 is extensively analyzed by Fenik 1968:49–54 and 159–89; Thornton 1984:86–92 makes the same point but divides the sequences differently and must explain too many omissions to keep the recurring pattern clear.

47. I have listed this scene as though it is modeled on the basic type scene, and in a very general way, it is; but there is a long section about the horses of Achilles (426–542) which seems a digression. Fenik 1968:159–60 sets this passage aside from the repeated type scene basic to book 17, but acknowledges that it does reflect this structure.

48. Stanley 1993:176–78 shows how carefully structured 543–96 are as a subsection of this unit.

49. I have based my divisions most closely on Fenik 1968:159–89. There are only slight differences in the arrangements at the end of the book by Moulton 1977:73–75, Stanley 1993:175–81, and Edwards 1991.

50. There is a strange disjunctiveness in this simile; it does not seem that the calf is

dead but, rather, that the older animal is protecting the younger from attack (Leumann 1950: 242–43). Edwards 1991 on 3–6 notes that Menelaus in this book has the same type of sensitive and compassionate nature as Patroclus; see also Patzer 1996:120–22 and Willcock 2002:221–29.

51. For the other serial negative simile with a cumulative effect see 14.394 and Janko 1992.

52. This simile is composed from elements of the wind and tree similemes. The weakness of the young shoot is clear in 18.56 = 437, *Ody.* 14.175, and *Ody.* 6.162; compare the strength of heartier trees in 4.482, 5.560, 13.178, 13.389 = 16.482, and 14.414.

The strongest examples of destructive winds are 16.765 and 14.398; parallels to weak objects stirred by the wind are a cornfield, chaff, and dust (2.147, 5.499, and 13.334).

53. Fenik 1968:52–53 argues that similes are alternative means of emphasizing the Trojan charge in rebuke scenes, thus providing another juncture at which the tradition would suggest a simile to the poet. See also 164–65, concerning the customary simile at 17.109.

54. Edwards 1991 on 260–61 notes the broadening of the scope carried by the self-question of the poet, the simile, and the actions of Zeus.

55. For the careful matching of tone to narrative, compare the simile at 18.318; Moulton 1977:73–75 and 105–6 links these two similes as conscious parts of a pattern developing throughout book 17. See also Moulton 1981:1–8 and Edwards 1991 on 17.132–36.

56. Note how simile and narrative develop simultaneously when Ajax strides along the foremost fighters, then the boar in the simile scatters the dogs and men, and on return to the narrative Ajax now scatters his opponents.

57. Edwards 1991 on 256–59 notes that this simile is used only for Meriones and always following a line like 258 (2.650). This is a good example of the close tie between content and simile in the tradition.

58. Cf. 4.452 and 17.747. Noise is the object of comparison; the resistance of the Greeks to the Trojans is implicit in the loudness of the surge.

59. Underlined by lines 451–55 (see 11.193–94 and 208–9).

60. The images gathered by Friis-Johansen 1967:191–200 show that after Homer the fight over Patroclus' body was considered a separate episode; often the named characters match the story as it is told by Homer.

61. Compare the similar tone of overhanging death in 13.437; see Fraenkel 1921:56.

62. The closest parallel to this simile in setting and content is *Ody.* 22.302. It is difficult to establish a series of variations for this simileme because there are so few examples and they appear in such different contexts: 7.59, 13.531, 16.428, and *Ody.* 16.217.

63. *Ody.* 22.402 is the only parallel simile and provides a further developed version of the simileme.

64. For recent discussion of the difficulties in dealing with 543–93 see Fenik 1968:183n3 and Stanley 1993:176–78.

65. Fraenkel 1921:29 makes clear that the narrow comparison to the single *Vergleichungspunkt* is far from the full contribution of this simile to the scene; in fact, the poet fails to keep simile and narrative separate (cf. 4.75). The same ambiguous effect is found when gods are compared to birds; see Fenik 1968:182 and Scott 1974:77.

66. For the tone of this simile compare 4.130. Persistence is the key; the mention of "blood" could tie this simile more closely to the narrative, but the reduction of Menelaus' war efforts to the attack of a single fly effectively lessens the impact.

67. Leaf 1902:657–73 finds 11.657 pointless in content and weak in expression in comparison to 11.548. But these two examples may show more about the simileme than any others. In each passage a major warrior withdraws reluctantly (see Beye 1984:7–13 for the most forceful analysis of these similes as occurring in parallel locations). When the poet chooses the lion simileme, he is using a highly traditional topic and then extends it with elements from the simileme that underline the lion's reluctance. He chooses different words for the first two lines, but could well feel that he had made no addition to the basic elements of the simileme. In book 17 he omits the color of the lion in the first line as well as the identification of his prey as cattle, but both can be easily assumed from phrasing that the audience knew (see 18.161; and in any case *boon* is provided in 659). In 17.658 the lion is worn down rather than driven back; the difference is slight, but it reflects the difference in strength of Menelaus vs. Ajax in book 11. Otherwise the next six lines are identical, probably reflecting the poet's previous use of these lines to form elements from the lion simileme into an effective simile.

The swiftness of the eagle's attack is emphasized in 15.690, 21.252, 22.308, and *Ody.* 24.538, as is common in bird similes (Scott 1974:77–79). Here Fraenkel 1921:106 objects to the lack of parallelism between simile and narrative, and Macleod 1982 on 24.78–82 and Edwards 1991 on 17. 674–78 point out further inconcinnities. As in those cases, Homer is using a point in the narrative to attach a simile—here, Menelaus' sharp gaze. But once he has established a framework for a simile, he draws upon the elements from the simileme that will focus on his broader theme—the developing strength of Menelaus against the weaker Trojans.

68. As parallels of 11.737 see 18.207, 21.522, and 22.410. Edwards 1991 on 736–41 and Richardson 1993 on 522–25 sense that Homer is building this series of similes to a culmination. The use of repeated similemes to enhance a developing narrative can be easily accommodated to the psychology of an oral poet.

Kirkon is used only at 11.755 and 22.139; *irex* is commoner (see 16.582 and *Ody.* 13.86).

69. This boar is wounded and still defends himself; most boar similes—even those in which the boar will die—show stronger resistance: 8.338, 11.324 and 414, 12.41 and 146, 13.471, and 17.281. There is no proper parallel to the dam simile; usually the force of the river rushes over or breaks through the dam and devastates the land; see Scott 1974:76–77 and 17.263.

70. See the discussion of simile clusters in chap. 2. Edwards 1991 on 725–61 notes that each of the individual scenes closely follows the developing action (and in the case of 725 even prefigures the narrative action).

71. Thornton 1984: 91–92; Edwards 1991 on 736–41.

72. The following studies have been especially useful in this section: Fraenkel 1921; Reinhardt 1961:308–48; Fenik 1968; Baltes 1983; Janko 1992; Stanley 1993:166–74.

73. Close identification of Patroclus with Achilles is deeply rooted in the text. Whitman 1958:199–203; Lowenstam 1981:174–77; Nagy 1999:292–36.

74. This is then repeated almost verbatim at 16.36–45. See Janko 1992:309–10 for a discussion of the broader sources of responsibility for Achilles' plans. At 16.87–96 Achilles himself sets the preservation of his honor as the major goal of the plan; at this point he attempts to define a line beyond which Patroclus should not go and which he will be unable to recognize in the heat of battle.

75. Janko 1992:310–11: "The Trojans are at first alarmed, but Sarpedon is soon asking who this warrior is, and Glaukos knows it is Patroklos (280, 423, 543)."

76. *Iliad* 16.46–48, 103, 119–21, 458–61, 644–55, and 688–91.

77. *Iliad* 16.20–35, 249–52, 440–43, 707–9, and 837–42.

78. *Iliad* 16.140–44, 152–54 (see Janko 1992), 249–56, and 686–67.

79. Whitman 1958:281–82 and Fenik 1968:190–218.

80. Janko 1992 divides at 277, thus creating a threefold pattern of simile and preparation/exhortation (156ff., 212ff., and 259ff.), but the organization seems clearer when the responsibility is fully passed to Patroclus at 257. This is supported by the *men-de* opposition in 253 and 257. See also Stanley 1993:166–74.

81. Reinhardt 1961:340–48; Baltes 1983:40–42.

82. See the detailed discussion of this intensifying structure reflected in the similes by Baltes 1983.

83. Monsacré 1984:91–92 cites the womanly qualities characteristic of Patroclus: preparing food, healing, and gentleness—although only to an appropriate extent; see Crotty 1994:55n13.

84. The critical nature of this moment was presented through a sequential series of highly warlike similes in 15.592–637.

85. Scott 1974:130–40 discusses the repeated similes. This discussion gives major importance to the freestanding nature of the similes in the poet's storehouse of previously used materials. There is, however, no presumption in that study that Homer could not use such similes to mark similar moments at a parallel narrative moment—or even recall an earlier parallel moment in the poems; see Whitman 1958:279–80 and Moulton 1977:103–4.

86. See Janko 1992 on 16.7–10.

87. Significantly, this limitation is removed at the start of section 3, just before Patroclus kills Sarpedon (466–76).

88. For discussion of the limitations that prevent Patroclus from playing the role of Achilles see Armstrong 1958.

89. This is the one of the rare similes in which the action (vomiting the blood and gore of their prey) has completely passed by the narrative moment (men entering battle); cf. 11.293, 11.474, 12.41, 12.146, 15.271, 16.752, and 21.573. Fraenkel 1921:73–75 sees this as the poet's desire to give a lively intention for the wolves' act. Nimis 1987:23–33 and Janko 1992 on 156–63, however, suggest that this simile may replace the meal before battle.

90. Three of the epithets for the Myrmidons emphasize their ability in war: *ehchesimorous* (*Ody.* 3.188); *tachypoloi* (23.6); and *philoptolemoisi* (16.65 and 23.129).

91. Scott 1974:31–33.

92. There is no good explanation for Hector's flight at 367, especially after his firmness

at 363. Leaf 1902 on 364 and Fenik 1968:193-94 recommend excising one set of the offending lines. Whitman 1958:151-52; Moulton 1977:34-35; Thalmann 1984:71; and Janko 1992 on 364-93 defend the text from various perspectives.

93. This is a loosely organized simile; see especially Kakridis 1960:250-53, with the bibliography in his notes, and Kirk 1977:6. Probably the two parts of this simile should be united into a single image promising the greatest menace for the children as well as the unsuspecting man who stumbles into the situation. See also discussions by Kakridis 1971:138-40; Marcovich 1962; and Erbse 2000:266-68.

94. The lack of examples makes it hard to structure a simileme for insects. There are only three relevant parallels of potentially harmful insects in the Homeric poems. The insects at 12.167 remain only a potential threat but are prepared to defend their home and young; those at 16.259 actually attack. In contrast, unfocused bees who flit from flower to flower at 2.87 are symbols of weakness; see also 2.469 and 16.641.

95. Moulton 1977:33-38 identifies this storm simile as the beginning of a three-part chain that closely parallels the narrative. The topic for these similes may arise from the notion of light as salvation against the darkness of defeat; see 15.741, 16.39, and 17.645. While there are not a sufficient number of parallels to construct a full cloud simileme, there is one indication that Zeus is the controller of the clouds at 5.522. Cf. Whitman 1958:151-53; Fenik 1968:192; Janko 1992 at 16.384-93; and Nannini 2003:34-38.

96. Leaf 1902 excises 364-71; see also Fenik 1968:1933-34. Thalmann 1984:17-18 shows how this section with its simile is part of a ring structure that emphasizes the important moment "when the Trojans' earlier triumph is canceled by their rout." On the details of the simile see Janko 1992 on 16.364-65.

97. See Scott 1974:76-77 on river similes. Certain elements seem derived from a simileme of rushing, destructive rivers, even though there are not enough examples to establish an outline of the full form: the storm comes from Zeus, the season is given, several rivers feed the flow, the river is full, the rivers rush from the mountains, they run toward the sea, and they break through the properties of men.

98. It is unclear to what or to whom in the narrative this simile applies; see discussion by Scott 1974:55-56; Moulton 1977:35-37; and Janko 1992 on 384-93. The literal point of comparison is the noise of the Trojan horses in retreat, but the narrative contains some features that seem contradictory to elements of the simile. A three-line section stresses Zeus as the agent in this unit of the poem; this is perhaps the strongest implicit parallel in the narrative. Van der Valk 1963-64:II:475 reaches too far in finding a generalized morality dominating the defeat of the Trojans.

99. Scott 1974:75.

100. "Lists of victims' names almost always precede a hostile intervention, often resulting from divine help" (Janko 1992 on 415-18; cf. Fenik 1968:68-69).

101. There seems to be a vulture simileme that is used for a variety of purposes but commonly describes the attack of a hero swooping after smaller prey (13.531, 16.582, 17.460, *Ody.* 22.302). It is striking that this simile describes equally powerful opponents; see Baltes 1983:37-38.

102. Scott 1974:78.

103. Fenik 1968:204; Baltes 1983:36–39.

104. This simile is repeated at 13.389. It may be a sign that the plan of Zeus continues at 17.744, when Patroclus becomes the log that is made into a beam or a ship timber.

105. For the most bloodthirsty representations of the simileme see 5.136, 5.161, 11.172, 11.548 = 17.657, 12.299, 15.630, 17.61, and *Ody.* 6.130; for similar language see 18.579–84 (Shield).

106. For parallel similes from the vulture simileme, see note 101 earlier in this chapter.

107. The *aiganee* seems to be a javelin used for sport; see 15.358, 2.774, and *Ody.* 4.626 = *Ody.* 17.168. The addition of this peaceful alternative is the first of several in the concluding sections of book 16 which emphasize poetically that this battle is not totally the result of human initiative but, rather, is under the control of Zeus.

108. *Orumagdos ororei* describes both woodcutters and warriors (Aristarchus). Janko 1992 on 633–34 suggests that this simile implies the presence of Zeus: "The sound echoes far *because* it is in the glens. As often in the simile, this detail implies an observer; in fact both we and Zeus are watching."

109. See 16.259 and 12.167; see also Scott 1974:74.

110. See the parallel simile at 2.469.

111. See Fenik 1968:211–12 and Leinieks 1973:102–7, esp. 104.

112. 16.192.

113. Hence the factual correctness but inappropriateness of Leaf's 1902 complaint in his introduction to book 16, p. 155: "It is strange that, after we have been led to expect the final fight between Patroklos and Hector (see particularly 755–64), the scene should suddenly change to a general mellay, lasting apparently a long time." But for the pattern of this narrative see Fenik 1968:209–14.

114. See Scott 1974:72 and Moulton 1979:287. The lightheartedness of this scene seems to arise not from the simileme but from the rhetorical twist to the subject given by Patroclus; see Lloyd 2004, esp. 86–87.

115. Reinhardt 1961:347–48.

116. Parallel similes presenting a lion that is either wounded or killed are 5.136, 5.554, 12.41, 12.299, 17.725, and 20.164.

117. Schnapp-Gourbeillon 1981:82; Baltes 1983:41–42.

118. There is no exact parallel to this simile, but its elements are seen in such similes as 3.23, 7.256, 16.823, and *Aspis* 402. Fraenkel 1921:62 and Baltes 1983:40 (including n28) see this simile as a unique expansion of the simileme.

119. Parallel similes with destructive clashes of winds are 9.4, 11.305, 13.795, and 15.624. See Fraenkel 1921:37; see also Baltes 1983:42–43, corrected by Janko 1992 on 765–69.

120. Baltes 1983:45 notes that the aorists in 823–26 force the audience to read about a fight whose winner has already been determined. This is the only simile in the Homeric poems where a lion and boar confront one another (cf. *Aspis* 168–77 and Fraenkel 1921:62); in fact, nowhere else is the boar, a defensive fighter, killed by a predatory beast. Thus it is significant that Hector is cast as the lion and Patroclus as the boar. See Schnapp-Gourbeillon 1981:46; Baltes 1983:44; Janko 1992 on 823–26; and Beck 2005:179–80.

121. See Lohmann 1970:115–17 and 159–61 and Janko 1992 on 830–63.

122. E.g., 16.156, 269, 384, 487, and 765.

123. Scott 1974:74–75.

124. It is clear that Sarpedon is a stronger and more threatening opponent that Cebriones, but Sarpedon is fated to die and thus is vulnerable in a way that Cebriones is not.

125. This organization is symptomatic of Owen 1946 and commentary style, but Stanley 1993:101–85 is more focused on the connections between larger sections of narrative.

126. This analysis makes clear the special richness and significance of the run of books from *Iliad* 13–18, when the plan of Zeus must be acknowledged and dealt with by the heroes.

CHAPTER SIX
The Creative Poet and the Co-creating Audience

1. Berg and Haug 2000:8; West and West 1999:72n1.

2. Armstrong 1958. The arming of Agamemnon does contain one simile, but it is not developed to equal the fire simile in book 19.

3. For full discussion of fire imagery in the *Iliad* see Whitman 1958:128–53.

4. Nannini 2003: 29–31.

5. Moulton 1974b:394 describes similes as "innovative variations of traditional material by an individual poet for his aesthetic purpose."

6. Hampe 1952:10–13.

7. Scott 1974:87.

8. Scott 1974:79–80.

9. Shannon 1975:84.

10. See chap. 5 for discussion of the structure of book 13.

11. The oak is the most commonly cited tree in the Homeric poems. It serves as a building element, a tree that will be blasted by lightning, and seemingly a general-use tree. The pine is used for building and appears only conjunction with the oak. The poplar (*acherois*) appears only in the present formula for three trees. Thus, these trees seem to have little implicit connotation.

12. Buxton 2004: 152.

13. Cf. 12.132.

14. Scott 1974:87.

15. See 5.161, 16.752, 17.725, and 20.164; 12.41 and 12.299.

16. See the chart on the tree simileme.

17. Nimis 1987:32 describes this moment of co-creativity well: "If we can characterize narrative in a preliminary fashion as a succession of textual swathes, the interrelationships among these various units and the flow from one textual unity to another will be determined by a number of coded factors. Notions of narrative 'sequences,' 'motifs,' 'patterns,' etc., are common interpretative devices which are used to account for these interrelationships. . . . This grouping together of a series of actions into a single 'scene' which has a significance beyond its discrete components is an important part of the interpretive process by which readers produce meaning."

18. For discussion of Homer's handling of thematic needs that conflict with prestated goals and plans see Scodel 1998 and 1999:77–83.

19. Scott 1987.

20. Previously this type of criticism has been practiced only at a basic level. For example, Lee 1964:28–29 maintains that similes in the *Iliad* are often intrusive, since they can easily be removed with no detriment to their passages and such excision often improves the passages' sharpness and simplicity. I am arguing that Homer seeks complexity through the adaptation of the tradition. It is not surprising that similes are formally detachable from their passages, given that they are placed in the narrative by a decision separate from their adaptation, but these separate decisions do not necessitate a failure of each simile to enrich its passage.

21. See 11.113, 129, 172, and 239. For supporting discussion of this whole paragraph see Erbse 2000.

22. Edwards 1991 on 17.657–67.

23. See, among others, Arend 1933; Armstrong 1958; and Hansen 1972.

24. Goody 1987:83: "Once a speaker has delivered his first recital, which has been 'learnt' in an informal manner, he stores what he has given (or improvised) and then tends to reproduce his original version. He does not memorize someone else's recitation (certainly not in a verbatim manner), but he does memorize (after a certain fashion) his own."

25. Nimis 1987:51–55.

26. Scott 1974:140–61.

BIBLIOGRAPHY

Alden, M. 2000. *Homer Beside Himself: Paranarratives in the Iliad.* Oxford.
Ameis, K. F., and C. Hentze. 1897. *Anhang zu Homers Ilias.* 2 vols. Leipzig.
Amory, A. 1963. The Reunion of Odysseus and Penelope. In *Essays on the* Odyssey, edited by C. H. Taylor. Bloomington. 100–36.
Andersen, O. 1976. Some Thoughts on the Shield of Achilles. *Symbolae Osloenses* 51:5–18.
———. 1978. *Die Diomedes Gestalt in der Ilias.* Oslo.
Arend, W. 1933. *Die typischen Scenen bei Homer.* Berlin.
Armstrong, J. I. 1958. The Arming Motif in the *Iliad. American Journal of Philology* 79:337–54.
Atchity, K. J. 1977. *Homer's Iliad: The Shield of Memory.* Carbondale.
Austin, N. 1966. The Function of Digressions in the *Iliad. Greek, Roman, and Byzantine Studies* 7:295–312.
———. 1975. *Archery at the Dark of the Moon.* Berkeley.
Bakker, E. J. 1993. Discourse and Performance: Involvement, Visualization and "Presence" in Homeric Poetry. *Classical Antiquity* 12:1–29.
———. 1995. Noun-Epithet Formulas, Milman Parry, and the Grammar of Poetry. In *Homeric Questions*, edited by J. P. Crielard. Amsterdam. 97–125.
———. 1997a. *Poetry in Speech: Orality and Homeric Discourse.* Ithaca.
———. 1997b. The Study of Homeric Discourse. In *A New Companion to Homer*, edited by I. Morris and B. Powell. Leiden. 284–304.
———. 1999. How Oral Is Oral Composition? In *Signs of Orality*, edited by A. Mackay. Leiden. 24–47.
Bakker, E. J., and N. van den Houten. 1992. Aspects of Synonomy in Homeric Diction: An Investigation of Dative Expressions for "Spear." *Classical Philology* 87:1–13.
Baltes, M. 1983. Zur Eigenart und Funktion von Gleichnissen im 16. Buch der Ilias. *Antike und Abendland* 29:36–48.
Bannert, H. 1981. Phoinix' Jugend und der Zorn des Meleagros: Zum Komposition des neunten Buches der Ilias. *Wiener Studien* 15:69–94.
———. 1988. *Formen des Wiederholens bei Homer: Beispiele für eine Poetik des Epos.* Vienna.
Bartsch, S., and Elsner, L. 2007. Special Issue on Ekphrasis, edited by S. Bartsch and L. Elsner. *Classical Philology* 102.
Bassett, S. E. 1938. *The Poetry of Homer.* Berkeley.
Beck, D. 2005. *Homeric Conversation.* Washington, D.C.
Becker, A. S. 1990. The Shield of Achilles and the Poetics of Homeric Description. *American Journal of Philology* 111:139–53.
Berg, N., and Haug, D. 2000. SO Debate: Dividing Homer (Continued): Innovation vs. Tradition in Homer—an Overlooked Piece of Evidence. *Symbolae Osloenses* 75:5–23.

Bethe, E. 1914–27. *Homer, Dichtung und Sage.* Vol. 3. Leipzig.
Beye, C. R. 1984. Repeated Similes in the Homeric Poems. In *Studies Presented to Sterling Dow on His Eightieth Birthday*, edited by A. Boegehold et al. Durham, N.C. 7–13.
Bliss, F. R. 1968. Homer and the Critics: The Structural Unity of *Odyssey* Eight. *Bucknell Review* 16:57–73.
Borchhardt, H. 1977. Frühe griechische Schildformen. In *Kriegswesen 1: Schutzwaffen und Wehrbauten*, edited by H. Buchholz and J. Wiesner. Göttingen. 1–56.
Braswell, B. K. 1971. Mythological Innovation in the *Iliad*. *Classical Quarterly* 21:16–26.
———. 1982. The Story of Ares and Aphrodite: Theme and Relevance to *Odyssey* 8. *Hermes* 110:129–37.
Bremer, J. M. 1985. Four Similes in *Iliad* 22. In *Papers of the Liverpool Latin Seminar 5*, edited by F. Cairns. 367–72.
———. 1987. The So-called Götteraparat in *Iliad* XX–XXII. In *Homer, Beyond Oral Poetry*, edited by J. Bremer, I. J. F. de Jong, and J. Kalff. Amsterdam. 31–46.
Brown, C. G. F. 1989. Ares, Aphrodite, and the Laughter of the Gods. *Phoenix* 43: 283–93.
Brown, H. P. 2006. Addressing Agamemnon: A Pilot Study of Politeness and Pragmatics in the *Iliad*. *Transactions of the American Philological Association* 136:1–46.
Burkert, W. 1960. Das Lied von Ares und Aphrodite. *Rheinisches Museum für Philologie* 103:130–44.
Buxton, R. 2004. Similes and Other Likenesses. In *The Cambridge Companion to Homer*, edited by R. Fowler. Cambridge, U.K. 139–55.
Calhoun, G. M. 1935. The Art of Formula in Homer — "epea pteroenta." *Classical Philology* 30:215–27.
Catling, H. W. 1977. Panzer. In *Kriegswesen 1: Schutzwaffen und Wehrbauten*, edited by H. Buchholz and J. Wiesner. Göttingen. 74–118.
Coffey, M. 1957. The Function of the Homeric Simile. *American Journal of Philology* 78:113–32.
Combellack, F. M. 1959. Milman Parry and Homeric Artistry. *Comparative Literature* 11:193–208.
Cook, E. F. 2003. Agamemnon's Test of the Army in *Iliad* Book 2 and the Function of Homeric *akhos*. *American Journal of Philology* 124:165–98.
Crotty, K. 1994. *The Poetics of Supplication: Homer's* Iliad *and* Odyssey. Ithaca.
Damon, P. 1961. Modes of Analogy in Ancient and Medieval Verse. *University of California Publications in Classical Philology* 15:261–334.
Danek, G. 2002. Traditional Referentiality and Homeric Intertextuality. In *Omero tremila anni dopo*, edited by F. Montanari. Rome. 3–19.
———. 2004. Der Schiffskatalog der Ilias: Form und Funktion. In *Ad Fontes! Festschrift for Gerhard Dobesch*, edited by H. Heftner and K. Tomaschitz. Vienna. 59–72.
Dickson, K. 1995. *Nestor: Poetic Memory in Greek Epic.* New York.
Dimock, G. 1989. *The Unity of the* Odyssey. Amherst.
Dougherty, C. 2001. *The Raft of Odysseus: The Ethnographic Imagination of Homer's* Odyssey. Oxford.

Dubel, S. 1995. L'arme et la lyre: Remarques sur le sense du bouclier d'Achille dans *l'Iliade*. *Ktema* 20:245–57.
Dunkle, J. R. 1981. Some Notes on the Funeral Games, Iliad 23. *Prometheus* 7:11–18.
Edwards, M. W. 1975. Type Scenes and Homeric Hospitality. *Transactions of the American Philological Association* 105:51–72.
———. 1987. Topos and Transformation in Homer. In *Homer: Beyond Oral Poetry*, edited by J. M. Bremer, I. J. F. de Jong, and J. Kalff. Amsterdam. 47–60.
———. 1991. *The* Iliad: *A Commentary: Volume V: Books 17–20*. Cambridge, U.K.
———. 2002. *Sound, Sense, and Rhythm: Listening to Greek and Latin Poetry*. Princeton.
Elliger, W. 1975. *Die Darstellung der Landschaft in der griechischen Dichtung*. Berlin.
Erbse, H. 1961. Betrachtungen über das 5. Buch der Ilias. *Rheinisches Museum für Philologie* 104:156–89.
———. 1998. Achilleus, Patroklos und Meleagros. In *Psyche: Festschrift für Karin Alt zum 7. Mai 1998*. Stuttgart.
———. 2000. Beobachtungen über die Gleichnisse der Ilias Homers. *Hermes* 128:257–74.
Erp Taalman Kip, A. Marie van. 2000. The Gods of the *Iliad* and the Fate of Troy. *Mnemosyne* 53:387–402.
Felson-Rubin, N. 1987. Penelope's Perspective: Character from Plot. In *Homer: Beyond Oral Poetry*, edited by J. M. Bremer, I. J. F. de Jong, and J. Kalff. Amsterdam. 61–83.
Fenik, B. 1968. *Typical Battle Scenes in the* Iliad: *Studies in the Narrative Techniques of Homeric Battle Description*. Wiesbaden.
———. 1974. *Studies in the* Odyssey. Wiesbaden.
———. 1978. *Homer, Tradition and Invention*. Leiden.
———. 1986. *Homer and the Niebelungenlied: Comparative Studies in Epic Style*. Cambridge, U.K.
Fillmore, C. J. 1982. Frame Semantics. In *Linguistics in the Morning Calm*. Seoul: Linguistic Society of Korea.
Finnegan, R. 1977. *Oral Poetry: Its Nature, Significance, and Social Context*. Cambridge, U.K.
Fittschen, K. 1973. *Der Schild des Achilleus, Arch Hom II.N.1b*. Göttingen.
Foley, H. P. 1978. "Reverse Similes" and Sex Roles in the *Odyssey*. *Arethusa* 11:7–26.
Foley, J. M. 1990. *Traditional Oral Epic*. Berkeley.
———. 1991. *Immanent Art: From Structure to Meaning in Traditional Oral Epic*. Bloomington.
———. 1995. *The Singer of Tales in Performance*. Bloomington.
———. 1997. Traditional Signs and Homeric Art. In *Written Voices, Spoken Signs*, edited by E. J. Bakker and A. Kahane. Cambridge, U.K. 56–82.
———. 2002. *How to Read an Oral Poem*. Urbana.
———. 2005. Fieldwork on Homer. In *New Directions in Oral Theory*, edited by M. C. Amodio. Tempe. 15–41.
Fraenkel, H. 1921. *Die homerischen Gleichnisse*. Göttingen.
Friedrich, R. 1981. On the Compositional Use of Similes in the *Odyssey*. *American Journal of Philology* 102:120–37.

Friedrich, W.-H. 1956. *Verwundung und Tod in der Ilias*. Göttingen.
Friis-Johansen, K. 1967. *The Iliad in Early Greek Art*. Copenhagen.
Gaisser, J. B. 1969. A Structural Analysis of the Digressions in the *Iliad* and the *Odyssey*. *Harvard Studies in Classical Philology* 73:1–43.
Goatly, A. 1997. *The Language of Metaphors*. London.
Goody, J. 1987. *The Interface between the Written and the Oral*. Cambridge, U.K.
Goold, G. P. 1960. Homer and the Alphabet. *Transactions of the American Philological Association* 81:272–91.
Griffin, J. 1980. *Homer on Life and Death*. Oxford.
———. 1986. Homeric Words and Speakers. *Journal of Hellenic Studies* 106:36–57.
Güntert, H. 1919. *Bedeutungsgeschichtliche Untersuchungen auf dem Gebiet der indogermanischen Sprachen*. Halle.
Hainsworth, J. B. 1962. The Homeric Formula and the Problem of Its Transmission. *Bulletin of the Institute of Classical Studies* 9:57–68.
———. 1968. *The Flexibility of the Homeric Formula*. Oxford.
———. 1970. The Criticism of an Oral Homer. *Journal of Hellenic Studies* 90:90–98.
———. 1993. *The Iliad: A Commentary: Volume III: Books 9–12*. Cambridge, U.K.
Hainsworth, J. B., A. Heubeck, and S. West. 1988. *A Commentary on Homer's Odyssey: Books I–VIII*. Vol. 1. Oxford.
Hammer, D. C. 1997. "Who Shall Readily Obey?": Authority and Politics in the *Iliad*. *Phoenix* 51:1–34.
———. 2002. *The Iliad as Politics: The Performance of Political Thought*. Norman.
Hampe, R. 1952. *Die Gleichnisse Homers und die Bildkinst seiner Zeit*. Tübingen.
Hansen, W. F. 1972. *The Conference Sequence, Patterned Narration and Narrative Inconsistency in the Odyssey*. Berkeley.
Hardie, P. R. 1985. Imago Mundi: Cosmological and Ideological Aspects of the Shield of Achilles. *Journal of Hellenic Studies* 105:11–31.
Haubold, J. 2000. *Homer's People: Epic Poetry and Social Formation*. Cambridge, U.K.
Heffernan, J. A. W. 1993. *Museum of Words: The Poetics of Ekphrasis from Homer to Ashbery*. Chicago.
Heiden, B. 1998. The Placement of "Book Divisions" in the *Iliad*. *Journal of Hellenic Studies* 118:69–82.
Hermann, G. 1877. De iteratis apud Homerum. In *Opuscula* 8. Leipzig.
Hoekstra, A. 1965. *Homeric Modifications of Formulaic Prototypes: Studies in the Development of Greek Epic Diction*. Amsterdam.
Holmes, B. 2007. The *Iliad*'s Economy of Pain. *Transactions of the American Philological Association* 137:45–84.
Hubbard, T. K. 1992. Nature and Art in the Shield of Achilles. *Arion* 2:16–41.
Ingalls, W. Attitude toward Children in the *Iliad*. *Échos du monde classique* 17:13–34.
Jachmann, G. 1958. *Der Homerische Schiffskatalog und die Ilias*. Cologne.
Janko, R. 1992. *The Iliad: A Commentary: Volume IV: Books 13–16*. Cambridge, U.K.
Jensen, M. S. 1999. Dividing Homer: When and How Were the *Iliad* and the *Odyssey* Divided into Songs. *Symbolae Osloenses* 74:5–91.

Jong, I. J. F. de. 1985. Fokalisation und die Homerischen Gleichnisse. *Mnemosyne* 38:257–80.

———. 1987. *Narrators and Focalizers: The Presentation of the Story in the* Iliad. Amsterdam.

———. 2001. *A Narratological Commentary on the Odyssey*. Cambridge, U.K.

Kakridis, J. T. 1960. Das Wespengleichnis im P der Ilias. *Hermes* 88: 250–53.

———. 1971. Sphekessin eoikotes execheonto (P 259–67). In *Homer Revisited*. Lund.

Kirk, G. S. 1966. Formular Language and Oral Quality. *Yale Classical Studies* 20:153–74.

———. 1977. *Homer and the Oral Tradition*. Cambridge, U.K.

———. 1985. *The Iliad: A Commentary: Volume I: Books 1–4*. Cambridge, U.K.

———. 1990. *The Iliad: A Commentary: Volume II: Books 5–8*. Cambridge, U.K.

Kouklanakis, A. 1999. Thersites and Odysseus: The Social Order. In *Nine Essays on Homer*, edited by M. Carlisle and O. Levaniouk. Lanham. 35–53.

Krischer, T. 1971. *Formale Konventionen der homerischen Epik*. Munich.

Kullmann, W. 1960. *Die Quellen der Ilias (Troischer Sagenkreis)*. Wiesbaden.

———. 1984. Oral Poetry Theory and Neoanalysis in Homeric Research. *Greek, Roman, and Byzantine Studies* 25:307–23.

Lakoff, G., and M. Turner. 1989. *More Than Cool Reason: A Field Guide to Poetic Metaphor*. Chicago.

La Motte, M. de. 1716. *Reflexions sur la critique*. 2d ed. Paris.

Lardinois, A. 2000. Characterization through Gnomai in Homer's *Iliad*. *Mnemosyne* 53:641–61.

Latacz, J. 1977. *Kampfparänesse, Kampfdarstellung und Kampfwirklichkeit in der Ilias, bei Kallinos und Trytaios*. Munich.

Leaf, Walter. 1900 and 1902. *The Iliad of Homer*. 2 vols. London.

Lee, D. J. N. 1964. *The Similes of the* Iliad *and the Odyssey Compared*. Melbourne.

Leinieks, V. 1973. A Structural Pattern in the *Iliad*. *Classical Journal* 69:102–7.

Lesky, A. 1961. *Göttliche und menschliche Motivation im homerischen Epos*. Heidelberg.

Leumann, M. 1950. *Homerische Wörter*. Basel.

Lloyd, M. 2004. The Politeness of Achilles: Off-record Conversation Strategies in Homer and the Meaning of Kertomia. *Journal of Hellenic Studies* 124:75–89.

Lohmann, D. 1970. *Die Komposition der Reden in der Ilias*. Berlin.

———. 1997. The "Inner Composition" of the Speeches in the *Iliad*. In *Homer: German Scholarship in Translation*, edited by G. M. Wright and P. V. Jones. Oxford. 239–57.

Lonsdale, S. H. 1989. Hesiod's Hawk and Nightingale (*Op*. 202–12): Fable or Omen? *Hermes* 117:403–12.

———. 1990. *Creatures of Speech, Lion, Herding, and Hunting Similes in the* Iliad. Stuttgart.

Lord, A. B. 1960. *The Singer of Tales*. Cambridge, Mass.

———. 1962. Homer and Other Epic Poetry. In *A Companion to Homer*, edited by A. J. B. Wace and F. H. Stubbings. London. 179–214.

———. 1991. Words Heard and Words Seen. In *Epic Singers and Oral Tradition*. Ithaca.

Lord, M. L. 1967. Withdrawal and Return: An Epic Story Pattern in the Homeric Hymn to Demeter and in the Homeric Poems. *Classical Journal* 62:241–48.

Lowenstam, S. 1981. *The Death of Patroklos: A Study in Typology*. Königstein.
Lynn-George, M. 1988. *Epos: Word, Narrative and the* Iliad. Atlantic Highlands.
Mackie, D. J. 1999. Scamander and the Rivers of Hades in Homer. *American Journal of Philology* 120:485–501.
Macleod, C. W. 1982. *Homer: Iliad. Book 24*. Cambridge, U.K.
Mancuso, H. 1915. De Similitudinibus Homericis Capita Selecta, Particula I. *Rivista di Filologia* 43:56–66.
Marcovich, M. 1962. On the *Iliad*, XVI, 259–265. *American Journal of Philology* 83:288–91.
Marinatos, S. 1960. *Crete and Mycenae*. New York.
Marquardt, P. 1985. Penelope Polytropos. *American Journal of Philology* 106:32–48.
Martin, R. P. 1989. *The Language of Heroes: Speech and Performance in the* Iliad. Ithaca.
———. 1997. Similes and Performance. In *Written Voices, Spoken Signs*, edited by E. J. Bakker and A. Kahane. Cambridge, U.K. 138–66.
Mattes, W. 1958. *Odysseus bei den Phaiaken*. Würzburg.
McGlew, J. F. 1989. Royal Power and the Achaean Assembly at *Iliad* 2.84–393. *Classical Antiquity* 8:283–95.
Michel, C. 1971. *Erläuterungen zum N der Ilias*. Heidelberg.
Minchin, E. 1991. Speaker and Listener, Text and Context: Some Notes on the Encounter of Nestor and Patroklos in *Iliad* 11. *Classical World* 84:273–65.
———. 1992. Scripts and Themes: Cognitive Research and the Homeric Epic. *Classical Antiquity* 11:229–41.
———. 1999. Describing and Narrating in Homer's *Iliad*. In *Signs of Orality*, edited by A. Mackay. Leiden. 49–64.
———. 2001a. *Homer and the Resources of Memory: Some Applications of Cognitive Theory to the* Iliad *and the* Odyssey. Oxford.
———. 2001b. Similes in Homer: Image, Mind's Eye, and Memory. In *Speaking Volumes, Orality and Literacy in the Greek and Roman World*, edited by J. Wilson. Leiden. 25–52.
Monsacré, H. 1984. *Les larmes d'Achille: Le héros, la femme et la souffrance dans la poésie d'Homère*. Paris.
Moog-Grünewald, M. 2001. Der Sänger im Schild. In *Behext von Bildern? Ursachen, Funktionen, und Perspekiven der textuellen Faszination durch Bilder*, ed. by H. J. Drügh and M. Moog-Grünewald. Heidelberg.
Morrison, J. V. 1992. *Homeric Misdirection: False Predictions in the* Iliad. Ann Arbor.
Moulton, C. 1974a. The End of the *Odyssey. Greek, Roman, and Byzantine Studies* 15:153–69.
———. 1974b. Similes in the *Iliad. Hermes* 102:381–97.
———. 1977. *Similes in the Homeric Poems*. Göttingen.
———. 1979. Homeric Metaphor. *Classical Philology* 74:279–93.
———. 1981. The Speech of Glaukos in *Iliad* 17. *Hermes* 109:1–8.
Muellner, L. C. 1990. The Simile of the Cranes and Pygmies: A Study of Homeric Metaphor. *Harvard Studies in Classical Philology* 93:59–101.
Mülder, D. 1910. *Die Ilias und ihre Quellen*. Berlin.
Murray, G. M. 1907. *The Rise of the Greek Epic*. Oxford.

Nagler, M. N. 1967. Towards a Generative View of the Oral Formula. *Transactions of the American Philological Association* 89:269–311.
———. 1974. *Spontaneity and Tradition: A Study in the Oral Art of Homer*. Berkeley.
Nagy, G. 1996. *Poetry as Performance: Homer and Beyond*. Cambridge, U.K.
———. 1997. The Shield of Achilles: Ends of the *Iliad* and Beginnings of the Polis. In *New Light on a Dark Age*, edited by S. Langdon. Columbia, Mo. 194–207.
———. 1999. *The Best of the Achaeans*. Rev. ed. Baltimore.
Nannini, S. 2003. *Analogie e Polarità in Similitudine: Paragoni iliadici e Odissiaci à confronto*. Amsterdam.
Nicolai, W. 1973. *Kleine und grosse Darstellungseinheiten in der Ilias*. Heidelberg.
Nimis, S. A. 1987. *Narrative Semiotics in the Epic Traditon: The Simile*. Bloomington.
Notopoulos, J. A. 1949. Parataxis in Homer: A New Approach to Homeric Literary Criticism. *Transactions of the American Philological Association* 80:1–23.
———. 1957. Homeric Similes in the Light of Oral Poetry. *Classical Journal* 52:323–28.
Olson, S. D. 1995. *Blood and Iron: Stories and Storytelling in Homer's Odyssey*. Leiden.
Ong, W. J. 1982. *Orality and Literacy: The Technologizing of the Word*. London.
Ortony, A. 1979. Beyond Literal Similarity. *Psychological Review* 86:161–80.
Owen, E. T. 1946. *The Story of the Iliad*. London.
Page, D. L. 1959. *History and the Homeric Iliad*. Berkeley.
———. 1973. *Folktales in Homer's Odyssey*. Cambridge, Mass.
Paivio, A. 1983. The Mind's Eye in Arts and Science. *Poetics* 12:1–18.
Parry, A. 1957. Landscape in Greek Poetry. *Yale Classical Studies* 15:3–29.
———. 1971. *The Making of Homeric Verse: The Collected Papers of Milman Parry*. Oxford.
Parry, M. 1928. *L'épithète traditionelle dans Homère: Essai sur un problème de style homérique*. Paris.
Patzer, H. 1971. *Dichterische Kunst und Poetisches Handwerk im homerischen Epos*. Wiesbaden.
———. 1996. *Die Formgesetz des Homerischen Epos*. Stuttgart.
Podlecki, A. J. 1971. Some Odyssean Similes. *Greece and Rome* 18:81–90.
Primavesi, O. 2004. Der Held im Gleichnis: Zehn Ansichten der Odyssee. In *Grosse Texte alter Kulturen: Literarische Reise von Gizeh nach Rom*, edited by H. Martin. Darmstadt. 131–51.
Pucci, P. 1987. *Odysseus Polutropos: Intertextual Readings in the Odyssey and the Iliad*. Ithaca.
Rabel, R. J. 1990. Agamemnon's Aristeia: *Iliad* 11.101–21. *Syllecta Classica* 2:1–7.
———. 1991. Agamemnon's *Iliad*. *Classical Journal* 32:103–17.
———. 1993. Cebriones the Diver: *Iliad* 16.722–76. *American Journal of Philology* 114:339–41.
———. 2005. *Approaches to Homer, Ancient and Modern*. Swansea.
Redfield, J. M. 1994. *Nature and Culture in the Iliad: The Tragedy of Hector*. Extended ed. Durham, U.K.
Reinhardt, K. 1961. *Die Ilias und ihr Dichter*. Göttingen.

Rengakos, A. 1995. Zeit und Gleichzeitigkeit in den homerischen Epen. *Antike und Abendland* 41:1–33.

———. 1998. Zur Zeitstruktur der Odyssee. *Wiener Studien* 111:45–66.

Richardson, N. J. 1987. The Individuality of Homer's Language. In *Homer: Beyond Oral Poetry*, edited by J. M. Bremer, I. J. F. de Jong, and J. Kalff. Amsterdam. 165–84.

———. 1993. *The Iliad: A Commentary: Volume VI: 21–24*. Cambridge, U.K.

Riffaterre, M. 1978. *Semiotics of Poetry*. Bloomington.

Rosner, J. A. 1976. The Speech of Phoenix: Iliad 9.434–605. *Phoenix* 30: 314–27.

Rubin, D. C. 1995. *Memory in Oral Traditions: The Cognitive Psychology of Epic, Ballads, and Counting-Out Rhymes*. Oxford.

Russo, J. A. 1963. A Closer Look at the Homeric Formulas. *Transactions of the American Philological Association* 94:235–47.

———. 1966. The Structural Formula in Homeric Verse. *Yale Classical Studies* 20:219–40.

———. 1982. Interview and Aftermath: Dream, Fantasy, and Intuition in *Odyssey* 19 and 20. *American Journal of Philology* 103:4–18.

Russo, J. A., M. Fernández-Galliano, and A. Heubeck. 1992. *A Commentary on Homer's Odyssey: Books XVII–XXIV*. Vol. 3. Oxford.

Schadewaldt, W. 1943. *Iliasstudien*. Leipzig.

———. 1965. *Von Homers Welt und Werk: Aufsätze und Auslegungen zur homerischen Frage*. 4th ed. Stuttgart.

Schank, R. C. 1999. *Dynamic Memory Revisited*. Cambridge, U.K.

Schank, R. C., and R. P. Abelson. 1977. *Scripts, Plans, Goals, and Understanding: An Inquiry into Human Knowledge Structures*. Hillsdale, N.J.

Scheliha, R. 1943. *Patroklos: Gedanken über Homers Dichtung und Gestalten*. Basel.

Schnapp-Gourbeillon, A. 1981. *Lions, héros, masques: Les représentations de l'animal chez Homère*. Paris.

Schoeck, G. 1961. *Ilias und Aithiopis. Kyklische Motive in homerischer Breching*. Zurich.

Scodel, R. 1982. The Autobiography of Phoenix: Iliad 9.444–95. *American Journal of Philology* 103:128–36.

———. 1998. The Removal of the Arms, the Recognition with Laertes, and Narrative Tension in the *Odyssey*. *Classical Philology* 93:1–17.

———. 1999. *Credible Impossibilities: Conventions and Strategies of Verisimilitude in Homer and Greek Tragedy*. Stuttgart.

Scott, J. A. 1921. *The Unity of Homer*. Berkeley.

Scott, W. C. 1971. A Repeated Episode at Odyssey 1.125–48. *Transactions of the American Philological Association* 102:541–51.

———. 1974. *The Oral Nature of the Homeric Simile*. Leiden.

———. 1987. Teaching Homer from the Top Down: The Telemachy. In *Approaches to Teaching World Literature*. New York.

———. 1997. The Etiquette of Games in Iliad 23. *Greek, Roman, and Byzantine Studies* 38:213–27.

———. 2005. The Patterning of the Similes in Book Two of the *Iliad*. In *Approaches to Homer, Ancient and Modern*, edited by R. J. Rabel. Swansea. 21–53.

———. 2006. Similes in a Shifting Scene: *Iliad*, Book 11. *Classical Philology* 101:103–4.
Scully, S. P. 2003. Reading the Shield of Achilles: Terror, Anger, Delight. *Harvard Studies in Classical Philology* 101:29–47.
Segal, C. 1962. The Phaeacians and the Symbolism of Odysseus' Return. *Arion* 1:17–64.
———. 1972. *The Theme of the Mutilation of the Corpse in the* Iliad. Leiden.
Shannon, R. S. 1975. *The Arms of Achilles and Homeric Compositional Technique*. Leiden.
Shive, D. 1987. *Naming Achilles*. Oxford.
Snell, B. 1960. *The Discovery of the Mind*. New York.
Snodgrass, A. M. 1998. *Homer and the Artists: Text and Picture in Early Greek Art*. Cambridge, U.K.
Stambury-O'Donnell. 1995. In *The Ages of Homer*, edited by J. B. Carter and S. P. Morris. Austin. 315–34.
Stanford, W. B. 1958. *The* Odyssey *of Homer*. 2d ed. London.
Stanley, K. 1993. *The Shield of Homer: Narrative Structure in the* Iliad. Princeton.
Taplin, O. 1980. The Shield of Achilles within the *Iliad*. *Greece and Rome* 27:1–24.
———. 1990. Agamemnon's Role in the *Iliad*. In *Characterization and Individuality in Greek Literature*, edited by C. Pelling. Oxford. 60–82.
———. 1992. *Homeric Soundings: The Shaping of the* Iliad. Oxford.
Tatum, J. 2003. *The Mourner's Song: War and Remembrance from the* Iliad *to Vietnam*. Chicago.
Thalmann, W. G. 1984. *Conventions of Form and Thought in Early Greek Epic Poetry*. Baltimore.
———. 1988. Thersites, Comedy, Scapegoats, and Heroic Ideology in the *Iliad*. *Transactions of the American Philological Association* 118:1–28.
Thiel, H. van. 1982. *Iliaden und Ilias*. Basel.
Thornton, A. 1984. *Homer's* Iliad*: Its Composition and the Motif of Supplication*. Göttingen.
Tsagarakis, O. 1969. The Achaean Wall and the Homeric Question. *Hermes* 97:129–36.
———. 1982. *Form and Content in Homer*. Wiesbaden.
Valk, H. M. H. A. van der. 1963–64. *Researches on the Text and Scholia of the* Iliad. Leiden.
Vernant, J. P. 1991. *Mortals and Immortals: Collected Essays*. Princeton.
Webster, T. B. L. 1960. *From Mycenae to Homer*. London.
West, M. L. 1969. The Achaean Wall. *Classical Review* 19:256–60.
———. 1997. *The East Face of Helicon: West Asiatic Elements in Greek Poetry and Myth*. Oxford.
West, M. L., and S. West. 1999. Comment. In *Dividing Homer, Symbolae Osloenses* 74 (1999) 5–91, edited by M. S. Jensen. 68–73.
Whitman, C. H. 1958. *Homer and the Heroic Tradition*. Cambridge, U.K.
Wilkins, E. G. 1919. A Classification of the Similes of Homer. *Classical World* 13:147–50 and 134–59.
Willcock, M. M. 1964. Mythological Paradeigma in the *Iliad*. *Classical Quarterly* 14:141–54.
———. 2002. Menelaos in the *Iliad*. In *Epea pteroenta: Beiträge zur Homerforschung: Festschrift für W. Kullman*, edited by M. Reichel and A. Rengakos. Stuttgart. 221–29.

Williams, B. 1993. *Shame and Necessity*. Berkeley.
Winter, F. J. 1956. *Die Kampfszenen in den Gesängen M N O der Ilias*. Frankfurt.
Wyatt, W. F., Jr. 2002. Agamemnon's Deception. *Syllecta Classica* 13:1–18.
Young, D. 1967. Never Blotted a Line? Formula and Premeditation in Homer and Hesiod. *Arion* 6:279–324.

INDEX

Achilles: Apollo/Agenor pursued by, 65, 67, 70–71, 76; aristeia of, 103, 126, 146, 154, 175, 176; arming scene of, 174–76; armor of, 21, 72, 73; bird similes for, 51–52, 73, 74; choosing between definitions of heroic code, 234n121; conflicting forces within, 156; contrasting heroic models to, 105; evening star compared with spear point of, 32–33, 73, 74–75; fire similes for, 69, 74, 153, 175; god similes for, 69, 74; Hector fails to take horses of, 149, 150, 154; Hector fought and killed by, 66, 68, 71–73, 75, 77, 175; Hector's body dragged by, 72, 75; Hector takes armor of, 145, 148, 149, 151, 154; ignorance of Patroclus' death, 149–50; invincibility of, 218n66; lion similes for, 74, 76; Lycaon killed by, 65, 66, 67–68, 69; Patroclus involved in events that lead to his death, 81; Patroclus likened to little girl by, 158, 169; Patroclus prohibited from acting as replacement for, 167; on Patroclus' visit to Nestor, 80, 88; as pawn in hands of gods, 66; Poseidon and Athena protect and encourage, 66; preservation of honor as goal of, 156, 241n74; river Xanthus attempts to drown, 65–66, 68, 69–70, 77; similes in book 22 contrast Hector with, 42, 72–75, 81, 220n85; strategem is misconceived, 156–57, 168; as "swift-footed," 15, 19–20. *See also* Shield of Achilles

Aeneas: Apollo encourages, 148; Diomedes wounds, 102, 103, 107, 109; Hector contrasted with, 129; Idomeneus fought by, 139, 140–41, 178; lion similes for, 106, 107; returns to battle, 107, 111, 128; similes for in book 5, 106–7; twins killed by, 179–80

Aeneid, The (Virgil), 1

Agamemnon: aristeia of, 79, 80, 81, 83–84, 103, 182, 222n114; arming of, 1, 21, 79, 82, 88, 222n105; books 1 and 2 as continuing characterization of, 44, 214n7; breastplate of, 1, 82, 83; Diomedes rebuked by, 104–5; fire similes for, 50, 84; god similes for, 54–55; lion similes for, 83–84; misinforms troops about his dream, 44, 60, 61–63, 64, 90; musters Greek troops for Catalogue, 56; in organization of book 11, 79, 80; retreat of, 82, 86–87, 96, 173, 230n77; review of Greek troops by, 11, 45; scene surrounding killings of, 172–73; scepter of, 62; similes for Hector contrasted with those of, 86; similes for in book 2, 16–17, 42; speech of instruction to his troops, 90–91; wounding of, 79, 84, 92, 93, 230n77

Agenor, 67, 70–71, 76

Ajax: boar similes for, 148, 151, 153, 240n69; challenges between Hector and, 139, 143; Epicles bashed in head by, 127, 128; falls back before Trojans, 107; fighting of, 79, 81, 82; Hector disabled with stone by, 92–93; Hector stopped from despoiling Amphimachus' body by, 135; lion similes for, 86, 148, 152, 153, 186; as model hero, 105; Patroclus' body pulled free by, 146, 147, 149, 151, 154; rushing river similes for, 86; Trojans scattered by, 87, 88; urges his men to take heart, 91

257

Alcathous, 134, 140
Alden, M., 208n16
Amphimachus, 135–36
Anderson, O., 230n75
Andromache, 72, 77, 87
Animal similes. *See* Bird similes; Boar similes; Farm animal similes; Insect similes; Lion similes; Wolf similes
Antilochus, 134, 149, 151, 152, 155
Aphrodite: conflict with Athena, 67, 104; Diomedes wounds, 102, 103, 104; Zeus prevents from entering battle, 132
Apollo: in Achilles' confrontation with Agenor, 70, 76; Aeneas encouraged by, 148; Aeneas healed by, 107, 128; attempts to aid Trojans in book 17, 155; Diomedes charges against, 106–7; on Diomedes fighting gods, 104; Greek wall swept away by, 95; Hector healed by, 128–29; Hector rebuked by, 146; Patroclus opposed by, 164, 166–67; Poseidon urges into battle, 67
Ares: Athena persuades to leave battle, 106, 111; and Athena trade insults, 67; Diomedes as agent of, 107; Diomedes wounds, 102, 103, 104, 109, 228n42; Hector compared to, 84, 143, 144, 187; Meriones compared to, 148; Patroclus compared to, 156; pulls veil of night over battle, 107; rallies Trojans, 102, 107, 110, 111
Arming scenes, 21, 174–76
Armstrong, J. I., 16
Artemis, 67, 70
Asios, 95, 96, 97, 99, 100, 140, 178–79, 236n17
Athena: Achilles protected and encouraged by, 66; Ares persuaded to leave battle by, 106, 111; asks Odysseus to urge Greeks back to assembly, 62–63; conflict with Aphrodite, 67, 104; conflict with Ares, 67; Diomedes as agent of, 107; Diomedes given ability to distinguish men from gods by, 104, 109, 228n48; Diomedes healed by, 103, 106; and Hera journey to battlefield, 108–9, 179; Odysseus compared to father by, 123, 124; Odysseus supported by, 113, 114, 116–17, 118–19, 125, 232n96; Stentor's chariot driven by, 109; in struggle over Patroclus' body, 150–51; Zeus sends her to encourage Greeks, 154, 155
Audience: creative poet and co-creating, 174–88; participation in Homeric similes, 8–10, 31–37
Automedon, 150, 152, 153, 155, 168

Bakker, E. J., 14, 211n35
Baltes, M., 243n120
Berg, Nils, 174
Bethe, E., 235n3
Bird similes: for Achilles, 51–52, 73, 74; analysis of occurrences in *Iliad* and *Odyssey*, 202–3; Artemis flees like a dove, 70, 219n73; chart, 202–3; in clustering of similes in *Iliad* 2.455–83, 49, 50–52; deleting and adding motifs to, 210n20; eagle omen in *Iliad* book 13, 139; for Greek army in *Iliad* book 2, 60; for Greeks in *Iliad* book 17, 152; for Hector, 144, 187; for Menelaus, 151, 153, 240n67; for Meriones, 141–42; in *Odyssey* book 5, 122; in *Odyssey* book 22, 114, 115, 116, 231n89; for Patroclus and Sarpedon, 162, 163, 242n101; for Poseidon, 135, 142, 143–44; Trojans likened to hawks, 151; warriors compared to birds of prey, 51
Boar similes: for Ajax, 148, 151, 153, 240n69; analysis of occurrences in *Iliad* and *Odyssey*, 193–96; chart, 193–96; for Idomeneus, 141; for Leontius and Polypoetes, 97, 226n16; for Odysseus and Diomedes, 86; for Patroclus, 165, 167, 169–70, 243n120; as simile family, 22, 28; standard

258 · Index

components of, 29–31; in wounding scenes, 93
Bremer, J. M., 220n85
Catalogue of the Greek army, 43–44, 49, 56, 58, 60–61, 153, 183
Catling, H. W., 207n.5
Catullus, 1
Cebriones, 165–66, 169
Character: Homer's use of similes for delineation of, 42–93; independently functioning characters in *Iliad*, 89–90; and plot as mutually reinforcing in traditional storytelling, 42
Complexity, similes for, 155–70
Crag similes, 48–49

Dark-watering spring similes, 158, 159, 161, 170
Deiphobus: encounter with Meriones, 135, 136; Idomeneus threatens, 139, 140; introduction of, 134; Meriones becomes opponent of, 141–42
Dickson, K., 213n1
Dimock, G., 232n98
Diomedes: ability to distinguish men from gods, 104, 109, 228n48; Aeneas wounded by, 102, 103, 107, 109; Agamemnon rebukes, 104–5; Aphrodite wounded by, 102, 103, 104; Ares wounded by, 102, 103, 104, 109, 228n42; aristeia of, 94, 103, 105–6, 109, 112, 126; boar similes for, 86; charges against Apollo, 106–7; crosses line between mortal and divine, 107, 110; god similes for, 108; ineffectuality of, 103, 104; lion similes for, 106, 108, 229n58; as main character of book 5, 102; as model hero, 103, 105; as obedient to authority, 104, 105, 110–11; opportunity for honor has passed, 110; rushing river similes for, 106; three entrances of, 102, 105–6, 111, 229n56; wounding of, 79, 80, 103, 106

Direct description, 91, 96, 155
Doloneia, 79
Dove similes, 70, 75, 219n73

Ekphrases, 1
Epipolesis, 45
Eurypylus, 78, 156
Expository digressions, 4

Farm animal similes: in clustering of similes in *Iliad* 2.455–83, 49, 55–56; for fallen warriors, 177; for Greek army in *Iliad* book 2, 60; for Menelaus and body of Patroclus, 55–56, 146, 147, 148, 149, 152; in *Odyssey* book 22, 114, 115; variety of tones of, 237n32; in wounding scenes, 93
Father similes, 123–24
Fawn similes, 69, 72, 183
Fenik, B., 220n85, 221n102, 224n3, 229n66, 235n8, 239n53
Fillmore, C. J., 24
Fire similes: for Achilles, 69, 74, 153, 175; for Achilles' arming scene, 174–76; for Agamemnon, 50, 84; analysis of occurrences in *Iliad* and *Odyssey*, 190–92; in army mustering scenes, 45; for battle in *Iliad* book 17, 149; chart, 190–92; in clustering of similes in *Iliad* 2.455–83, 49–50, 58–59, 215n23; for Hector, 135, 143, 144, 153, 187, 236n9; for Idomeneus, 137; in *Odyssey* book 5, 124; as simile family, 22, 28; for Trojan fighting, 135, 151; for Trojan watchfires, 33–34; two basic types of, 49; for warriors, 186
Fish similes, 67–68, 69, 93, 107, 115, 161
Flower similes. *See* Leaves and flower similes
Foley, J. M., 20, 210nn 14, 18, 213n55, 234n120
Fraenkel, H., 212nn 43, 49, 239n65
Friedrich, W.-H., 236n17

Gathering storm similes, 160, 162, 166, 169
Gestalt structures, 24, 211n33
Glaucus, 12–13, 100, 104, 105, 146, 148, 155
Goatherd similes: in army mustering scenes, 45; in clustering of similes in *Iliad* 2.455–83, 49, 52–54
Gods: descend to battlefield in *Iliad* book 21, 65, 67; Diomedes crosses line between mortal and divine, 107, 110; insult and strike one another, 67, 68, 70; as managing affairs to suit themselves, 68, 110; Odysseus' escape protected by, 121–22; Zeus attempts to prevent from entering battle, 132. *See also* God similes; *and by name*
God similes: for Achilles, 69, 74; for Agamemnon, 50, 84; analysis of occurrences in *Iliad* and *Odyssey*, 197–99; chart, 197–99; in clustering of similes in *Iliad* 2.455–83, 49, 54–55; for Diomedes, 108; for Hector, 84, 143, 144, 187; for Idomeneus, 137; for Meriones, 137, 148; for Patroclus, 156, 164; as simile family, 22, 28; for warriors, 107, 186
Goody, J., 245n24
Griffin, J., 16, 220n87

Hainsworth, J. B., 221n103, 222nn 114, 116, 223n125, 224n4, 225n7, 226nn 21, 26
Harpalion, 142
Haug, Dag, 174
Hector: Achaeans recoil in fear from, 7–8; Achilles' armor taken from Patroclus by, 145, 148, 149, 151; Achilles drags body of, 72, 75; Achilles fights and slays, 66, 68, 71–73, 75, 77, 175; Ajax disables with stone, 92–93; alternative comparisons for, 56; Apollo heals, 128–29; Apollo rebukes, 146; armor of, 82, 83; Automedon pursued by, 168; in battle with Patroclus, 166–67, 169–70; bird similes for, 144, 187; bravery as fatal, 87; in catalogue of Trojans in book 12, 96, 101, 225n14; challenges between Ajax and, 139, 143; cluster of similes for entrance of, 57; as complicit in seeking risk, 88; dilemma of hero understood by, 71–72; diminishing strength of, 152, 154–55; eagle and snake omen ignored by, 97–98, 99, 226n20; end of day of glory of, 145; entrance in book 11, 57, 80, 82, 84–85; with face like the swift night, 99, 101; fails to control battle in book 13, 133, 142; fails to retrieve Imbrius' body, 135, 136–37; fails to take Achilles' horses, 149, 150, 154; fire similes for, 135, 143, 144, 153, 187, 236n9; flees before Patroclus, 159–60, 162, 163; Glaucus rebukes, 146, 155; god similes for, 54–55, 84, 143, 144, 187; Greek wall breached by, 95, 98, 101, 127–28; hunting similes for, 84–85; introduction in book 12, 96, 100; last charge of, 151; as leader of Trojan army, 95, 99, 101, 135; lion similes for, 88, 96, 129, 153, 166, 170, 225n11, 243n120; list of accompanying warriors, 88, 222n111; Menelaus confronts, 147; in organization of book 11, 79, 80; as pawn in Zeus' plan, 166; physical description as he advances on Greek ships, 55; runs away, 71, 73, 75; similes for Agamemnon contrasted with those of, 86; similes in book 22 contrast Achilles with, 42, 72–75, 81, 220n85; as snowy mountain, 143; as victim of heroic code, 71, 75; wind similes for, 84, 85, 96, 101; wounding of, 131; Zeus as protector of, 81, 95, 99
Heiden, B., 12
Hephaistos: Achilles' armor made by, 72, 73; river Xanthus forced to retreat by, 65, 66, 69, 70, 77; target of Diomedes rescued by, 106, 227n41
Hera: Artemis beaten by, 67; and Athena journey to battlefield, 108–9, 179;

defeat of Troy as goal of, 66; Diomedes as agent of, 107; takes shape of Stentor, 109; on Zeus and Sarpedon's death, 162; Zeus distracted by, 131; Zeus prevents from entering battle, 132

Heroic code: Achilles and Hector respond to differently, 81; Achilles' challenge to, 94, 111, 234n121; contrasting heroic models, 105; as defensive ethical system, 68; distorting effect of, 100; divine domination and, 68, 110; Hector as tragic victim of, 71, 75; Shield of Achilles and, 6

Hesiod, 59

Homer: complexity of language of, 18; creative poet and co-creating audience, 174–88; formulaic language adapted by, 40–41; multivalent meanings limited by, 21; oral nature of Homeric verse, 14–17; threaded speech in, 33; traditional language inherited by, 34. *See also* Homeric similes; *Iliad*; *Odyssey*

Homeric similes: audience participation of, 8–10, 31–37; background of, 14–41; basic motifs in *Iliad* and *Odyssey*, 189–205; book divisions and, 10–13; books 1 and 2 of *Iliad* distinguished, 11, 16–17; for character and plot delineation, 42–93; clusters, 57–58, 186, 187; for complexity in *Iliad* book 16, 155–70; as constructed to suit context, 8; in contrasting parallel scenes, 90–93; development within, 6–7; as easily recognized, 6; for enhancing and bringing essential features of narrative into focus, 127; as exceptional in complexity and originality, 187; exclusion in shaping individual, 37–38; as expository digressions, 4; as expression of individual poet and product of preexisting motifs, 18–19; extended, 15, 36, 182, 184, 187; families of, 17, 19–31, 37, 39; as guides through series of type scenes in *Iliad* book 17, 145–55; to interpret typical actions in *Odyssey* book 22, 112–18; juxtaposed, 43, 46, 47, 52, 78, 88, 170, 215n17, 224n129; markers of, 8, 33, 174; for marking shift of scene in *Iliad* book 11, 78–89; within the narrative, 174–80; narrative enhanced by, 8; for narrative theme delineation, 94–129; and oral nature of Homeric verse, 14–17, 26, 209n6; parallel similemes to create unified theme in *Iliad* book 5, 102–12; phrase selection in, 185; placement of, 16–17; poet's choice in forming individual, 181–84; point of view in, 39; in problem books of *Iliad*, 130–73; repeated, 22, 25, 26, 28, 144, 174, 184, 237n28, 241n85; as retarding action and inviting reflection, 112; reversed, 234n120; seven identically repeated similes, 22, 26, 28; short, 25, 35–37, 39, 185, 186–87, 213n60; for showing thematic contrast in *Iliad* books 21 and 22, 65–78; simileme concept illuminates standard problems of, 38–41; for studying paratactic composition, 182; subject matter of, 17; thematic similes in *Odyssey* book 5, 118–26; unity of narrative and, 188

Horse similes, 26, 129, 235n122

Hunting similes, 84–85

Hymn to Apollo, 18

Idomeneus: Aeneas fought by, 139, 140–41, 178; aristeia of, 53–54, 134, 139–41, 178; Asios killed by, 140, 178–79; boar similes for, 141; entrance of, 137, 178, 236n20; fire similes for, 137; god similes for, 137; Meriones meets, 134, 137; Othryoneus killed by, 140, 178

Idyll (Theocritus), 1

Iliad (Homer): bird similes in, 202; book divisions of, 10–13; creative poet and co-creating audience in, 174–88; fire

Iliad (Homer) *(continued)*
similes in, 190–91; god similes in, 197–98; independently functioning characters in, 89–90; insect similes in, 205; lion and boar similes in, 193–96; oral nature of, 14–17; poetic techniques compared with *Odyssey*, 234n120; as poetic whole, 181; problem books of, 130–73; similes used for character and plot delineation, 42–93; similes used within the narrative, 174–80; similes used for narrative theme delineation, 94–129; traditional devices in, 16; tree similes in, 204; wind and wave similes in, 200–201. *See also* entries by book; characters by name

Iliad (Homer), book 2: battle books contrasted with, 171; catalogue of the Greek army, 43–44, 49, 56, 58, 60–61, 153, 183; characterization by similes in, 43–65; clustering of similes 2.455–83, 49–58, 216n36; irony as major literary device of, 64; leadership as theme of, 44, 60; location of similes in, 183; narrative means other than similes in, 61–64; number of similes in, 43; role of similes in, 59–65; similes of, 44–59; tone shift between book 1 and, 181; two narrative units of, 43

Iliad (Homer), book 5: alternative means of telling story, 111; Diomedes as main character of, 102; four basic units of, 102; moves from man to god, 110; parallel similemes to create unified theme in, 102–12; similes in, 102–3, 110–12

Iliad (Homer), book 11: battle books contrasted with, 171; complexity of, 78, 90; coordination of similes and narrative themes in, 89; density of similes in, 43; ekphrases in, 1–2; location of similes in, 87, 89; major problem of, 81; new day of fighting begins in, 42; number of similes in, 43; pivotal nature of, 78, 89, 221n102; similes for marking shift of scene in, 78–89; structure of, 79–80, 88; too many characters in, 81; two sections of, 183

Iliad (Homer), book 12: battle books contrasted with, 171; direct focus on single theme in, 94–102; the Greek defensive wall, 94–95, 96, 101, 126, 127–28, 131, 224n4; mutually reinforcing themes of, 95; nontraditional similes in, 98–99; six sections of, 95–99; stones picked up by Ajax and Hector in, 127–28; sudden shift in tone of, 101–2; Zeus sends wind from Mt. Ida in, 95, 98, 100–101

Iliad (Homer), book 13: as battle book, 171; beginning of, 131–32, 144; conclusion of, 131, 144; cross-purposes as theme of, 132; as introductory to major segment of epic, 171; lack of organization in, 132; number of similes in, 135; as part of unit that does not end till book 15, 131, 144, 171; seen as retarding story, 130–31; short similes at end of, 187; similes for ordering conscious chaos in, 130–45; Teucer's killing of Imbrius in, 135, 140, 176–78; two sections of, 133–35

Iliad (Homer), book 16: appearance-reality discrepancy underlies, 169; as battle book, 171; design of similes in, 168–70; four basic units of, 157–58; as house of mirrors, 155, 167; main problem of, 168; as pivotal book in larger structure, 171; sequential similes in, 170; similes for complexity in, 155–70

Iliad (Homer), book 17: as battle book, 171; closing similes reflect narrative developments in, 153; cluster of similes for fixing scene in memory, 187; critical concerns about, 145–46; each unit centers on different hero, 152; emotion in, 155; as introductory to major segment of epic, 171; number of similes in, 145; similes as guides through series of type scenes in, 145–55; six units of, 146

Iliad (Homer), book 21: fire versus water contrast in, 234n116; four disillusioning actions in, 65, 76–77; mutual reinforcement of book 22 and, 76–78; questioning of war's effectiveness in, 66, 67–68; similes and differing plot structures of book 22 and, 90; similes for showing thematic contrast in, 65–71; transition to book 22 from, 71; worth of human life as theme of, 69

Iliad (Homer), book 22: complexity of, 71; linear structure of, 77; mutual reinforcement of book 21 and, 76–78; similes and differing plot structures of book 21 and, 90; similes for showing thematic contrast in, 71–78; transition between book 21 and, 71

Imbrius, 135, 136, 176–78

Insect similes: analysis of occurrences in *Iliad* and *Odyssey*, 205; bees in *Iliad* 2.87, 44–45; chart, 205; in clustering of similes in *Iliad* 2.455–83, 49; for defenders of Greek wall in *Iliad* book 12, 97, 226n18; flies circling milk pail, 163–64, 169, 170, 172, 186; for Greek army in *Iliad* book 2, 60; juxtaposed with leaves and flower simile in *Iliad* 2.468 and 2.469, 52; for Menelaus, 151; for Myrmidons, 160, 161, 166, 170, 242n94; in *Odyssey* book 22, 114–15

Janko, R., 236n9, 238n35
Jensen, M. S., 12
Jong, I. J. F. de, 220nn 85, 87

Kirk, G. S., 216n28, 229n58
Krischer, T., 16

Lakoff, G., 209n6
Lamb similes, 73, 76

La Motte, Houdar de, 1
Leaf, Walter, 130–31, 214n15, 221n102, 238n45, 240n67, 243n113
Leaves and flower similes: in clustering of similes in *Iliad* 2.455–83, 49, 52; connotations of, 216n26; for Greek army in *Iliad* book 2, 60
Lee, D. J. N., 245n20
Leontius, 97, 101
Lessing, Gotthold Ephraim, 208n18
Libation Bearers, The (Aeschylus), 9
Lion similes: for Achilles, 74, 76; for Aeneas, 106, 107; for Agamemnon, 83–84; for Ajax, 86, 148, 152, 153, 186; analysis of occurrences in *Iliad* and *Odyssey*, 193–96; in army mustering scenes, 45; for Automedon, 152; chart, 193–96; for Diomedes, 106, 108, 229n58; directions they do not take, 182; for Greeks in *Iliad* book 17, 150, 152; for Hector, 88, 96, 129, 153, 166, 170, 225n11, 243n120; for Menelaus, 56, 147, 148, 151, 152, 153, 240n67; for Odysseus, 115–16, 118; in *Odyssey* 6.130 and 12.299 compared, 23–24; for Patroclus, 162, 163, 165, 166, 169; for Penelope in *Odyssey* 4.791, 31–32, 183, 212n49; for Sarpedon, 98, 226nn 24, 25; Sarpedon compares Greeks to lions, 107; short simile at *Iliad* 24.572, 35–36; as simile family, 22, 28; standard components of, 29–31; for twins killed by Aeneas, 180; for warriors, 86, 182, 183, 184, 186; in wounding scenes, 93

Lohmann, D., 16
Lonsdale, S. H., 212n43, 221n98, 223nn 118, 125, 229n67
Lord, Albert, 14, 218n57
Lycaon, 65, 66, 67–68, 69

Mackie, D. J., 218n58
Martin, R. P., 16
Meleager, 4

Menelaus: Athena gives strength to, 151; bird similes for, 151, 153, 240n67; Hector confronted by, 147; Helenus' arrow bounces off of, 142; insect similes for, 151; lion similes, 56, 147, 148, 151, 152, 153, 240n67; mother cow simile for, 55–56, 146, 147, 148, 149, 152; similes for attempt to retrieve Patroclus' body, 57; wind similes for, 147; wonders whether he should stand against advancing Hector, 155

Meriones: Ares compared with, 148; bird simile for, 141–42; encounter with Deiphobus, 135, 136; god similes for, 137, 148; and Idomeneus encourage one another, 137, 139; introduction of, 134; and Patroclus' body, 57, 153

Metonymic pathways, 20, 210n18

Minchin, E., 212n46, 213nn 60, 63, 215n20

Moulton, C., 216n36, 220n87, 236n17, 242n95, 244n5

Muellner, L. C., 213n60

Myrmidons, 159, 160, 161, 166, 169, 170

Nagler, M. N., 24, 25, 211n33

Nannini, S., 234n120

Narrative: similes as supporting narrative strategies, 8, 11, 75, 130; similes for delineation of theme, 94–129; the simile within, 174–180; unity of simile and, 188

Nestor, Patroclus' visit to, 79, 80, 81, 88–89, 156

Nimis, S. A., 25–26, 215n17, 244n17

Notopoulos, J. A., 210n11, 212n55

Oak trees, 27, 244n11

Odysseus: Athena's support for, 113, 114, 116–17, 118–19, 125, 232n96; bases of power of, 113; boar simile for, 85–86; chooses between Calypso and Penelope, 94, 120, 127; craftsman similes for, 125; deaths inflicted in *Odyssey* 22, 116, 231n93; escapes from Calypso's island, 118–26; indomitable spirit of, 120; lion similes for, 115–16, 118; rallies the Greeks, 63; suitors defeated by, 112–18; Trojans scattered by, 87; visit to Autolycus in *Odyssey* book 19, 2–4; wounding of, 79, 81

Odyssey (Homer): bird similes in, 51, 203; Demodocus' song of Ares and Aphrodite, 4; Demodocus' tale of Troy, 234n113; farm animal similes in, 56, 114, 115; fire similes in, 50, 192; god similes in, 198–99; insect similes in, 205; lion and boar similes in, 196; lion simile for Penelope in 4.791, 31–32, 183, 212n49; oral nature of, 14–17; poetic techniques compared with *Iliad*, 234n120; as poetic whole, 181; traditional devices in, 16; tree similes in, 204; two beginnings of, 181; wind and wave similes in, 201. *See also* Odysseus; entries by book

Odyssey (Homer), book 5: number of similes in, 121; terms of hero's choice to return made clear in, 94; thematic similes in, 118–26; three sections of, 120–21; two themes of, 118

Odyssey (Homer), book 22: forces greater than heroic code in, 94; as most Iliadic book, 112; similes to interpret typical actions in, 112–18; six units comprise, 114

Oral nature of Homeric verse, 14–17, 26

Oral Nature of the Homeric Simile (Scott), 15

Othryoneus, 140, 178

Owen, E. T., 221n102, 224n4

Paivio, A., 209n6

Paratactic composition, 181–82

Paris, 21, 26, 56, 105, 143, 235n122

Parry, Milman, 14, 19

Patroclus: Achilles as ignorant of death of,

149–50; Ajax pulls free body of, 146, 147, 151, 154; aristeia of, 103, 158; Athena in struggle over body of, 150–51; attacks Troy's walls, 164–67; in battle with Hector, 166–67, 169–70; Cebriones killed by, 165–66, 169; crosses limit Achilles set for him, 157, 163; death of, 156, 165, 166–67; emotions run deep, 79; god similes for, 156, 164; Greeks fight for body of, 145, 187; Hector flees before, 159–60, 162, 163; Hector takes Achilles' armor from, 145, 148, 149, 151, 154; initial charge of, 159–62; limitations of, 158–59, 168, 170; lion similes for, 162, 163, 165, 166, 169; Menelaus and body of, 55–56, 146, 147, 148, 149, 152; in organization of book 11, 79, 80; as pawn in Zeus' plan, 166; Sarpedon killed by, 156, 158, 162, 169, 170, 172, 179; Sarpedon's armor stripped by, 164, 168; sheds tears like mountain spring, 158, 169, 170; unreachable goal of, 156–57; unwarlike similes for, 158–59; visit to Nestor, 79, 80, 81, 88–89, 156; wounding of, 79, 166
Plot: and character as mutually reinforcing in traditional storytelling, 42; Homer's use of similes for delineation of, 42–93
Polydamas, 95, 96, 97–98, 226n20
Polypoetes, 97, 101
Poseidon: Achilles protected by, 66; Adamas' spear rendered harmless by, 142; Alcathous paralyzed by, 134, 140; anger at death of Amphimachus, 136; Antilochus guarded by, 134; Apollo urged into battle by, 67; battle's course reversed by, 99; bird simile for, 135; chaos ensues when he takes over battle, 131–32; Greeks encouraged by, 131, 133, 134, 135, 138–39, 149, 176; Greek wall swept away by, 95; on Hector as leader of opposition, 133; on Hector fighting like fire, 143; Idomeneus challenged by, 137; Odysseus escapes from, 121, 122, 233n107; speech against Zeus, 132–33; Teucer encouraged by, 135, 140, 177
Pucci, Pietro, 23–24

Quarrel scenes, 90

Rabel, R. J., 223n118
Racehorse similes, 73, 76
Redfield, J. M., 208n17, 210n14, 221n97
Reinhardt, K., 230n74
Richardson, N. J., 219nn 72, 80, 220n89
Riffaterre, M., 26
Roaring river similes. *See* Rushing river similes
Rumor, 62
Rushing river similes: for Ajax, 86; in army mustering scenes, 45; for Diomedes, 106; for Hector, 135, 162; for Trojan withdrawal, 160, 242n97; for warriors, 86

Sarpedon: battle over body of, 163, 170, 172; bird similes for, 162, 163, 242n101; breaks piece of Greek wall, 95, 101; bull simile describing last moments of, 55; burial of, 164; death of, 156, 158, 162, 169, 170, 172, 179; Hector and Trojans rebuked by, 107; Hector implicitly contrasted with, 96; lion similes for, 98, 226nn 24, 25; Patroclus strips armor from, 164, 168; as skilled ally of Hector, 99; statement to Glaucus, 100, 226n25; tree similes for fall of, 162–63, 170, 179; warlike similes introduce, 98
Scales of Zeus, 71, 73
Scene: similes for contrasting, 90–93; similes for marking shift of, 78–89
Scepter of Agamemnon, 62
Schadewaldt, W., 78, 208n19, 221n102
Scodel, R., 207n14
Semantic frames, 24
Seven against Thebes (Aeschylus), 1

Index · 265

Shield of Achilles: ancient audience's interpretation of, 10; antitheses as structure for, 5; as basic to book 18's larger theme, 5; as creation of the poet, 2, 6; as expository digression, 4; fire simile for, 174–75; as prototype for later poets, 1; simultaneous movements in organizing structure of, 4–5; special problems regarding, 2

Shield of Heracles, The, 1

Shipbuilder similes, 162, 170, 179

Similemes, 18–31; defined, 19; evidence for existence of, 37; excluding elements from, 38; flexibility of, 25, 37; limited number of contexts of, 26–27, 37; as nonverbal, 19, 28, 37; problems of Homeric composition illuminated by, 38–41; traditional stock of, 90, 184. *See also* Homeric similes

Snow similes, 97, 98, 100, 226n22

Stanford, W. B., 231n92

Stanley, K., 10, 12, 220n89, 222n115, 227n39

Star similes, 32–33, 73, 74, 105, 106, 221n95

Storm similes, 160, 162, 166, 169

Telemachus, 112, 113, 116, 123, 234n113

Teucer, 135, 140, 176–78

Thalmann, W. G., 242n96

Theme: direct focus on single theme in *Iliad* book 12, 94–102; Homeric similes for narrative theme delineation, 94–129; parallel similemes to create unified, in *Iliad* book 5, 102–12; thematic similes in *Odyssey* book 5, 118–26

Theogony (Hesiod), 59

Thersites, 63–64

Tlepolemus, 107

Tree similes: analysis of occurrences in *Iliad* and *Odyssey*, 204; for Asios' death, 140, 178–79; chart, 204; complementary and contradictory components of, 25; connote death, 108; directions they do not take, 182; for Imbrius'

death, 136, 177–78; for Leontius and Polypoetes, 97, 101; narrative contexts of, 26–27; oak tree as most common, 244n11; for Sarpedon's fall, 162–63, 170, 179; as simile family, 22–23; for twins killed by Aeneas, 180; woodcutter simile and, 27–28

Turner, M., 209n6

Type scenes, 16, 26, 40, 145–55, 174, 182

Typical actions, similes to interpret, 112–18

Unified theme, parallel similemes to create, 102–12

Valk, H. M. H. A. van der, 217n39

Wave similes: analysis of occurrences in *Iliad* and *Odyssey*, 200–201; in army mustering scenes, 45; for battle scenes, 184, 186; chart, 200–201; for gathering of Greek army in *Iliad* book 2, 45–46, 60; as simile family, 28

Weapons, similes for describing gleam of, 32–33

West, Martin L. and Stephanie, 174

Wind similes: analysis of occurrences in *Iliad* and *Odyssey*, 200–201; in army mustering scenes, 45; for attacking warriors, 108, 137–38, 184; chart, 200–201; as continuing subject in *Iliad* book 12, 100–101; deleting and adding motifs to, 210n20; for gathering of Greek army in *Iliad* book 2, 45–47, 60; for Greeks in *Iliad* book 17, 152; for Hector, 84, 85, 96, 101; for Menelaus, 147; in *Odyssey* book 5, 122, 233n109; as simile family, 22, 28; for Trojan fighting, 135, 143; in wounding scenes, 93; Zeus sends wind from Mt. Ida, 95, 98, 100–101

Wolf similes: for Myrmidons, 159, 160, 162, 166, 170; for warriors, 135

Woodcutter similes, 27, 162, 163, 170, 243n108
Wounding scenes, 93

Xanthus (river), 65–66, 68, 69–70, 77, 218n57

Zenodotus, 224n129, 227n30
Zeus: Achilles' prayer for Patroclus denied by, 159; as active force in battle, 82–83; Asios reproaches, 97; attempts to keep gods out of battle, 132; diverts his attention from battlefield, 138, 235n6; divine deception of, 131; end of Hector's role in plan of, 145; in escape of Achilles' horses, 149, 150, 154; "Golden Chain" speech of, 132, 138; Hector and Patroclus as pawns in plan of, 166; Hector protected by, 81, 95, 99; on Hector taking Achilles' armor, 148, 154; Iris as agent of, 82, 222n110; Odysseus protected by, 118, 232n104; in Patroclus' ignoring limit Achilles set for him, 157; Patroclus' mind dominated by, 164; plan to shift momentum to Trojans, 78, 79, 80, 82, 89, 95, 99, 126; Poseidon's speech against, 132–33; prophecy about Hector, 129; reversal of plan of, 142, 144, 171; on Sarpedon's death, 162; scales of, 71, 73; sides with Greeks, 150; storm controlled by, 160, 161–62, 166, 169; underlying favor for the Greeks of, 98; wind sent from Mt. Ida by, 95, 98, 100–101

www.ingramcontent.com/pod-product-compliance
Lightning Source LLC
Chambersburg PA
CBHW030310080526
44584CB00012B/515